Introduction to Interactive Computer Graphics

Introduction to Interactive Computer Graphics

JOAN E. SCOTT

JOHN WILEY & SONS
A Wiley-Interscience Publication
New York   Chichester   Brisbane   Toronto   Singapore

Library of Congress Cataloging in Publication Data:

Scott, Joan E.
  Introduction to interactive computer graphics.

  "A Wiley-Interscience publication."
  Bibliography: p.
  Includes index.
  1. Computer graphics. 2. Interactive computer
systems. I. Title.

T 385.S36   001.55   81-7621
ISBN 0-471-05773-8   AACR2
ISBN 0-471-86623-7   (pbk)

Printed in the United States of America

10 9 8 7 6 5

To my father,
Julius C. Parker

Preface

This book combines in a single volume both technical information about graphics systems and practical knowledge concerning their use. The intent of this comprehensive introduction is to make the concepts easy to understand, to suggest applications in various fields, and to give solid help in putting graphics to work in these fields. The explanations are written in clear, nonmathematical style. All technical terms are defined where they first occur in the text and the definitions are based on standard industry usage. References are provided for specialized topics beyond the scope of this book. Graphics equipment is described in terms of generalized capabilities rather than specific brands, but vendor lists of manufacturers and products are included. A complete index is provided for quick reference, because much of the material will be of continuing value to the reader in his or her work. With this format, the book is easy to read and understand, but has enough depth to serve as a reference.

Illustrations are used generously to increase comprehension. The principle of operation of each hardware device is shown in a simple line drawing. There are photographs of all types of equipment, as well as photographs of the results of many applications. Simple block diagrams clarify programming relationships. The section dealing with the management of a graphics installation uses checklists and contains sample forms.

For those who wish to become sophisticated users of computer-assisted design and for managers responsible for initiating and supervising graphics installations, this book will serve as a complete education. It is a precise but nonmathematical starting point for that overwhelming majority of working computer science professionals with no previous contact with interactive graphics. It is a tool that salesmen of computer systems or hardware can use to widen their scope of knowledge and can recommend to prospective customers as background information. Although not primarily designed as a textbook, this book can fill the critical need for an introductory college level text.

The technology of interactive graphics has now reached the level of maturity and can be a powerful tool for a much wider range of applications than is currently realized. By bringing the information on graphics together into a single practical guide, I hope that this volume may contribute to the field's ongoing development.

I gratefully acknowledge the help of the many companies who supplied information and illustrations. I am especially indebted to Fluor Engineers Houston Division who provided my initial experience with graphics. I thank my husband Dan for his active cooperation and my mother for her care of my daughter, who was born during the writing.

JOAN E. SCOTT

Houston, Texas
May 1981

Contents

PART THREE   A PRACTICAL TOOL

Introduction to
Interactive
Computer Graphics

PART ONE
Hardware

CHAPTER 1

Input Devices at the Work Station

Input devices are the user's tools for creating results with a graphics system. An input device captures data and makes them available to the graphics program. The program processes the input data and determines the resulting effect on the visual display, if any. In other words, there is a strict separation of input operations and output operations, with the graphics program supervising the link between them. This separation is the key to the superiority of interactive computer graphics over traditional drawing methods, where the final result depends entirely on the skill of the person holding the pen or pencil. The intervention by the graphics program between input and output makes it possible for the computer system to assist the human operator in small ways, such as straightening the lines he or she draws, or in complex ways, such as performing extensive calculations.

The input devices at a computer graphics work station fall into three major categories—light pens, analog devices, and keyboard devices.

A light pen seems to be a magic pen, leaving a trail of light behind on the screen. Actually, the pen does not emit light, but detects the presence of light on the screen. Light pens are used as input devices on only sophisticated graphics systems because of the need for extensive support programming, not the relative cost of the light pen hardware. The physical construction and operation of the light pen are relatively simple.

The majority of interactive input devices are analog-to-digital convertors. This simply means that they sense some physical quantity (usually generated by a human hand), such as speed, acceleration, force, position, direction, distance, and rotation, and then convert it into a numeric quantity that the computer can accept. These analog devices include digitizers, joysticks, trackballs, and dials.

3

A keyboard enters letters, numerals, and other characters by sending digital codes to the computer. A button that is not part of an alphanumeric keyboard can capture only one data item, the fact that it has been pushed. Likewise, a simple switch can make only one data item available to the computer, whether its current position is on or off. The meanings associated with the button and switch input data are determined within the graphics program. A voice data entry system is in effect a super keyboard that enters complete words and phrases from a limited vocabulary by recognizing human speech.

1.1. LIGHT PENS

The *light pen* is a multiple-purpose input device that has the physical size and shape of a fountain pen so it can be held comfortably in the operator's hand (Figure 1.1). The light pen's primary function is to point at graphic objects shown on a refreshed cathode-ray tube (CRT). The secondary use for a light pen is to locate positions within the displayed area. This positional input, called *tracking*, is accomplished by moving a cursor cross-hair symbol, by interacting with a special array of dots, or by some other means. These

Figure 1.1.   Light pen. Courtesy of Information Control Corporation.

two basic functions can be adapted to yield more sophisticated interactive input techniques as described in Chapter 6.

Figure 1.2 is a block diagram showing light pen operation. A refreshed CRT is the only type of display that can be used with a light pen because the light pen responds to the instantaneous peak in brightness for a point in the image that occurs when the electron beam excites the CRT phosphor at that point. The average brightness of the steady image seen by a human observer is much less than this peak. A light pen operates best with a phosphor that has a high ratio of peak to average brightness.

The light pen's field of view must be restricted to a small area on the screen surface so the pen can point to a single character or a small graphic object. A simple circular opening in the tip of the pen permits entrance of light from a cone-shaped region in space. This corresponds to a small circular area on the

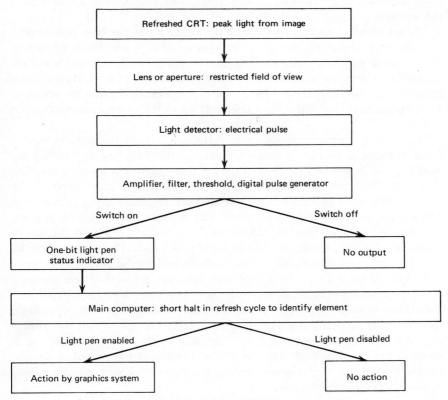

Figure 1.2. Block diagram of light pen operation.

screen if the pen is held perpendicular to and close to the screen. A lens system in the pen tip provides more definite control of the field of view, especially if the light pen is designed to be held at a distance from the phosphor screen. The operator is assisted in accurately aiming the pen from a distance by a finder beam, a small circle of light that is projected through the lens system from a source inside the pen. This circle defines the exact area on the screen that is viewed by the pen.

Light entering the pen reaches a high-speed light detector that reacts by generating an electrical pulse. Solid-state detectors of the phototransistor and the photodiode types are small enough to be located inside the pen itself and the resulting electrical pulse is carried by cable to the auxiliary electronics unit. Most display devices are compatible with solid-state detectors, but an extremely high-performance CRT requires the faster response that can be obtained with a photomultiplier tube. This vacuum tube is too bulky and delicate to be inside the pen, so it is located in the auxiliary unit instead. Light is carried to the tube by a fiber-optics conductor connecting the pen to the auxiliary unit.

The electronics unit contains several devices to refine the light pen output. The electrical signal originated by the light detector is amplified, filtered to eliminate the effects of room lighting, and compared to an adjustable voltage threshold to separate interference from the desired signal. A digital pulse generator responds to the leading edge of the electrical pulse by setting a 1-bit digital code that indicates a light pen *hit* to the graphics system's main computer.

The graphics system operator controls the light pen by turning a switch on for a moment to identify a single element in the image or by holding the switch in the on position for the duration of drawing or moving activities. The switch can be located on the body of the pen within easy reach of the operator's finger or in the tip of the pen so it can be turned on by pressing the pen against the CRT glass. The switch accomplishes its purpose by opening and closing a physical shutter that covers the opening in the tip of the pen or by electrical control inside the auxiliary electronics unit. The result is that the light pen produces output only when it is activated by the graphics operator.

A typical response time for a solid-state light pen is less than one-millionth of a second and a photomultiplier-tube light pen gives even faster feedback. This is important because correct interpretation of a light pen hit depends on the computer receiving the digital signal quickly enough to halt the display process so the specific element being refreshed by the electron beam at that moment can be identified. The identity of the element is passed to the appropriate part of the graphics program for action based on commands previously entered by the operator.

The display process is restarted following the brief halt for element identification and the entire image is refreshed many times per second until another halt occurs. The operator cannot possibly release the activator switch in time to prevent another hit on the same element. This problem is avoided automatically by a method of enabling and disabling the light pen under program control by the computer. No action is taken in response to a hit while the light pen is disabled. The way the enable/disable function is applied depends on whether the light pen is being used for an individual pointing action or a continuous drawing or moving action. The same enable/disable function that prevents erroneous repeated hits can also be used to make a displayed element invisible to the light pen. The operator can use graphics system commands to interactively set the visibility or invisibility of elements, and the system itself can make messages, grid guidelines, and similar elements invisible to the light pen. This control is accomplished by placing a disable code at the beginning of the element's display description in computer memory and placing an enable code at the end.

The light pen has both advantages and disadvantages in comparison to the other popular general-purpose input device, the tablet and cursor combination.

One important consideration is that the light pen is heavily dependent on software support for its useful operation as an interactive graphics input device. The light pen's primary pointing function depends on close coordination between hardware activity and the execution of the program that controls the display process. The tracking function is an extension of the pointing function made possible through elaborate programming.

The light pen has two unique properties. It is the only device that is primarily suited for pointing at graphic objects and it is the only device other than the touch panel that physically touches the screen surface. The advantage of these properties is the natural and direct way the operator can interact with the displayed image by pointing to an object as he looks at it. The disadvantage is that accurate aiming is difficult if the pen itself blocks the operator's view.

The resolution of a light pen is poor in comparison to the resolution of a tablet and cursor. This is the combined result of the light pen's relatively large field of view and the display screen's limited image sharpness. This lack of precision makes the light pen inappropriate for accurate sketching and it presents a problem when the light pen must discriminate among several tightly spaced elements in the image.

Light pen tracking is successful only when the operator moves the pen at an almost constant speed, because any abrupt motion will cause the pen to lose contact with the cross-hair image. The cross hair is displayed at the point where tracking terminated until the operator reestablishes contact by aiming the light pen at the cross-hair image and resumes tracking from there.

1.2. DIGITIZERS

A *digitizer* accurately measures the position of a point within a two-dimensional area and codes the measurement into *xy* coordinates, suitable for computer processing. The digitizer input device normally consists of two separate components, a stationary flat surface and a hand-held positioning tool. The flat surface is called a digitizer *tablet* when it is about the same size as a tablet of writing paper (usually 11×11 in.) and it is called a digitizer *board* or *table* when it is as large as a traditional drafting board (typical size 42×60 in.). The positioning tool is either a slender instrument with a sharp point for surface contact, which is known as a *stylus* or *pen*, or it is a flat, boxy object with a cross-hair sight, which is known as a *cursor* or *mouse*.

The word "cursor" expresses two different concepts in computer graphics terminology. A *cursor device* is a particular kind of digitizer positioning tool, whereas a *cursor symbol* is a small, special shape such as a cross or square that is displayed to indicate the currently active point within the design. The context in which the word is used normally makes the intended meaning clear. However, there is some potential for confusion since one of the most popular input techniques is the use of a cursor (device) to interactively control the position of the cursor (symbol) on the screen.

Figures 1.3 through 1.6 show typical variations of digitizer equipment. In addition to the range of sizes for the digitizing surface and the two basic types of positioning tools, many specialized equipment options are available to suit a wide range of applications. The flat surface is usually a durable, solid material, but a translucent material is also available. This option makes it possible to 'project a 35-mm slide photograph or a microfilm image on the back of the digitizer surface. The surface can also be backlighted to aid in entering data from an X-ray film or similar transparent media. Every positioning tool must have at least one switch or button to selectively activate the digitizing process, but some cursors have as many as twelve additional buttons to enter numeric data or program commands. Alternatively, a detached alphanumeric keyboard may be used as a digitizer accessory.

A digitizer is a versatile input device that enables the operator to exercise control over the interactive graphics system. Some prevalent digitizer uses include moving the cursor symbol on the screen to interact with existing elements in the image or to add new elements; entering system commands or nongraphic data through a tablet menu; and converting an existing pictorial document, such as a map, engineering drawing, or photograph, into computer data. A pencil line is 0.005 inch wide, so precise tracing work requires a high-resolution digitizer and adequate lighting to enable the operator's eyes to accurately discern a line of this thickness. The hand–eye coordination needed to control the cursor symbol with a digitizer is easy to learn and quickly mastered.

Certain operational features are common to all digitizers regardless of the details of their construction. First, a digitizer measures the absolute location of a point in relation to the permanent frame of reference provided by the flat surface, in contrast to devices such as the joystick, which measure changes in location. Second, the output produced for each point is a pair of *xy* coordinates measured in the units of resolution of the digitizer. Resolution is generally within the range of 100 to 1000 units per inch on the flat surface. Third, the point coordinates expressed in digitizer units can easily be converted by the computer to any unit of measure that is meaningful for the application, such as miles on an aerial photograph or map. The operator sets up the conversion factors at the beginning of digitizer operation and thus creates a well-defined relationship between the digitizer surface and the design area in the computer data base. Fourth, the digitizer surface does not have any fixed relationship to the image area on the screen. It is generally impractical to install a transparent digitizer over the screen because of this absence of any natural association between the two devices. Fifth, a digitizer can be successfully operated in either the *on-line* or *off-line* mode. The immediate visual feedback provided through on-line operation of a digitizer with a graphics system is essential in creative design applications. Off-line operation is widely accepted as a cost-effective method of extracting a large volume of data from a pictorial document for input to strictly numeric calculations or for later editing with an interactive graphics system.

The details of construction for five major subsets within the broadly defined set of digitizer input devices are discussed in Sections 1.2.1 through 1.2.5. These subsets are identified (according to their method for measuring position) as electromagnetic, touch-sensitive, sonic, incremental, and light-detector digitizers.

1.2.1. Electromagnetic Digitizers

The majority of commercially available digitizers are based on the principle of an electric or magnetic field that is generated through one component and detected through the other component. The two components are the flat surface and the positioning tool, a pen or cursor. An electronic control unit originates the field-producing signal and interprets the feedback signal to determine location. The most frequently seen implementation is a flat sur-

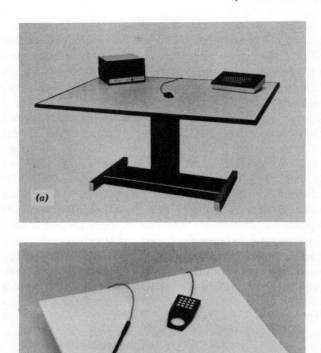

Figure 1.3.   Electromagnetic digitizers. (a) Table. (b) Tablet. Courtesy of GTCO Corporation.

face consisting of a protective covering over a finely spaced grid made with many tiny, taut wires or a printed circuit board. For example, an 11-inch square surface with a high resolution of 0.001 inch requires a grid of 11,000 × 11,000 crisscrossing conductors. The control unit applies digitally coded pulses to the conductors. The pen picks up the pulses from the horizontal and vertical conductors closest to it and transmits them by wire to the control unit, where they are decoded to uniquely determine the pen's location. Generally, all conductors in the entire surface are pulsed in sequence. A variation by one manufacturer limits the area that is active at any given time to a 1-inch square surrounding the pen. An electronic feedback system ensures that the active area surrounds the pen position at all times.

Another approach to measuring position with an electromagnetic field is to replace the grid with a single coil located under the digitizer surface. This coil is attached to a mechanical gantry that is moved by two electric motors operating under the control of a feedback system. The pen detects the field generated by the coil and returns a signal to the digitizer control unit, which uses this signal to measure the pen's location. The feedback system uses this location information to make the coil continuously follow the pen's movements. The location measurement is also available as input data for the graphics system.

1.2.2. Touch-Sensitive Digitizers

Several commercially available digitizers utilize an ordinary pen or pencil in conjunction with a touch-sensitive digitizer surface. The surface senses pen movements as resistive xy analog values that the control unit converts to digital xy coordinates. The surface is insensitive to the less intense pressure caused by a book or an arm resting on the digitizer surface. One benefit gained with this type of construction is that the pen is completely free to move without an attached wire. Another benefit is that the visible marks put on the source document serve as a permanent record of the digitized information.

1.2.3. Sonic Digitizers

Sound impulses, generated by an electric spark at the point of the pen and detected by two microphone sensors on the tablet, are used by the sonic

Figure 1.4.   Touch-sensitive digitizer. Courtesy of Elographics, Inc.

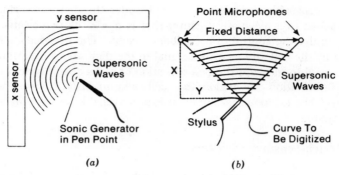

Figure 1.5. Sonic digitizers. (a) Microphone strips. (b) Point microphones. Courtesy of Science Accessories Corporation.

digitizer to determine the location of a point. The time intervals required for the sound to reach each of the two microphones are converted into distance measurements that yield the *xy* coordinates of the pen tip. There are two types of microphone equipment. The L-shaped configuration consists of two microphone bars joined at right angles. Each bar contains many tiny microphone elements mounted inside a protective metal strip. The sound emitted by the pen is picked up first by the microphone element on each bar that is nearest the pen's location. The calculation of the coordinates of that point is straightforward because one bar functions as an *x*-axis sensor and the other as a *y*-axis sensor. Since sound waves travel freely through the air in all directions from the pen point, a three-dimensional sonic digitizer is built by mounting a third microphone bar in the *z*-axis direction perpendicular to the two-dimensional digitizer surface.

The alternative type of equipment consists of two point microphones mounted at opposite ends of a straight metal bar. Again, the length of time between generation of the sound and detection by each microphone is converted into a measurement of the distance of the pen from each microphone. These distances are then mathematically converted into the *xy* coordinates of the point.

Either type of microphone apparatus can be placed on any convenient flat surface, such as a table, desk, drafting board, projection screen, or CRT screen. A variety of sound-generating pens and cursors are available, including a pen with a nonscratching plastic tip for use on a CRT screen. A sonic digitizer is not affected by a reasonable level of background noise. The only necessary precaution is to keep the path of the sound waves from being blocked by hands, arms, books, or any other object placed between the pen and the microphones.

1.2.4. Incremental Digitizers

The incremental digitizer, an older type of construction, is now primarily limited to use in conjunction with specialized measuring instruments such as stereoplotters as a means of automatically recording measurements, although it was once an important input device for computer graphics.

An incremental digitizer incorporates a rotary or linear encoder that uses mechanical, optical, magnetic, or brush-contact means to generate a distance-increment count that corresponds to the total distance traveled by the positioning tool across the digitizer surface. The resolution of an encoder can be as high as 0.001 inch, which means that the encoder counts 1000 increments per inch of distance. Independent measurements of the distances along the xy direction components are made by two encoders to determine both the distance and direction of positioning tool movement. An incremental digitizer is similar to a joystick, trackball, and dial in that it supplies information on distance and direction rather than absolute position.

One way to establish a frame of reference that can determine absolute position is to mount the encoders on the arms of a rigid brace affixed to the digitizer surface. The two encoders are linked to a cursor so they are activated when it is moved up or down and right or left. The cursor itself just provides a cross hair for visual alignment with the input point.

An incremental digitizer with a different approach is the Stanford Research Institute *mouse* [1]. The mouse is a hand-held device capable of rolling freely over any flat surface. It is attached by wire to an electronics unit. The two wheels mounted underneath the mouse are linked to two rotary encoders that count the increments of revolution for each wheel as the mouse rolls. This input device is not satisfactory for most digitizer applications because the two wheels are not constrained to motion parallel to the x and y directions. Also, it is impossible to determine absolute position with the mouse because it can be lifted from the surface and put down at any new location.

1.2.5. Light-Detector Digitizers

Touch panel and *touch input system* are the names utilized by the manufacturers for a type of digitizer that operates through light detection. The equipment physically resembles a picture frame. The open space in the middle is the active digitizer area, while the optical devices and associated electronics are mounted on the flat frame. A number of tiny light-emitting diodes (LEDs) are installed along one horizontal and one vertical edge of the frame. Light detectors are attached to the other two edges opposite the LEDs. The

Figure 1.6. Touch panel (light-detector digitizer). Reprinted with permission Magnavox Government and Industrial Electronics Company.

matrix of infrared light beams created by the LEDs is interrupted when the graphics operator places his finger or an ordinary pen on the active digitizer area. The photodetectors signal this interruption to the digitizer's electronic logic, which generates the coordinates of the touched point. The resolution of currently available touch panels is about 0.25 inch, a value that is extremely poor compared to those for other digitizers, but that is more than adequate for many input techniques, including option selection from a screen menu.

The touch panel is marketed mainly as an accessory for a plasma panel display (see Section 2.6). The frame holding the optical and electronic equipment is installed around the plasma panel so that the matrix of light beams is projected directly above the surface of the screen. The operator interacts with the graphics system by simply touching points of interest on the displayed image. This direct, intuitive method of communication is ideal for applications such as computer-aided education, where the users are not trained operators.

The feasibility of measuring three-dimensional position through a light-detector method has been demonstrated with a research project called the *twinkle box* [1]. The active digitizer space is an enclosure surrounded by four walls with a light-detector assembly mounted on each wall. A light-emitting stylus is used as the positioning tool. The *xyz* coordinates describing the location of the stylus tip are computed from the vertical and horizontal angular displacements measured by the detector apparatus.

1.3. JOYSTICKS, TRACKBALLS, AND DIALS

Joysticks, trackballs, and dials constitute one popular category of interactive graphics input devices. Used mainly for cursor-symbol control in lieu of a light pen, these devices can also fill other roles when included in a multiple-device graphics terminal.

Devices in this category fulfill the cursor-control function by dictating the movement of the cursor on the screen rather than by setting its position with absolute coordinates as is done by a digitizer. A joystick enables the graphics operator to indicate the direction, speed, and duration of the motion, while a trackball or pair of dials allows him to enter the direction and distance of movement. Cursor motion stops immediately when the operator removes his hand from the input device although there is no on/off switch and the device remains ready for use at all times. All cursor movements are accumulated by the graphics program so the coordinates of the cursor location are always available within the computer. The accuracy of the resulting cursor position is limited because changes in cursor position due to this type of input device are measured in units of resolution on the screen, not in the units of measurement defined for the graphics application data base. A typical screen has roughly 1000×1000 units of resolution.

Members of this category are also used as auxiliary input devices to change the scale of a displayed object by lengthening or shortening it, to alter the color of an object, or to continuously vary the value of any mathematical quantity involved in a specific graphics application.

Each input device in this group has two components, a handle and a sensor. The sensor passes input data in the form of an analog signal or an incremental count to a detached electronic control unit that converts the data into a suitable digital format and transmits them to the graphics system computer. The names "joystick," "trackball," and "dial" refer to the different kinds of handles (Figure 1.7). At least four types of sensors can be combined with these handles to construct a practical input device.

A *joystick* is a shaft approximately 1 to 4 inches in height that is vertically mounted in a base. It can be pulled or pushed with the fingers in any arbitrary direction made up of forward–backward and right–left components. The joystick is the fastest and least accurate cursor-control device in this category, since typically it can move the cursor across the full width of the screen in 1 second. There are three commonly used joystick–sensor combinations. The most popular and economical type for interactive graphics is the *displacement joystick*. The operator tilts this joystick in the desired direction by as much as a 30-degree angle from its upright position. Speed of cursor

Figure 1.7. Input devices. (a) Joystick. (b) Trackball. (c) Dial. Photographs courtesy of Measurement Systems, Inc., Norwalk, Connecticut.

movement is proportional to the magnitude of the angle. The typical displacement joystick has an automatic spring-return feature so that it returns to vertical when the operator releases it. The joystick naturally moves in any direction with equal ease for free-form control, but it can be equipped with mechanical detents that guide the stick along x-axis and y-axis lines unless slightly more finger pressure is applied. Data related to a third dimension can be entered through an optional rotating knob mounted on the top of the joystick. A potentiometer (variable resistor) mechanism is the sensor in a

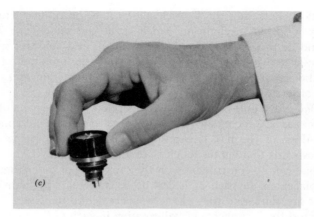

(c)

Figure 1.7.   Continued

displacement joystick. The potentiometer sensor describes the angle of the joystick by measuring the angular displacement in the four component directions (forward, backward, right, left) and generating four analog signals. A total of six analog signals are generated by a three-dimensional joystick.

A *force-operated joystick* provides extremely fast response and greater accuracy than other types. It is also known as an *isometric joystick* because the handle feels stiff and there is no noticeable deflection, although the joystick does cause the cursor to move in response to pressure from the operator's fingers. Releasing pressure immediately stops the cursor. One advantage of the force-operated joystick is that momentary bumps against the handle move the cursor one unit of resolution at a time for precise positioning. Cursor speed during normal operation is directly proportional to the force applied to the joystick. There is a wide range of responsiveness from the minimum finger pressure required to initiate cursor movement to the pressure that causes maximum cursor speed. The force-operated sensor generates two analog voltages that correspond to the amount of force applied to the joystick in the x-axis and y-axis component directions. A hand grip mounted across the top of the stick enables the operator to control a third dimension by exerting a torque on the joystick. An additional analog voltage is generated to indicate this twisting force.

The *switch-activated joystick* is a third type of construction, but it is rarely used for interactive graphics. The base of the joystick is connected to as many as eight switches, corresponding to directions along eight points of the compass. Other arbitrary directions cannot be measured by the switch-type sensor. Tilting the joystick in any direction causes the switch closest to that direction to be turned on and to remain on as long as the joystick stays in the tilted position. Releasing the joystick allows it to be returned to a vertical position by a spring mechanism, which turns the switch off. A graphics system could be programmed to move the cursor at a constant speed in the direction indicated by the activated switch, but the limitation of motion to eight directions severely restricts the freedom of interaction that is the main advantage of joystick control.

A *trackball* is a simple rotating sphere operated with the palm of the hand. This device has a 3-inch ball mounted on rollers inside a cabinet so that about one-third of the ball is exposed through the top of the cabinet. A trackball responds to a lighter touch than a joystick.

A trackball can be constructed with the same type of potentiometer sensor as the displacement joystick or it can be constructed with four optical encoders that are similar to the sensors in incremental digitizers. The optical encoders count the increments of ball rotation in each of the four component directions and generate four streams of data-carrying pulses. Associated electronic circuits convert the pulse streams into digital data indicating distance and direction of trackball rotation. The distance that the cursor moves on the screen is directly proportional to the number of revolutions of the ball, while the direction of cursor motion corresponds to the direction of rotation. The ratio of cursor distance to trackball rotation can be adjusted to suit the graphics application and the preference of the operator. The cursor can be moved across the screen with as little as three revolutions for normal usage or as many as 300 revolutions for ultrafine control. Higher precision results in slower operation because the operator must physically turn the ball more revolutions. The accuracy of cursor control with the trackball, as with the joystick, is limited by the resolution of the display. Nevertheless, the trackball is generally preferred over the joystick for highly accurate positioning or for pointing to an object in a dense display area because the operator can perform more gradual movement.

A *dial* is a one-axis cursor-control device. The handle is usually an ordinary rotating knob, but it can take other forms, such as a lever that moves back and forth. A dial with a potentiometer sensor operates like a single-axis joystick. Turning the knob clockwise moves the cursor in one direction, turning it counterclockwise moves the cursor in exactly the opposite direction, and releasing it stops the cursor. A spring return brings the knob back to its center position automatically upon release. Cursor speed is proportional to the degree of knob rotation away from the center position. A more popular kind of dial is a simple knob that rotates continuously in either direction to activate a mechanical or optical encoder that counts the increments of revolution. Counting halts when the knob is released and the knob simply sits still. The distance traveled by the cursor depends on how many degrees the knob is turned.

Effective cursor control can be provided by two dials, one for motion along the x-axis and the other for motion along the y-axis. One widely used configuration consists of two dials mounted at right angles to each other on the side of a graphics terminal keyboard (Figure 1.8). These dials are referred to as *thumb wheels* because the toothed edge of each dial is easily rotated by the operator's thumb. Thumb wheels are ideal for easy and accurate cursor movement along straight lines, but are much less useful than a joystick or trackball for motion in a diagonal direction or along a curved path.

1.4. KEYBOARDS, BUTTONS, AND SWITCHES

Keyboards, buttons, and switches are a group of important input devices that are available in a variety of configurations to suit different purposes. Almost all graphics terminals incorporate a full alphanumeric keyboard as a standard feature (Figure 1.9). Some early graphics systems utilized the keyboard as the sole input device through positioning by typing the numeric coordinates of each point and selecting a displayed object by typing its name. However, these keyboard techniques do not promote man–machine cooperation, so other input devices have supplanted the keyboard for positioning and selecting. The alphanumeric keyboard is generally the most efficient method

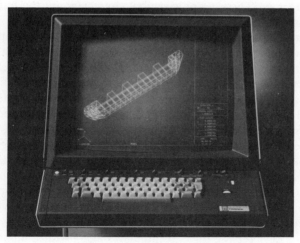

Figure 1.8. Thumb wheels on graphics terminal (to the right of the keyboard). Upper wheel is for vertical cursor control; lower wheel is for horizontal cursor control. Courtesy of Tektronix, Inc.

Figure 1.9. Keyboard with alphanumeric characters (center), program function keys (top two rows), cursor control keys (top right), and number pad (bottom right). Courtesy of Aydin Controls.

for entering nongraphic data into the graphics system data base. Therefore, the keyboard is an essential input device since the great majority of practical applications involve graphic objects that have associated nongraphic data such as part numbers, material specifications, and explanatory notations.

The shift key on a typewriter is used to choose between lowercase and uppercase letters, but on a keyboard input device it can be utilized instead to select between an alphabet of uppercase letters only and a set of graphic-symbol characters. These graphic-symbol characters are the building blocks for the creation of pictures in some limited graphics systems.

A keyboard input device should have the same size key caps, the same spacing between keys, and the same key-response feeling as a standard electric typewriter so that a graphics operator who is trained in touch-typing can get full benefit from his skill. A keyboard that is smaller or less well constructed than the standard is difficult for a person with large hands to operate and it is not rugged enough to be reliable when subjected to constant use. Automatic repeat mode is an optional keyboard feature that can be handy, especially to speed up the creation of a graphic design built with graphic-symbol characters. Generation of repeated characters at the rate of about ten per second begins when any key stays down for a short time after the initial strike and continues for as long as the key remains down.

A configuration that is extremely useful for entering a large volume of all-numeric data is the twelve-key numeric pad that contains a rectangular arrangement of keys for the digits 0 through 9 along with a minus sign and a decimal point. It can be an independent input device or it can be placed on the extreme right-hand side of a full keyboard to supplement or replace the typewriter arrangement of digits across the top row.

Many graphics terminal keyboards have a set of five special keys for cursor control. Pressing one of these keys causes the cursor to move up or down in a vertical column or left to right in a horizontal row, as indicated by the direction of the arrow on the top of the key. The cursor moves diagonally if two keys for perpendicular directions are pressed simultaneously. The cursor changes position by stepping one space at a time for as long as the key is depressed. A single strike of the center key marked "home" causes the cursor to immediately return to a programmed origin position. Stepping movement is relatively slow because the cursor requires 8 seconds to go from one edge of the screen to the other at a typical rate of ten spaces per second on a screen that is eighty spaces wide. Key-controlled cursor movement is satisfactory only for a graphics system in which a single alphanumeric character or a graphic-symbol character of equivalent size is the smallest unit of resolution on the screen that the operator can manipulate. The cursor symbol in such a system is usually a block occupying a one-character area.

A graphics system can be controlled by typing command statements on a standard keyboard, but program function keys offer a faster way to give commands to the system with fewer errors because a single key stroke enters a complete command statement. A typical program function keyboard contains sixteen or thirty-two keys mounted on a self-contained console (Figure 1.10). Alternatively, a single button or a small group of buttons can be mounted on some other input device such as a digitizer where they will be more accessible for frequently used program-command operations (Figure 1.11).

"Key" and "button" are synonymous names that apply to a special type of

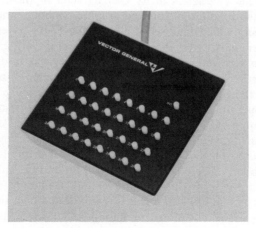

Figure 1.10. Program function keyboard with lamps. Courtesy of Vector General.

Figure 1.11.   Cursor with twelve extra buttons. Courtesy of Summagraphics Corporation.

momentary switch that rebounds after being depressed. The term "switch" is generally used in computer graphics terminology to mean an input device that remains in one of two possible positions until changed by the operator. A message is sent to the computer when a key is pressed or a switch is reversed. This message indicates the fact that data entry has occurred and it contains a code to identify the specific key or switch responsible for that entry. A keyboard that is specifically designed for entering alphanumeric data generates messages utilizing one of several standard codes, such as the American National Standard Code for Information Interchange (ASCII). ASCII uses an 8-bit code to represent the letters, numbers, punctuation marks, and special characters in its 128-character alphabet. In contrast, a keyboard designed to enter customized graphic-symbol characters can be set up to generate any selected subset of all possible 17-bit codes.

The computer must give the graphics operator verification that each character code is received correctly. The customary way to do this is to echo each alphanumeric character by adding it to a character string displayed in a special area on the screen. The graphics system does not process the input data until the operator has entered a meaningful string, visually checked it, and indicated approval by pressing a control key labeled "enter." Program function keys can provide independent feedback if each key is made out of translucent, colored plastic with a lamp inside or if a tiny lamp is mounted adjacent to each key. These lamps are turned on and off individually by the computer in response to the input data received. Generally, a program function is activated by one key strike and is discontinued by a subsequent strike of the same key. The advantage of illuminated keys is that the graphics operator can quickly determine which program functions are currently active by looking at the keyboard itself rather than tediously deciphering messages on a display screen.

1.5. VOICE DATA ENTRY SYSTEMS

Voice data entry (VDE) enables the graphics operator to input design information or system commands using speech, the most natural human communications method. Speech recognition equipment can replace or supplement graphics input devices such as an alphanumeric keyboard, a set of program function keys, and a tablet menu. VDE is most useful in interactive graphics applications where the data are captured or created by a single person and then entered into the computer. Figure 1.12 shows a graphics operator utilizing VDE equipment to give system commands and to add numeric information in conjunction with positional information entered through a large digitizer. This equipment results in more efficiency and fewer errors because the eyes of the user can remain on the source document while his or her hands are on the cursor. Any other method would force this operator to continually switch his or her attention between the data source and the input device.

The graphics operator makes an utterance that the VDE system recognizes as belonging to a predefined vocabulary. The matching input data for that

Figure 1.12. Graphics operator using voice data entry in conjunction with a digitizer table. Photograph courtesy of Interstate Electronics Corporation, Anaheim, California.

vocabulary item are returned to the operator as alphanumeric characters on a visual display. The operator speaks a code word such as "go" to signal that the result is correct, or "cancel" to indicate that it is incorrect. The VDE unit transmits the verified input to the computer system as characters in exactly the same way a keyboard transmits when the "enter" key is pressed. The recognition process depends on the comparison of each utterance to words appearing in a stored vocabulary table. This vocabulary table is created or modified by using the VDE equipment along with a keyboard input device. A graphics system command or data item is typed and then the related spoken word is repeated ten times by the operator. A pattern classifier within the system uses these ten repetitions to determine the characteristics of the word and transform it into a pattern in 240- or 512-bit format, depending on the system design. The resulting patterns are stored in a vocabulary table that has a length limit varying from 32 to 900 items depending on the pattern format and the capacity of the speech recognition microcomputer. Mass storage such as tape cassettes or a disk unit can be used to store multiple tables containing different items for use by a single operator or several different tables containing the same items for multiple operators. The appropriate vocabulary table is loaded into the microcomputer at the beginning of each graphics design session.

Figure 1.13 is a block diagram of the VDE equipment. Each user station consists of a headset microphone designed to minimize stray noise pickup, a small control console, and a visual display. The display may be a small alphanumeric LED device with the capacity for sixteen to thirty-two characters or it may simply be a character string appearing on an alphanumeric or graphics CRT that belongs to the graphics system. One or more user stations are connected to an interface unit that converts the analog signal from the microphone into digital format and sends the raw data to the speech recognition processor. The processor is a general-purpose microcomputer running the program that creates and matches the digital word patterns. The results are transmitted from the microcomputer to the main computer supporting the graphics application.

VDE systems have been in use since 1975 for applications other than graphics and are now marketed as an optional part of graphics systems by at least one major turnkey vendor, Synercom Technology.

VENDOR LIST

Information provided by these companies was used in the preparation of Chapter 1. This is not intended to be a complete list of all suppliers.

Typical Configuration

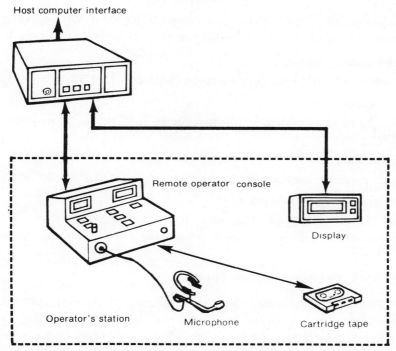

Figure 1.13. Block diagram of voice data entry equipment. Courtesy of Threshold Technology, Inc.

LIGHT PENS

Information Control Corporation, 9610 Bellanca Avenue, Los Angeles, CA 90045 (213) 641-8520

Sanders Associates, Inc., Daniel Webster Highway South, Nashua, NH 03061 (603) 885-5280

DIGITIZERS

Electromagnetic Digitizers

Altek Corporation, 2150 Industrial Parkway, Silver Spring, MD 20904 (301) 622-3906

GTCO Corporation, 1055 First Street, Rockville, MD 20850, (301) 279-9550

Houston Instrument, One Houston Square, Austin, TX 78753 (512) 837-2820

Instronics Inc., Suite 204, Bridge Plaza, Ogdensburg, NY 13669 (315) 393-7550

Summagraphics Corporation, 35 Brentwood Avenue, Fairfield, CT 06430 (203) 384-1344

Talos Systems, Inc., 7419 E. Helm Drive, Scottsdale, AZ 85260 (602) 948-6540

Tektronix, Inc., P.O. Box 500, Beaverton, OR 97077 (503) 638-3411

Touch Sensitive Digitizers

Elographics, Inc., 1976 Oak Ridge Turnpike, Oak Ridge, TN 37830 (615) 482-4038

Sonic Digitizers

Science Accessories Corporation, 970 Kings Highway West, Southport, CT 06490 (203) 255-1526

Incremental Digitizers

Altek Corporation, 2150 Industrial Parkway, Silver Spring, MD 20904 (301) 622-3906

Light Detector Digitizers (Touch Panels)

Carroll Mfg. Co., 1212 Hagan, Champaign, IL 61820 (217) 352-5438

Magnavox Display Systems, 2131 South Coliseum Boulevard, Fort Wayne, IN 46803 (219) 482-4411

JOYSTICKS, TRACKBALLS, AND DIALS

Aydin Controls, 414 Commerce Drive, Fort Washington, PA 19034 (215) 542-7800

Genisco Computers, 17805-D Sky Park Circle Drive, Irvine, CA 92714 (714) 556-4916

Measurement Systems, Inc., 121 Water Street, Norwalk, CT 06854 (203) 838-5561

Megatek Corporation, 1055 Shafter Street, San Diego, CA 92106 (714) 224-2721

Sanders Associates, Inc., Daniel Webster Highway South, Nashua, NH 03061 (603) 885-5280

Tektronix, Inc., P.O. Box 500, Beaverton, OR 97077 (503) 638-3411

KEYBOARDS, BUTTONS, AND SWITCHES

Aydin Controls, 414 Commerce Drive, Fort Washington, PA 19034 (215) 542-7800

Genisco Computers, 17805-D Sky Park Circle Drive, Irvine, CA 92714 (714) 556-4916

Sanders Associates, Inc., Daniel Webster Highway South, Nashua, NH 03061 (603) 885-5280

Tektronix, Inc., P.O. Box 500, Beaverton, OR 97077 (503) 638-3411

Vector General, 21300 Oxnard Street, Woodland Hills, CA 91364 (213) 346-3410

VOICE DATA ENTRY SYSTEMS

Interstate Electronics Corporation, P.O. Box 3117, Anaheim, CA 92803 (714) 635-7210

Threshold Technology Inc., 1829 Underwood Boulevard, Delran, NJ 08075 (609) 461-9200

CHAPTER 2

Interactive Display Devices

The display screen is the most prominent piece of equipment in a graphics system because the system's most dramatic result is the computer-generated picture. In fact, a system cannot be described as interactive unless it responds to the operator's actions with immediate visual feedback.

The two major approaches to generating an image are stroke-writing and raster. A stroke-writing device draws lines to create an image, while a raster device uses an array of closely spaced dots to form a picture. A portion of this chapter is devoted to each of these two methods, explaining the characteristics of the hardware, the basic operations involved in producing the image, and the format of the data transferred from the computer to the display device.

Regardless of whether a device uses the stroke-writing or raster method, it can maintain a display for prolonged viewing by two different means. A refreshed tube continuously regenerates the image, whereas a storage tube physically retains the picture until it is erased. The design of software for a graphics system depends on whether a storage or refreshed display is utilized. Also, the capabilities of the display method influence the way a user interacts with the computer. Information concerning storage and refreshed displays is presented throughout this chapter.

2.1. STROKE-WRITING SCREENS

A draftsman produces even the most complex picture by drawing one line at a time. A stroke-writing CRT displays a picture in the same manner by drawing individual lines having any length and oriented at any angle and by drawing alphanumeric characters as collections of short lines. A stroke-writing display can be identified by any of several synonymous adjectives, such as *calligraphic, vector, xyz,* and *random scan.* The stroke-writing display device has an associated electronic unit known as a *vector generator.* To draw a line, the endpoint coordinates are supplied by the computer to the vector generator, which converts them into the *xy* analog voltages that drive the deflection system in the CRT. These voltages control the direction of the electron beam, causing it to trace a path on the phosphor screen that corresponds to the position of the line in the image. Most display systems also include character generators, circle generators, and so forth.

Stroke-writing screens are commonly divided into two types, *storage* and *refreshed* displays. The difference in the two types is not how the image is drawn on the screen, but how it is maintained for viewing over an extended period of time. *Persistence* is the length of time that a phosphor continues to produce light after it is excited by the CRT electron beam. A long-persistence phosphor in a storage tube holds the visible image for as long as an hour after a single trace. The image on a refreshed display is maintained through repeated excitation of a short-persistence phosphor by a continuous, regular tracing cycle. Each line in the display must be retained until it is drawn again on the next cycle, typically $1/30$ to $1/60$ second later, but it is not retained any longer. The operator of the graphics terminal will see the image *flicker* if the picture is not refreshed frequently enough to match the persistence of the phosphor, but he will see *ghosts* of the old image along with the new image if the persistence is too long compared to the refresh rate. At least one supplier (Hewlett-Packard) offers a *variable persistence tube* that enables the graphics operator to adjust the duration of light production to match the refresh rate for a particular application and allows him to switch the tube to operation as a storage display. This variable persistence is achieved by varying the strength of the electron beam.

The phosphor in a storage tube must be excited by a voltage that exceeds a certain threshold value for the long-persistence image to occur. The phosphor has short persistence when excited by a low-intensity beam. This characteristic makes it possible for a storage tube to display a *refreshed cursor*, a cross-hair symbol that moves in response to actions by the graphics operator, as well as a modest amount of other refreshed lines.

2.2. STORAGE DISPLAYS USING STROKE-WRITING SCREENS

The *direct-view storage tube* was introduced as an oscilloscope screen by Tektronix, Inc., in 1962. Since then this display device has become so popular in computer graphics that now it is an unofficial industry standard.

The storage tube is frequently mentioned in advertisements for other display devices to compare performance features or to emphasize compatibility of new displays with existing applications.

A storage device is constructed with all the usual CRT components plus a secondary cathode located between the electron gun and the screen (Figure 2.1). The primary electron gun produces the *writing beam* that strokes the graphic pattern on the phosphor screen. The secondary cathode continuously emits a diffuse stream of low-energy electrons, known as the *flood beam*, that causes the stored pattern on the screen to glow. To erase the stored pattern, the energy of the flood beam is raised high enough to cause the entire screen to reach storage excitation, and then the voltage applied to the screen is reduced to zero to allow the phosphors to return to normal. A complete erasure takes about 1 second. Selective erasure of unwanted portions of the image without disturbing the rest of the display is impossible.

The resolution of a storage tube (up to 4000 × 3000 displayable points on a 19-inch diagonal screen) meets or exceeds the resolution of any other type of display device. The drawing speed of a storage tube writing beam is relatively slow (5000 inches per second), but this is not significant since the patience of the operator is the only limitation on the total amount of information displayed. In contrast, a refreshed display is limited to the informaton that can be stroked within a single refresh cycle. The storage tube's image consists of points and lines all displayed with the same intensity in a single color, so the only way to add emphasis is to use lines of various thicknesses. The line width is controlled by the graphics program, which directs the CRT to stroke two or more adjacent lines to represent a single vector. The storage tube is bright enough for viewing under subdued lighting, although it is not nearly as bright as a refreshed screen, either the stroke-writing or raster type.

The use of a storage display involves two basic functions. First, the image of each graphic object added to the design by the operator is immediately stroked by the CRT as an addition to the existing image on the screen. Second, when the graphics operator makes any change in the design other than a simple addition or he selects a different view of the design, the screen area is completely erased and the CRT makes one trace of the entire new image to

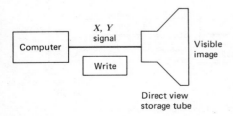

Figure 2.1. Direct view storage tube operation.

update the display. Both of these functions are initiated by some operator action, so the storage screen is dormant while the computer system is waiting for the operator's next action. A storage-screen graphics system can be designed for a low rate of data transfer from the computer to the terminal. This means that several terminals can be supported by one minicomputer, that the terminal does not need a microprocessor or memory device, and that relatively slow communications lines can transmit the data to terminals located away from the computer. Therefore, the investment in system hardware is minimized. However, a configuration based on the low average demand is inadequate when a large amount of data must be supplied to the terminal as quickly as possible for an update. The operator is forced to wait several seconds or more while the new picture is drawn line by line on the screen.

An *electrostatic storage tube* is a CRT that uses the stroke-writing method to create an electron charge pattern on a screen made of silicon–silicon oxide material. A scanner reads the stored pattern and transforms it into a video signal, and then the video signal drives a refreshed raster CRT to produce a visible image. The electrostatic storage tube involves a more complicated set of equipment (Figure 2.2) than the direct-view storage tube, but the visible image it produces on the video display is much brighter. Also, the electrostatic storage tube has selective erase capability and produces up to 32 different intensity levels.

2.3. REFRESHED DISPLAYS USING STROKE-WRITING SCREENS

A refreshed display is a necessity for simulated motion applications such as cartoon animation and scientific studies in chemistry, physics, and engineering. A refreshed display can provide dynamic viewing capabilities for a three-dimensional computer model of a complicated object. Any task that involves extensive interaction between a human and a computer is facilitated by the

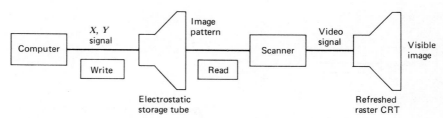

Figure 2.2. Electrostatic storage tube operation.

fast response of a refreshed display system, either the stroke-writing or raster type.

A stroke-writing refreshed display system is shown as a block diagram in Figure 2.3. It operates in the following manner. The interactive graphics system builds a data base that contains a complete description of the model and a display file that holds the current view of the model. The display file is placed in *refresh memory*, a storage area in either the main computer or the graphics terminal. The display processor reads the contents of refresh memory and sends instructions to the vector and circle generators, which convert geometric descriptions into the xy analog voltages to control the deflection of the electron beam. The entire image is stroked during each refresh cycle. A refreshed display does not have an erase operation; instead, the interactive graphics system changes the image by replacing the contents of the display file.

The length of time required for the CRT to trace all the lines in an image depends on the moving speed and drawing speed of the beam and on the complexity of the image. A refreshed CRT generates strokes much faster than a storage tube so beam speeds such as 600,000 inches per second for drawing and 1,000,000 inches per second for moving are achieved. The maximum image complexity is determined by a trade-off between the number of individual vectors and the total length of all vectors. One long line can be drawn much more quickly than several short lines with the equivalent total length. Circles and other curves are time-consuming because they are displayed as approximations composed of short lines or even dots. Alphanumeric characters are also composed of many short strokes. For example, a display system with a 30 cycle per second refresh rate that is capable of stroking 30,000 total inches of long vectors can only stroke 5000 1-inch vectors and can generate only 3000 characters.

A display with a *free-running refresh rate* simply strokes the entire image and then immediately begins to stroke it again. The length of time required for a refresh cycle is directly dependent on the complexity of the image. The display flickers if the refresh cycle is too long, thereby limiting the amount of information that can be presented.

Most displays have a *fixed refresh rate* such as 30 or 60 cycles per second. This rate is matched to the phosphor persistence so flicker cannot occur. The refresh cycle can be controlled by an internal timing device or by coupling it to the phase of the electric current supply. The amount of information that can appear on the screen is limited to the lines that the CRT can trace during the time allotted for one refresh cycle. It is possible for the display processor to miss the last part of an excessively long display file because it returns to the start of the file at the beginning of each refresh cycle.

A refreshed, stroke-writing CRT is comparable to a raster screen in image

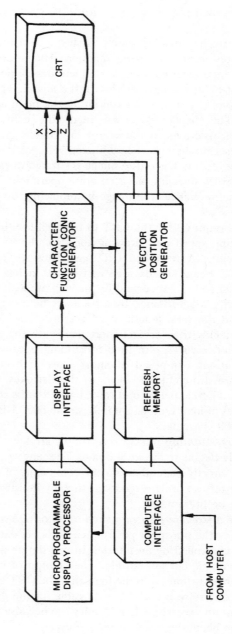

Figure 2.3. Block diagram of a refreshed stroke-writing tube system. Courtesy of Aydin Controls.

32

brightness and is superior to it in image resolution, with up to 4000 × 4000 displayable points compared to the maximum raster array of 1000 × 1000. A monochrome monitor can display lines of various brightness levels through control of the electron beam voltage.

The *beam penetration* method is used to produce multicolor stroke-writing displays. This type of CRT has a single electron gun and a screen that is coated with layers of two or more different phosphors separated by a thin layer of dielectric. The color of each vector in the image depends on the velocity of the beam when that vector is stroked. Figure 2.4 is a block diagram of a beam penetration display system. In a typical system, a screen with two phosphors (red and green) produces a display consisting of four different colors (red, orange, yellow, and green). The digital-to-analog convertor receives a description of each vector that includes a color code (2 binary digits) along with the endpoint coordinates. The color code indicates one of four different steps in anode voltage. The anode voltage determines the velocity of the beam produced by the electron gun. At the lowest velocity, the beam penetrates only the first layer and that phosphor emits light of a characteristic red color. At the next higher velocity, the beam partially penetrates the second layer and some green light is mixed with the red to produce an orange appearance. The third next higher velocity produces yellow light. The highest velocity causes the beam to fully penetrate to the second layer and its green color predominates since the efficiency of the green phosphor is much higher than that of the red.

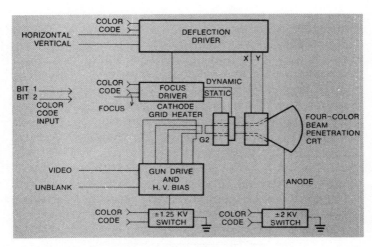

Figure 2.4. Four-color beam penetration CRT operation. Courtesy of CPS, Inc.

2.4. RASTER SCREENS

A raster screen creates a graphic image by displaying a large number of tiny dots having various brightness levels. These dots are called *picture elements* or *pixels*. They are arranged into a series of parallel, horizontal lines that cover the screen. This pattern of lines is the *scanning raster*.

The construction of CRT units used as stroke-writing and raster monitors is almost identical, but the principle of operation is different. The array of pixels on a raster screen is created in the following manner. The electron beam is magnetically deflected to trace one horizontal line. The voltage applied to the electron gun is continuously changed in response to the incoming video signal. The electron beam excites a dot of phosphor as it passes each point along the line. The brightness of the light produced by each dot is determined by the momentary intensity of the beam. Scanning proceeds from left to right at constant speed for each line and from top to bottom on the screen area. The beam is turned off or *blanked* when it reaches the end of a line, quickly positioned at the start of the next line, and turned on to resume scanning. Similarly, the beam is blanked after tracing the bottom line and quickly returned to the top of the screen.

Sequential scanning is the writing of each horizontal line in order from top to bottom. Sequential scanning allows the picture to flicker when the refresh rate is not high enough to match the persistence of the phosphor because the upper portion of the image fades while the lower portion is being intensified. *Interlaced scanning* (Figure 2.5) prevents flicker by tracing all the odd-

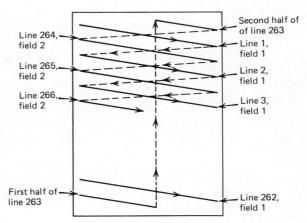

Figure 2.5.   Interlaced scanning pattern. Courtesy of De Anza Systems, Inc.

numbered lines first and then tracing the even-numbered lines, so that the screen surface is covered twice during each refresh cycle.

A full-color monitor utilizes the same raster pattern as a monochrome monitor, but each pixel is a triad of phosphor dots in three primary colors—red, green, and blue. Three separate video signals are supplied to the CRT to control the voltages applied to the three primary-color beams. In computer graphics applications each signal is transmitted over an individual coaxial cable, so it is not necessary to encode the color information into a single channel and later decode it in the receiver as is done in broadcasting. A graphics monitor is a simpler device than a television receiver because it does not need the antenna, tuner, audio circuitry, speaker, and so forth. A standard picture tube can be used as a raster CRT, but a higher resolution tube capable of displaying over 1000 horizontal lines is used for computer graphics applications that demand a well-defined complex image.

The raster method is naturally suited for displaying television pictures because a television camera originates the video signal by a raster scanning technique. However, the graphic information stored in the computer data base is not directly compatible with the raster display method, so an extensive conversion process is required to create a video signal to drive the CRT. The system of electronic equipment needed to support a raster monitor is shown in Figure 2.6. The cost of the CRT itself is only a fraction of the total hardware cost. A complete display system as illustrated is dependent on the host computer only for data base storage, an arrangement that produces the optimum display performance but involves the purchase of a significant amount of auxiliary hardware. To eliminate the need for some of this extra equipment, the main computer could do a portion of the data conversion, but this approach is not recommended because it places an excessive load on the central processor.

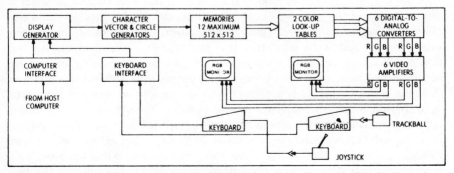

Figure 2.6. Block diagram of a refreshed raster tube system. Courtesy of Aydin Controls.

A full-color display system consists of the following components: display processor, character, vector, and circle generators, refresh memory, color lookup table, three digital-to-analog convertors, three video amplifiers, and a color monitor. This equipment configuration is shown in Figure 2.6. The display processor is a general-purpose microcomputer that is programmed to control the overall operation of the display system. The display processor is responsible for changing the data base descriptions of graphic objects into simple commands that can be executed by the character, vector, and circle generators. The microcomputer can also be programmed to provide optional display manipulation functions like zoom, pan, and scroll. The character, vector, and circle generators are read-only-memory (ROM) devices with built-in programs for computing all the raster points required to present the image on the screen. The raster points could be calculated by programs in the display processor, but specialized hardware generators are more efficient for these routine operations.

The digital data that identify the raster points are written into the refresh memory, a random-access-memory (RAM) device capable of rapid information retrieval. The amount of refresh memory required for a full-color display is kept within reasonable limits by storing the data describing each raster point as a short address for referencing a color lookup table. The table entry at that address contains full instructions for generating the appropriate hue-saturation-intensity combination for that pixel. The instructions (digital data) are transferred to the three digital-to-analog convertors that generate the voltages to control the intensity of the beam for each primary color. These three video signals are amplified and are then supplied to the color monitor to produce the display.

The continuous process of reading the refresh memory, referencing the color lookup table, and generating the three video signals for every pixel in the raster is repeated during each refresh cycle, usually thirty times per second. The contents of the refresh memory are not changed until the operator uses the graphics system to modify the image in the data base or to select a different view of the same image. At that time, the display processor and the character, vector, and circle generators convert the modified image into raster format and write new data into the refresh memory to *update* the display. Because extensive calculations are involved, updating cannot be accomplished more than two or three times per second, which is much slower than the refresh cycle. It is possible for an incomplete or incorrect picture to be displayed if refresh continues during update. One solution is to stop the refresh process and let the screen be blank for a brief time during an update. A more satisfactory solution is *double buffering*, the use of two refresh memory units. The digital data in one unit are displayed while the other unit is receiving new data. When the update is complete, the roles of the two refresh memory units are reversed so that the next refresh cycle begins the display of the new image.

The digital data stored in the refresh memory are the basis for the video signal in computer graphics. The simplest data format that can describe an image is 1 bit for each pixel in the image. The data are stored as an array known as a memory plane, memory channel, or *bit map*. One dimension of the array is the number of horizontal scan lines per frame and the other dimension is the number of pixels per line. Typical array sizes for computer graphics applications are 256×256, 512×256, 512×512, and 1024×1024. The computer system can change the value of any bit independently, making each pixel an *addressable* point. The *resolution* of the display processor system is the number of addressable points in the array. In contrast, the resolution of the CRT depends on the size of the phosphor spot that is excited by the electron beam and is expressed as the number of distinct lines that the CRT can display. A quality image can be produced only when the resolution of the CRT equals or exceeds the resolution of the digital data produced by the display processor.

The information stored as one bit per pixel can indicate only whether the pixel should be black (no intensity) or white (full intensity). A black-and-white display is adequate for many applications, especially for functions that replace ordinary pencil or ink line drawings, such as the interactive electrical design example discussed in the preceding section. The information needed to produce either gray-scale or color images can be stored if enough memory space is available. The term "gray-scale" refers to the use of multiple intensity levels on a monochrome monitor, regardless of whether the monitor's phosphor produces light that is white, green, or any other single color. Many systems use 3 bits per pixel to specify eight different shades of gray (Figure 2.7). Alternatively, 3 bits per pixel can indicate eight different colors (Figure 2.8).

The graphics system operator selects an intensity level or color when he

Intensity code			Displayed gray scale	
0	0	0	Black (no intensity)	
0	0	1	Gray	
0	1	0	Gray	Darker
0	1	1	Gray	↑
1	0	0	Gray	↓
1	0	1	Gray	Lighter
1	1	0	Gray	
1	1	1	White (full intensity)	

Figure 2.7. Eight shades of gray specified by three bits per pixel.

Red	Green	Blue	Displayed color
0	0	0	Black (no intensity)
0	0	1	Blue ⎫
0	1	0	Green
1	0	0	Red
0	1	1	Cyan ⎬ Full intensity
1	0	1	Magenta
1	1	0	Yellow
1	1	1	White ⎭

Figure 2.8.   Eight colors specified by three bits per pixel.

adds each graphic object to the data base. The operator's gray-scale or color selection is indicated through the multiple-bit code when the data base description is converted to the bit map. In general, N bits are sufficient to directly represent choices from among 2^N gray levels or colors. As a practical matter, however, direct coding seldom exceeds 6 bits for a selection of sixty-four colors.

A selection of up to 4096 colors can be conveniently handled through the use of a *color lookup table*. A typical table includes information for producing 64 colors that have been chosen from among 4096 different possibilities. The refresh memory contains 6 bits per pixel to describe the image. These 6 bits are used as the address of an entry within the table. A 12-bit color code located at that address provides 4 bits of intensity information for each primary color. Much less memory is required to store 6 bits per pixel for over 1,000,000 pixels (1024 × 1024 raster) and to maintain a table of 64 entries having 12 bits each than would be required to directly store 12 bits per pixel. The operator still has great flexibility in his or her use of color because there are 64 table entries available as various shades within a single color group or as a range of hues that covers the spectrum. Also, the operator can redefine the table entries at any time without changing the data base.

2.5. CHARACTER GRAPHICS SYSTEMS

Thus far this section discusses the operation of *full graphics* raster systems in which every pixel in the display is directly addressable by the computer graphics system. This means that the data conversion from the geometric format in the data base to the bit map is an approximation that is accurate to the nearest pixel. For this reason, a circle of any diameter drawn on a full graphics raster display has a reasonably smooth, rounded appearance. A *character graphics* raster system is a variation in which the smallest addressable unit is the area occupied by one alphanumeric character. This method severely limits the quality of the display for curved or irregularly shaped objects. Also, the entire character must have the same color or monochrome intensity.

A character graphics system includes a set of graphic characters (in addition to a full standard set of numbers, letters, and special characters) that are used like mosaic tiles to create patterns. Many low-cost systems designed for business forms and graphs, hobby use, and computer games include only a general set of graphic characters stored on a ROM electronic chip. A typical set includes horizontal, vertical, and diagonal line segments, shaded areas of various shapes, arrows, and so forth. More sophisticated systems intended for industrial control and computer-aided design applications have an additional set of customized graphic symbols. The potential user determines the required symbols and draws each one as a pattern of dots on grid paper. The equipment supplier then sets up these patterns on a programmable read-only-memory (PROM) chip.

There is no single, widely accepted size for the dot array that defines a character. Figure 2.9 shows typical characters, each a 7 × 9 pixel array containing both the pattern and the appropriate blank areas for spacing. Characters of this size can be arranged 85 per row with 51 rows per frame, for a total of over 4000 characters per frame on a system with an overall resolution of 512 × 512 pixels.

Some systems provide additional flexibility through an optional PROM chip for oversized characters that each occupy an area equivalent to 4 normal characters. The large-sized character set can include numbers and letters for emphasis in messages and complex user-defined graphic symbols.

One system that approaches a compromise between character graphics and full graphics has the usual pixel array (6 × 8) for each character, but it

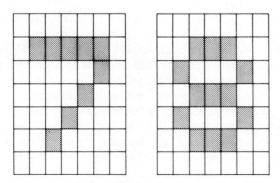

Figure 2.9. Typical pixel-array characters.

also has smaller blocks (3 × 2 pixel subsets of the array) that can be individually addressed by the computer system. The picture construction
capability provided by these blocks approximates the performance of a full
graphics system in which the computer can address each separate pixel.

Character graphics systems are popular because they are inexpensive, are
simple to program, and produce a display that suffices for many applications. The hardware for character graphics is less expensive than for full
graphics because character codes can be sent directly from the main computer to the character generator, eliminating the need for the display processor and the vector and circle generators in the configuration shown by
Figure 2.6. The task of converting the image into an array of raster dots is
reduced to a simple table lookup operation since each character code specifies a predefined pattern. The same character codes that define the image
can be transmitted to a matrix plotter (Section 3.2) to produce a paper copy
if the display system and the plotter have matching character sets, including
all customized symbols.

The way an application program utilizes character graphics is similar to
the way it formats printed output. An image can be loaded into the computer
in a noninteractive mode by preparing keypunched input specifying the location for each required character. Alternatively, a screen display can be produced interactively by entering the layout from a keyboard attached to the
CRT and visually checking the results. The terminal hardware assigns location coordinates and character codes for permanent storage in the main computer.

2.6. PLASMA PANEL DISPLAYS

The plasma panel is the only popular interactive display device that is not a
CRT. It is smaller, lighter, and more rugged than other screen units while
being comparable in performance and price. Plasma panels have been on the
market since 1971.

An exploded view of a plasma panel is shown in Figure 2.10. The
"plasma" referred to by the name of the device is neon gas that is sandwiched
between the two glass panels. Light is produced by electrical excitation of this
gas. Neon advertising signs operate on the same principle. A series of thin
conductive strips are attached to the inner surface of each glass sheet, running horizontally on one side and vertically on the other. These strips are the
x-axis and y-axis electrodes and each location where two electrodes cross is a
displayable point. The highest resolution currently available is an electrode
grid of 512 × 512. The electrodes are covered with a dielectric layer consisting of another sheet of glass coated with magnesium oxide. The seal be-

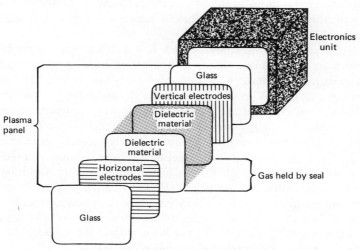

Figure 2.10. Plasma panel construction.

tween the glass sheets holds the inert gas inside the panel at a pressure of $1/2$ to 1 atmosphere and it keeps the glass sheets properly aligned. The solid-state electronic equipment shown schematically in Figure 2.11 is supplied with the plasma panel to support its operation.

To display a new point, a voltage pulse is applied to each of the two electrodes that correspond to the xy coordinates of the point. These pulses cause opposing charges to be stored on either side in the dielectric layer at the intersection. The potential between the dielectric layers, summed with the sustaining voltage constantly applied to the entire panel, ionizes the gas at that location, causing it to glow. Neon gas produces orange light. Each point can be erased by removing the stored charge from the dielectric layer. This is

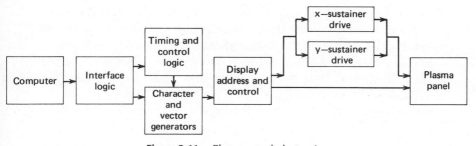

Figure 2.11. Plasma panel electronics.

done by applying a pulse to the two electrodes using a voltage that is out of phase with the sustaining voltage, briefly reducing the electrical potential at the point.

A plasma panel can be characterized as a monochrome, single intensity, raster format, stored image device with selective erase. A plasma panel has several features that make it unique among display devices. The screen is transparent, so images from 35-mm slides or microfilm can be projected from the rear to enhance the displayed image with a superimposed background. Unlike the slightly curved CRT screen, a plasma panel is flat. A flat screen is required for accurate results with a touch panel input device (Section 1.2.5). All other input devices except a light pen can also be used in conjunction with a plasma panel. Plasma panels are widely used in military applications because they can withstand shock, vibration, and other severe environmental conditions when properly packaged. A plasma panel is less susceptible to electrical or magnetic interference from nearby equipment because the operating voltages are much lower than the voltages used in the emission, focusing, and deflection systems of a CRT.

VENDOR LIST

Information provided by these companies was used in the preparation of Chapter 2. This is not intended to be a complete list of all suppliers.

STROKE-WRITING DISPLAYS

Beam-Penetration Color Refreshed Monitors

CPS Inc., 110 Wolfe Road, Sunnyvale, CA 94086 (408) 738-0530

Kratos Inc., 403 South Raymond Avenue, Bin 45, Pasadena, CA 91109 (213) 449-3090

Monochrome Refreshed Monitors

Adage, Inc., 1079 Commonwealth Avenue, Boston, MA 02215 (617) 783-1100

Aydin Controls, 414 Commerce Drive, Fort Washington, PA 19034 (215) 542-7800

Hewlett-Packard, 1501 Page Mill Road, Palo Alto, CA 94304 (213) 877-1282

Imlac Corporation, 150 A Street, Needham, MA 02194 (617) 449-4600

Megatek Corporation, 3931 Sorrento Valley Blvd., San Diego, CA 92121 (714) 455-5590

Sanders Associates, Inc., Daniel Webster Highway, South, Nashua, NH 03061 (603) 885-5280

Three Rivers Computer Corporation, Box 235, Schenley Park, Pittsburgh, PA 15213 (412) 621-6250

Vector General, Inc., 21300 Oxnard Street, Woodland Hills, CA 91364 (213) 346-3410

X-Ytron, Inc., 12323 Gladstone Avenue, Sylmar, CA 91342 (213) 365-0819

Monochrome Storage Monitors

Princeton Electronic Products, Inc., P.O. Box 101, North Brunswick, NJ 08902 (201) 297-4448

Tektronix, Inc., P.O. Box 500, Beaverton, OR 97077 (503) 638-3411

RASTER DISPLAYS

Monochrome and Color Refreshed Monitors

Aydin Controls, 414 Commerce Drive, Fort Washington, PA 19034 (215) 542-7800

Chromatics, Inc., 3923 Oakcliff Industrial Court, Atlanta, GA 30340 (404) 447-8797

Conrac Corporation, 1600 South Mountain Avenue, Duarte, CA 91010 (213) 359-9141

Genisco Computers, 17805-D Sky Park Circle Drive, Irvine, CA 92714 (714) 556-4916

Hewlett-Packard, 1501 Page Mill Road, Palo Alto, CA 94304 (213) 877-1282

Industrial Data Terminals Corporation, 1550 West Henderson Road, Columbus, OH 43220 (614) 451-3282

Intelligent Systems Corporation, 4376 Ridgegate Drive, Duluth, GA 30136 (404) 449-5961

Ramtek, 585 N. Mary Avenue, Sunnyvale, CA 94086 (408) 735-8400

Sony Video Products Company, 9 West 57th Street, New York, NY 10019 (212) 371-5800

Tektronix, Inc., P.O. Box 500, Beaverton, OR 97077 (503) 638-3411

Three Rivers Computer Corporation, Box 235, Schenley Park, Pittsburgh, PA 15213 (412) 621-6250

Videographics, 727 Dwight Way, Berkeley, CA 94704 (415) 549-0211

Plasma Panels

Interstate Electronics Corporation, 707 E. Vermont Avenue, Anaheim, CA 92803 (714) 772-2811

Magnavox Display Systems, 2131 South Coliseum Blvd., Ft. Wayne, IN 46803 (219) 482-4411

Display Processors

Child, Inc., P.O. Box 764, Lawrence, KS 66044 (913) 841-4096

Comtal Corporation, P.O. Box 5087, Pasadena, CA 91107 (213) 793-2134

De Anza Systems, Inc., 118 Charcot Avenue, San Jose, CA 95131 (408) 263-7155

Grinnell Systems Corporation, 2986 Scott Blvd., Santa Clara, CA 95050 (408) 988-2100

Ikonas Graphics Systems, Inc., 1200 Carlton Avenue, Raleigh, NC 27606 (919) 833-5401

Interpretation Systems, Inc., P.O. Box 1007, Lawrence, KS 66044 (913) 842-5678

Lexidata Corporation, 215 Middlesex Turnpike, Burlington, MA 01803 (617) 273-2700

CHAPTER 3

Lasting Results: Plots, Hard Copies, Photographs

Lasting results are necessary in almost every application of interactive computer graphics. The method of permanent output must be chosen carefully when planning a graphics system because it determines the quality and promptness of the final product. This chapter discusses the major output processes, the variations in equipment that are available, and the alternative operation methods. The variety of possibilities is important because the plotter is one of the most easily interchangeable components of a graphics system. Every general-purpose turnkey graphics system is offered with a particular plotter and hard copy unit as part of the package, but invariably other output equipment can be easily substituted if the customer insists. Matching the output equipment to the requirements of the application and to the physical configuration of the graphics system will lead to the optimum combination of desired performance and low cost.

3.1. PEN PLOTTERS

Since their introduction some 20 years ago, pen plotters have been so successful that there are now thousands of them in use throughout the world. The ancestors of today's computer-controlled (digital) plotters were direct acting *X-Y* instrument recorders with pen marking mechanisms, such as recording barometers and seismographs. Every digital pen plotter is basically a *servomechanism,* an automatic feedback control system for mechanical motion. The main components in the plotter servomechanism are shown in Figure 3.1.

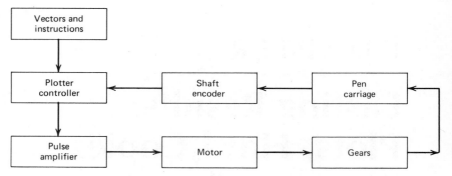

Figure 3.1. Pen plotter servomechanism.

The principle of a feedback control loop is incorporated in every pen plotter, although the identity of individual components may vary. The most popular arrangement is to have one direct current (dc) drive motor controlling movement along each axis, with the electric motor connected to the pen carriage by a system of gears, wire cables, or drive screws. A variation is the linear reluctance drive motor, which moves the pen carriage in any direction by the controlled interaction of magnetic forces. Changing the currents applied to electromagnets in the pen carriage assembly causes movement across a matrix pattern of ferromagnetic material that is implanted in the plotter bed.

Pen plotters are designed in three styles: flatbed (Figure 3.2), drum (Figure 3.3), and beltbed (Figure 3.4).

A *flatbed plotter* has a pen carriage that moves in the x and y directions simultaneously over the flat area where the paper is held smooth by an electrostatic charge. Movement of the pen in each direction is controlled by an

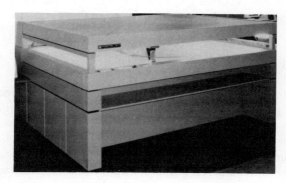

Figure 3.2. Flatbed plotter. Courtesy of Xynetics, Inc.

electric motor capable of causing fine movement in response to an electrical control signal. Small movements of the pen draw a series of tiny line segments to form all the lines, circles, and characters on the plot. If each pen stroke is small enough, the individual segments are not apparent to the human eye and even the curves look smooth. The length of time required for plotting depends more on how quickly the motors can start and stop the pen to change direction than on how fast the pen can move directly across the paper. This is because a typical plot contains many short lines, curves, and characters, but few long straight lines. The plotter includes a microcomputer that acts as the plotter controller to serve two functions—converting the program instructions into the series of tiny pen movements and generating the properly timed signals for the motors indicating the x- and y-direction movements.

In *drum plotter* operation, the pen still changes position in both the x and y directions relative to the surface of the paper, but it does so by the combined movement of the paper and the pen carriage. The paper is attached to a sprocket-feed mechanism on a roller similar to a typewriter platen. During plotting, the paper moves back and forth across the roller and the pen carriage moves in both directions along a straight line above the roller. Drum plotter equipment occupies less space than comparable flatbed equipment.

The *beltbed plotter* is a cross between the flatbed and the drum. A wide continuous belt covering both sides of the flat vertical plotting surface moves in conjunction with the pen carriage movement to produce a plot.

A *plot-back digitizer* is a hybrid input–output device that combines a flatbed pen plotter with a digitizer. (Digitizers are introduced in Section 1.2). An

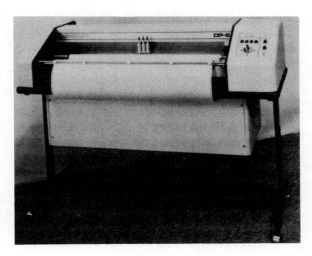

Figure 3.3. Drum plotter. Courtesy of Houston Instrument.

Figure 3.4.   Beltbed plotter. Courtesy of California Computer Products, Inc. (CalComp).

existing drawing or other data source is placed on the plotter's bed. To digitize, the operator manually aligns the plotter pen with the desired input point and presses a button. The device sends the coordinates of the point to the computer. When input is completed, the computer data can be plotted over the source document to verify the accuracy of the digitizing. The plot-back digitizer is best suited to low-volume applications, because the device is available for only one of its two functions at a time. Any simple flatbed plotter can be used for repeated plotting by placing a previously plotted drawing on the bed and carefully aligning the starting position of the pen. This technique can be used to compare and check drawing revisions if a different color ink is used for the second plot.

The pen plotter is unsurpassed in versatility. The writing instrument attached to the pen carriage can be a pressurized or nonpressurized wet ink pen, a ballpoint pen, a felt-tip pen, a scribe tip for coated material, or a cutter tip for strippable film. The continuous plotting media for drum plotters, in either rolls or fan-folded stacks, includes a variety of plain paper, printed grid paper, and transparent film. Almost any material can be used with a flatbed plotter, secured to the plotting surface by an electrostatic or vacuum hold-down system or simply by adhesive tape.

A distinction is sometimes made between incremental plotters and vector plotters. Every pen plotter is actually an incremental plotter because the image is formed by a multitude of small line increments. A vector plotter has a built-in microcomputer that handles vector, circle, and character generation in hardware, thus reducing the amount of plotter data preparation done by programs in the computer. The microcomputer may also be able to speed up the plotting rate with sophisticated control methods such as look-ahead variable acceleration, a technique to avoid stopping the pen between each pair of line increments.

3.2. ELECTROSTATIC PLOTTERS

The electrostatic process was invented in 1937 and had its commercial introduction for document copying in 1950. This process was first applied to computer output as a method of printing, resulting in a dramatic increase in speed compared to impact printers. Equipment soon became available making this fast electrostatic technique work for graphics plotting as well as for printing. Electrostatic plotters use one of two methods of applying the electrostatic charge to the paper, the matrix-writing technique or the photoconductive plate method.

The *matrix-writing technique* consists of producing an invisible image on the surface of the paper with a static electric charge, and then applying a liquid toner containing suspended carbon particles that become attached to the charged areas to create a visible image. Finally, the nonclinging excess toner is removed and the paper is quickly dried. The special paper has a dielectric coating to hold the charge. This plotting process is similar to the process used by copying machines, differing mainly in the method of creating the electrostatic image.

The plot is produced by a matrix technique consisting of a pattern of overlapping dots. Each black dot in the final image is the result of a charge placed on the paper by a tiny needle. As the paper rolls through the plotter, it passes under a bar extending the width of the paper that contains thousands of these stationary writing needles, equally spaced along two staggered rows. The plotter utilizes 1 bit of computer data to indicate whether or not voltage should be applied to each needle to place the electrostatic charge that forms a black dot in the image. The complete image is formed by plotting an entire line with the appropriate dots, advancing the paper slightly, then repeating the sequence. The data describing one plot line are referred to as a *raster scan* because the method of writing is comparable to the way an image is formed on a television screen by pixels in a series of horizontal lines. The potential speed of an electrostatic plotter exceeds the rate at which data can be prepared from the stored graphics design. A matrix plotter has simple construction since the writing is under electronic control and the only moving parts are for advancing the paper and drying the toner.

Matrix writing produces a sharp black on white image. Straight lines in either the horizontal or vertical direction appear solid because they are made up of overlapping dots, but diagonal lines and some curves have a distinct stairstep appearance that shows the approximation with dots. Text can be produced most efficiently using the plotter's standard character set. Each letter or number is a pattern within a rectangle of dots usually either 7×9 or 16×16 dots in size. These patterns are not just stick figures, but are especially designed for easy reading.

In the *photoconductive plate method,* the graphic image or the page of printing is produced as a whole on an internal rectangular CRT. The visible light from the CRT is transformed by a photoconductive plate into a charge on the paper. After an exposure time of several seconds, the toning and drying process is applied to the entire page of output. An alternate method of producing the visible image uses charged particles of dry ink that are bonded to the paper by heat. The plate method can produce pictures consisting of a range of gray shades, as well as black and white, by varying the strength of the electrostatic charge through control of the beam voltage that determines the intensity of the light from the screen phosphors. The size and quality of the plot in the plate method are limited by the dimensions and resolution of the CRT. The plate method is well suited for a hard copy plotter connected to a raster CRT interactive display because the same data format can be used for both the screen and the plotter.

A new variation on the electrostatic plate method is a plotter that utilizes a laser beam instead of a CRT electron beam to form the image. Full color output is produced by applying particles of seven pigments: cyan (dark blue), magenta (deep purplish red), yellow, red, green, blue, and black. Other colors can be simulated by intermixing the primary colors through halftoning under program control. The plot can be placed on either plain paper or transparency material for overhead projection. Some plate process equipment, either color or gray tone, is capable of copying a background form simultaneously with plotting the computer image to produce a composite result.

3.3. VECTOR TO RASTER DATA CONVERSION

The main drawback to all methods of electrostatic plotting is that the data describing the image must be in raster format. With most interactive graphics systems, it is a fairly straightforward process to change the design data into vector format suitable for a pen plotter. For electrostatic plotting, those same vectors are then sorted according to their location in the plot and separated into horizontal bands, and the vectors in each band are converted into pixel or matrix dot information. The volume of data is increased substantially by conversion into raster format, since the same amount of information is required for every point whether it is plotted or blank.

The vector to raster conversion can be done in the computer with a program provided by the plotter manufacturer or it can be done by a hardware raster conversion device. If the conversion program is run on a small minicomputer, the vector-to-raster process can take several minutes for a drawing that takes only seconds to plot. The conversion program runs faster on a larger computer, but the processing time and the amount of core required make the conversion process costly in resources used. The raster conversion device can handle vector to raster processing in about one-eighth the time required by a minicomputer. However, this hardware cannot handle the vector sorting, which must still be done by the computer.

The need for a hardware vector-to-raster converter is increased when the computer already has high utilization or when the plotting application is especially demanding because of heavy volume, high resolution, wide plots, or complex drawings. The vector-to-raster device is less necessary if most of the electrostatic output is printing that is handled by the built-in character generator. To minimize the initial plotter cost, the hardware converter can be omitted at first and added later if required to improve system performance.

3.4. GRAPHIC FILM RECORDERS

A *graphic film recorder* is simply a camera that photographs an internal CRT. Film recorders are also referred to as photoplotters. The principal components of a graphic film recorder are shown in Figure 3.5. The internal computer display screen is a black and white, single-line, raster scan CRT. This specialized CRT works in precisely timed coordination with the film transport, so that the film moves a tiny distance after each single line scan, until enough scans have been completed to expose the entire image. Direct color photoplotting is accomplished by transmitting white light from the CRT through a color filter assembly. One type of color filter assembly is a high speed rotating disk consisting of wedge-shaped filters in seven primary colors: red, green, blue, cyan (dark blue), magenta (deep purplish red), yellow, and neutral. The disk rotates at constant speed. The CRT single-line scans are timed to coincide with the passage of each color wedge above the CRT, so a primary color is formed

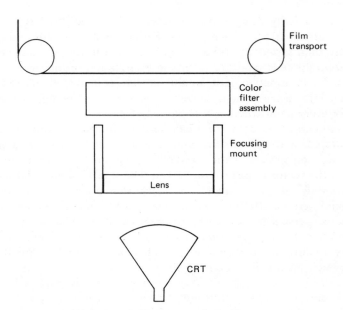

Figure 3.5.   Color film recorder construction.

during one flash of the desired light intensity. Other color hues are created by overlaying two or more primary colors, each flashed with a reduced light intensity proportional to the prominence of that color. The breakdown of the image by primary color and intensity is done in software prior to sending the data to the graphic film recorder.

Film transports that fit film sizes 16, 35, 70, and 105 mm, and Polaroid 4 × 5 in. and 8 × 10 in. are available for standard film recorders. The small image is desirable for projector slides, for permanent storage as microfiche and microfilm in place of bulky paper copies, and for computer-aided manufacturing of microscopic electronic components. Despite the small image, magnifying viewers and enlargement printers make it possible to use a microfilm as an original document or drawing.

There is a special large format film recorder that can record images as large as 42 × 60 in., which is equal to the output size of a large flatbed pen plotter. The sheet of film or photographic paper is mounted on a large rotating cylinder inside the film recorder. The computer divides the image into strips during output data preparation. Each image strip corresponds to a plot area that is several inches wide and 42 inches long. This length is equivalent to the circumference of the cylinder. A square CRT displays the image at a rate that is synchronized with the cylinder rotation so that one strip is exposed during each rotation. The CRT is mounted on an assembly so it can be moved into position for the next image strip a few inches further down the axis of the cylinder. This is repeated to produce the complete image. The large format recorder can be used to show drawing detail without the grain and loss of sharpness associated with photographic enlargement. This is done by plotting additional films of enlarged sections of the drawing through use of the recorder in conjunction with image processing programs that scale the graphics data.

3.5. ALTERNATIVE PLOTTER EQUIPMENT

The three major classes of equipment are pen plotters, electrostatic plotters, and film recorders, but there are also alternatives that do not fall into these classes. *Thermal plotting* is done by applying heat through an electrical resistor tip to temperature sensitive paper. Thermal printer/plotters have become popular as output devices for desktop microcomputer systems as a result of their reasonable cost and compact size. A *matrix impact printer/plotter* has an array of writing needles that press an inked ribbon against the paper to form dots. This is a low-cost, low-resolution device that can be used as a hard copy unit. The *ink-jet plotter* is another matrix device that forms the image by spraying dots of ink on the paper. The ink-jet plotter is a recent innovation, although ink-jet printers have been in use for several years. The plotter produces full color output through dots of red, blue, and green pigment arranged to create any desired effect. The ink-jet plotter is an addition to the range of color plotting equipment that also includes film recorders and laser electrostatic plotters.

An alternative to plotting in hard copy mode is the use of a Polaroid camera for CRT image recording. Once the camera is fitted with the proper hood and set for a particular screen, all the operator does is hold the camera against the display and squeeze the shutter release. A developed photograph of the image is available instantly.

The HRD-1 Laser Display/Plotter (Laser-Scan Laboratories Limited, Cambridge, England) is both a large-screen, high resolution interactive storage display and a precision film plotter. The display screen (1.0 × 0.7 m) provides the information handling capacity and size of a drafting board. The image appears as black (storage) and blue (refreshed) lines on an orange background. Gray-scale shaded pictures are possible through continuous control of the laser's intensity and high-speed stroking to fill areas. The storage image is obtained by writing with a laser on photochromic film while projecting the film image onto the screen. An image can be viewed for as long as 20 minutes before it fades away. The screen is cleared by advancing the film reel. The photochromic film is cycled repeatedly since the images eventually fade. The capacity for refreshed lines is limited, so the refreshed image is used for cursor-symbol display, highlighting, prompting, and so forth. The HRD-1 contains a station for laser writing on microfiche diazo film (148 × 105 mm) as permanent output. A complex architectural plan or map can be plotted in about a minute. High-quality, full scale drawings are produced from the film by photographic enlargement (10 × magnification).

3.6.   MODE OF OPERATION

Two decisions must be made regarding graphics system output—type of plotter equipment and mode of plotter operation. The preceding sections in this chapter describe the three major types of plotting devices and discuss the factors that influence the decision on equipment. This section introduces the topic of plotter operation.

When the plotter is connected directly to the same computer that is running the interactive graphics program, the mode of operation is *on-line plotting.* This direct operation is one of four possible methods for supplying data to the plotter equipment. The other methods are *off-line plotting,* which involves intermediate data storage, usually on magnetic tape, *remote plotting,* which depends on long distance data telecommunications, and *hard copy plotting,* which utilizes data obtained from the display screen rather than the computer. Figure 3.6 shows these four alternatives. Each mode of operation was developed to meet the needs of a particular application situation.

3.6.1.   Hard Copy Operation

The image on a display screen can be preserved as a permanent paper copy through the use of a plotter in the hard copy operation mode. The term "hard copy" emphasizes the distinction between the physical presence of the image on paper and the "soft" temporary visual image on the screen. A plot produced by any output method can be described as a hard copy. However, the term usually relates to providing direct output at the graphics terminal. Hard copy mode is designed as a fast way to reproduce on paper the same picture that is being viewed. A paper copy of the screen image is sometimes needed to record alternative views or intermediate steps, or to work with away from the terminal. A hard copy is generally used as a check print or rough preliminary output, with the final output produced on another plotter with greater resolution and larger plot size.

Hard copy operation mode consists of a plotter that is not in direct communication with the computer, but obtains the data for the plot image from

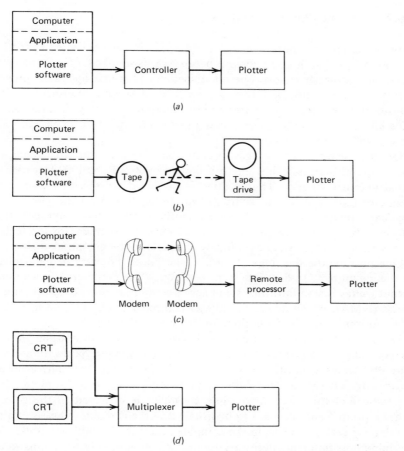

Figure 3.6. Plotter operation modes. (a) On-line. (b) Off-line. (c) Remote. (d) Hard copy.

the screen. A hard copy is produced from a storage tube by an electronic in-terrogation that results in a matrix of on/off point information. Producing a hard copy from a refreshed raster scan tube equipped with an output inter-face is a simple matter of sending the plotter the same video signal that up-dates the screen. Because the plot data from either a storage tube or a video tube are in a raster format, the plotter used for hard copies is generally raster type, such as a photoplotter, an electrostatic plotter using either the plate or the matrix method, or a matrix impact plotter. Pen plotters are not suitable for operation in this mode.

3.6.2. On-Line Plotter Operation

On-line plotter operation, where the plotter is directly connected to the host computer by cable, is often chosen because of its simplicity. It also has other advantages over alternative operation methods. On-line operation provides the fastest results because there are no time-consuming intermediate data-transfer steps between the plotter and the computer running the graphics application. It requires the lowest initial investment, only the purchase of a simple controller and the plotter.

On-line operation encourages locating the plotter in the same room with the computer because cable length is limited to 50 feet, or 1000 feet with optional long-line drivers. This location is preferred for several reasons. The computer room provides a security environment to protect the plotter from physical damage and to protect confidential output from improper distribution. Also, operations personnel, suitable power sources, fire protection, and other support services are already available in the computer room.

One possible disadvantage of on-line plotting is the extra demand placed on the computer. On-line data transfer through the peripheral device input/output routes is standard, but some newer computers provide direct memory access (DMA), which allows the plotter controller to obtain data at a faster rate and minimizes the CPU time for processing the transfer.

In on-line operation, the interface between the computer and the plotter is the controller. A *controller* is a data handler consisting of hardware and software that mates a specific computer to a specific plotter, both physically and electrically. The controller is usually purchased along with the plotter from the same manufacturer. An on-line controller is delivered in the form of either a printed circuit board to be installed in the computer chassis or a box suitable for rack mounting in the computer cabinet. A simple controller does the minimum functions necessary to ensure computer–plotter compatibility, mainly timing the data transfer. All other data preparation is done in the computer. Many on-line controllers are buffered, meaning that they have data holding areas that can accept very rapid input from the computer, then subsequently pass it on to the plotter at a steady, slower rate.

A *multiplexer* is a special type of controller designed for multiple interconnections between input data sources and output devices. The multiplexer takes care of addressing data to the proper destination and controlling each plotter individually. In a graphics system that requires a high volume of plotting, a multiplexer makes it possible for a single computer to be connected to two or more plotters. For an application with a plotting requirement that is low compared to the overall computational load, a multiplexer enables a single plotter to serve two or more computers. Multiplexing is also advantageous in applications where continuous plotting capability is a critical need, so the data flow can be switched between duplicate plotters as a backup in the event of equipment failure or shutdown for maintenance.

3.6.3. Off-Line Plotter Operation

It is characteristic of off-line plotting that the graphics data are transferred from the computer to the plotter through some removable storage volume, such as a magnetic tape, a hard disk pack, or a floppy diskette. In this operation the computer writes the data to storage and then the storage volume is moved by an operator to a separate set of equipment that reads the stored data and produces the plot. The computer can be in the same room as the reader and plotter or at some distant location. The operator plays a key role in this procedure because he or she decides whether to plot the stored data immediately, hold them for later processing, or use them repeatedly to produce multiple copies. The off-line procedure requires that the computer convert the graphics data from the interactive design format to the plotter format, as do all other modes of operation. However, a savings of computer time is the result of writing the data to storage as part of the conversion process as compared to retaining the plotter data on-line in the computer and then going through another process of sending it directly to the plotter.

Off-line plotting originated as a solution for input/output bottlenecks experienced with early model computers. Now the most important reason for off-line operation is that it significantly cuts computer costs by reducing the time spent on output processing. The cost of an additional tape or disk reader is soon recovered in computer savings if the plotting volume is high enough. Another reason for off-line operation is the opportunity to have a central facility where expensive equipment such as precision film recorders and full color plotters are installed for use by a number of separate graphics systems.

3.6.4. Remote Plotter Operation

The use of telecommunications to transfer the graphics data is the distinction between remote plotting and either on-line or off-line plotter operation. The data received at the remote site may go directly to the plotter in a manner similar to on-line operation or it may be placed on magnetic tape for off-line plotting. The cost of the equipment for sending and receiving the data, the modems, is relatively low, but the cost of telecommunications time is high.

Remote plotting is necessary when the graphics application program is being run on a distant computer through time-sharing. This situation occurs when computer time is purchased from a service bureau or when a centralized corporate computer is accessed by teleprocessing. Drafting and design systems are rarely supported by remote time-sharing since interactive response is impossible because of the restrictions imposed by telecommunications. (Communications are discussed in Section 4.2.)

Despite the disadvantages, remote time-sharing is practical for applications that use interactive graphics as an interface to an analytical program that requires the calculating power of a large computer because interactive response is not expected. For instance, many analytical programs deal with data that describe a model of a physical object or a conceptual model that can be represented graphically. Interactive graphics can be a means of visually checking the model set up by input data that were coded and keypunched or graphics can be directly involved in building the data model. Interactive graphics can also serve as an aid in understanding the results of a complex calculation by displaying the calculated outcome as another model. The remote user has a display screen, but he also needs a permanent record of the input and the results. Prompt, convenient output is supplied only by remote plotting. Examples of analytical programs suitable for time-sharing calculations and remote plotting are structural engineering, highway layout, and land survey mapping. Telecommunications is also desirable for fast drawing transmittal to a location distant from an interactive graphics installation.

VENDOR LIST

Information provided by these companies was used in the preparation of Chapter 3. This is not intended to be a complete list of all suppliers.

PEN PLOTTERS

California Computer Products, Inc. (CALCOMP), 2411 W. La Palma, Anaheim, CA 92801 (714) 821-2011

Data Technology, 4 Gill Street, Woburn, MA 01801 (617) 935-8820

Hewlett-Packard, 1501 Page Mill Road, Palo Alto, CA 94304 (213) 877-1281

Houston Instrument, 8500 Cameron Road, Austin, TX 78753 (512) 837-2820

Tektronix, Inc., P.O. Box 500, Beaverton, OR 97077 (503) 638-3411

Xynetics, Inc., 2901 Coronado Drive, Santa Clara, CA 95051 (408) 246-6500

Zeta Research, 1043 Stuart Street, Lafayette, CA 94549 (415) 284-5200

ELECTROSTATIC PLOTTERS

Gould, Inc., Instruments Division, 3631 Perkins Avenue, Cleveland, OH 44114 (216) 361-3315

Versatec, 2805 Bowers Avenue, Santa Clara, CA 95051 (408) 988-2800

COLOR PLOTTERS

Xerox Corporation, Xerox Square, Rochester, NY 14644 (716) 423-9200

Applicon, Inc., 154 Middlesex Turnpike, Burlington, MA 01803 (617) 272-7070

VECTOR-TO-RASTER CONVERTORS (PLOTTER CONTROLLERS)

Logic Sciences Inc., 6440 Hillcroft, Suite 412, Houston, TX 77081 (713) 777-8744

GRAPHIC FILM RECORDERS

California Computer Products, Inc. (CALCOMP), 2411 W. La Palma, Anaheim, CA 92801 (714) 821-2011

Constantine Engineering Laboratories Company (Celco), 70 Constantine Drive, Mahwah NJ 07430 (201) 327-1123

Dicomed Corporation, 9700 Newton Avenue South, Minneapolis, MN 55431 (612) 888-1900

Geo Space Corporation, 5803 Glenmont Drive, Houston, TX 77036 (713) 666-1611 (large-format recorder)

Laser-Scan Laboratories Limited, Cambridge Science Park, Milton Road, Cambridge CB4 4BH England Telephone 0223 69872 (HRD-1 Laser Display/Plotter)

HARD COPY DEVICES

Photophysics, Inc., 1601 Stierlin Road, Mountain View, CA 94040 (415) 968-2360

HARD COPY CAMERAS

Polaroid Corporation, 575 Technology Square, Cambridge, MA 02139 (800) 225-1618 (CU-5 camera with CRT hood)

MATRIX IMPACT PLOTTERS

Trilog, Inc., 16750 Hale Avenue, Irvine, CA 92714 (714) 549-4079

CHAPTER 4
Graphics Support

Computers, communications links, and storage devices make up the three general categories of support equipment. This chapter deals with support equipment only in the context of its role in sustaining the functions of input devices, display screens, and plotters. The same degree of detail given to the unique graphics components in Chapters 1, 2, and 3 is not given here because the subject is too broad, and extensive information on these hardware components is available elsewhere.

The value of all support equipment normally comprises more than half of the total hardware investment in the graphics system. Computers, communications links, and storage devices are not unique to graphics applications, but instead have a wide market in data processing for business, industry, and research. The influence of this mass market is reflected in competitive prices and continuous development efforts by the hardware suppliers. Technological advances in recent years have actually lowered the expense involved in supplying a given level of support services. What the future will bring is unknown, but all indications are that the progress in hardware technology will continue and that electronics (the source of past breakthroughs) will be joined by optics, crystallography, plasma physics, and polymer chemistry in providing future components for computer systems [2].

As a result of the progress in hardware manufacturing, the cost of hardware is now exceeded by the cost of software. This latter cost includes the software developed by vendors to accompany hardware, such as computer operating systems, communications procedures, and programs imbedded in microcomputer-based device controllers. It also includes applications programs and the practical working procedures developed by users of those applications programs. All together, these software components represent 90% of the cost of a finished, functional computer application, while hardware represents only 10% [2]. Also, software cost is more difficult to estimate and control, software is less reliable, and no revolutionary new ways of producing software can presently be seen. Thus the concensus is that this imbalance will increase. This is an argument for providing fully adequate support equipment for a graphics system, because skimping in this area can have serious ill effects on overall performance and it is false economy in light of the 90 to 10% cost split.

4.1. COMPUTERS

Providing computational support for an interactive computer graphics application is a broad topic, so attention is concentrated on the particular configurations that are most practical for graphics and on the influence of the computer on the overall success of the graphics application.

The software for interactive graphics can be installed and run on either a dedicated computer or a computer that is shared with other applications. The key difference between these two approaches is the priority of the graphics application and the resulting effect on the graphics user.

A *dedicated computer* is one that is devoted solely to graphics functions, including interaction with plotters and terminals. A dedicated computer is generally a minicomputer by a manufacturer such as Data General and Digital Equipment. The majority of minicomputers for graphics applications are sold through vendors of turnkey graphics systems, who purchase the computer at a discount price, combine it with peripherals, install their proprietary graphics software, and offer it to potential users as a complete package. Users who purchase graphics software that is not part of a turnkey system usually obtain a suitable minicomputer directly from the manufacturer. The dedicated computer for graphics is typically the user's first acquisition of a minicomputer and sometimes it is the user's only computer of any kind.

A *shared computer* is usually a larger machine from a manufacturer such as Control Data and IBM. These firms offer graphics software packages primarily as new or expanded applications for the computers belonging to their existing customers. The manufacturer either writes software specifically for this market or obtains distribution rights from the independent developer of a successful package. The major independent service bureaus also have proprietary graphics software installed on their large computers. These graphics systems are available for use through lease arrangements.

Large computers are designed to be shared and are equipped for this purpose with features to allocate the computer's resources and to prevent multiple users from interferring with each other. Several different organizations for a shared computer system are possible, including a multiprocesor system, a multiprogramming system, a network, and a parallel processor.

A *multiprocessor system* is a specialized hardware design consisting of several processor units that share a single main memory. The system can carry out calculations for two or more separate programs simultaneously or the calculations related to a single task can be programmed in a special way for simultaneous execution. Relatively few multiprocessor computers have been manufactured because they have not gained widespread acceptance.

A *multiprogramming system* is a single computer that can carry out two or more programs concurrently by giving alternating attention to each. Each program can utilize the full resources of the large computer although the elasped time for execution of a program is increased as a result of sharing the computer. Time-sharing, which is synonymous with multiprogramming, is a popular method for the effective utilization of a large computer. Some minicomputers also operate as multiprogramming systems and are therefore able to supply concurrent support to several graphics terminals and do other functions such as plotting as well.

A *network* is simply an interconnected arrangement of two or more conventional computer systems. Each of the network components is usually a self-sufficient computer system with processor, main memory, auxiliary storage, and peripherals for input and output. The communications links between computers in a network may be short connections between components in a single large computer installation or they may cover extremely long distances. For example, the Department of Defense sponsored ARPA network includes computers that are located in many parts of the United States [3].

A *distributed processing network* is characterized by the decomposition of applications into separate tasks that are assigned to the various network components on the basis of geography or capability. Both kinds of decomposition are used in graphics applications. An engineering firm with regional branch offices may have independent graphics systems in each office that are linked together in a network for the occasional transfer of portions of the data base or the rapid transmittal of finished drawings. This is an example of a geographically distributed network. An example of a capability-based distributed processing network is a dedicated minicomputer that supports several intelligent terminals. The microcomputer in each terminal has the important advantage of close association with the input and display devices, although it can handle only simple operations involving a limited amount of data. The central computer can execute complex programs and has extensive data storage, but it must divide its attention among several terminals. Division of tasks between the intelligent terminal's microcomputer and the dedicated minicomputer on the basis of these individual capabilities will result in the most satisfactory performance for the overall graphics system.

Conventional computers are *serial processors* because they carry out program instructions by executing a series of consecutive operations. In contrast, a *parallel processor* (also known as an array or vector processor) has a hardware design based on interconnected modules that enables it to execute many operations simultaneously. For example, a parallel processor could add sixty-four pairs of numbers to yield sixty-four sums as quickly as a conventional computer could add a single pair. Most supercomputers are intrinsically parallel processors, but low-cost parallel processor units are also available as attachments to conventional minicomputers and large computers. Computer graphics can be a suitable application for a parallel processor because graphic manipulations frequently necessitate performing the same operation on a multitude of point coordinates that describe a particular design. Also, many graphics operations are most easily handled through matrix algebra, which requires repetition of the same calculation for each element in a matrix.

The majority of computers are general-purpose machines that perform useful functions by executing specialized software. A graphics system must always include a general-purpose computer for overall control. However, performance is improved when certain important graphics techniques are removed from the software and implemented in special-purpose hardware instead. Techniques that have been accomplished with custom-designed computer processors include hidden-surface removal and video display data conversion. The Evans and Sutherland Picture System 2 is an example of a commercially available graphics system based on special-purpose computer hardware [4]. Its unique component is the Picture Processor, which has built-in functions to perform the high-speed matrix arithmetic, clipping, perspective projection, and other operations required for viewing dynamically changing images of two- and three-dimensional designs. (Viewing techniques are covered in Chapters 7 and 8.)

Extremely realistic-looking images with shadows, reflections, and texture can now be generated using software that requires many minutes of processing time on a large computer. Special-purpose hardware could potentially produce these images interactively. This alternative is becoming increasingly attractive as the cost drops for mass-produced microcomputer and memory chips because custom-designed processors can be assembled from these standard components.

4.2. COMMUNICATIONS

The man-machine conversation of interactive graphics requires the transfer of data from input devices to the computer and back to the display devices. Calculations involve the moving of data between the functional components of the computer. Some graphics applications utilize telecommunications to share data with distant computer installations or remote terminals. Responsiveness is the critical consideration in choosing a communication method to meet these various requirements. Any communication that is part of the normal operation of an interactive graphics system must occur so rapidly that the user receives a reply in 1 second or less. Most long distance communications methods are too slow to be considered interactive, although the user may be willing to tolerate a short wait to obtain the benefits of transferring data between widely separated locations.

All electronic data transmission is either analog or digital. The human voice is transmitted through a handset over an ordinary telephone line as an analog signal, specifically an alternating-current (ac) wave form with continuously varying value that represents sound waves. Computer data are naturally in digital form and can be conveniently represented as an ac wave form having just two values. The simpler digital signal can be carried over a telephone line with less distortion than an analog signal.

A one-way communications path is called a *channel*, and a two-way path formed by two channels is a *circuit*. Data enter the channel through a connecting device such as a telephone handset. An *acoustic coupler* is a piece of equipment that converts binary computer data into a series of audible tones. A handset placed in a cradle on the acoustic coupler picks up these tones and transmits them just like voice sounds. An acoustic coupler receives data by performing the reverse process. A *modem* is a direct connecting device that converts the binary signal originated by a computer into the proper ac digital signal for transmission or converts the ac signal to binary for reception. The name "modem" is a shortened form of "modulator–demodulator," the technical terms describing its two functions.

Communication speed depends on how fast data are generated from a computer source, converted by a modem, and transferred through a channel. Each of these rates can be stated in *baud*, a unit of measure in data transmission terminology equal to 1 bit of data per second for digital signals. Typical baud rates for data transmission over various channels are listed in Figure 4.1. A baud rate is also used to express a channel's *bandwidth*, its maximum data-carrying capacity.

Many different types of channels are available for the electronic com-

Dialed telephone line and acoustic coupler	300 baud
Dialed telephone line and modem	1,200 baud
Leased telephone line and modem	4,800 baud
Direct cable	9,600 baud
Direct cable with proprietary controller	300,000 baud
Internal computer bus	5,000,000 baud

Figure 4.1. Typical data transmission rates for various channel types.

munication of computer data. The rest of this section is devoted to explaining the characteristics and utilization of the most important ones.

Every computer has an internal channel called a *bus* that connects all the other major components in the system. Figure 4.2 shows the five primary functions of a bus in transferring data between pairs of components. First, it carries data items and instructions between the central processor and the main memory. Second, it transfers blocks of data between main memory and auxiliary storage. Third, it routes control commands from the central processing unit (CPU) to peripheral controllers and returns status codes from the controllers to the CPU. Fourth, it moves both control commands and data between the controllers and the peripheral devices. Fifth, it connects the computer system to external communication channels. These five functions each have different requirements for speed and data volume. The internal bus has the highest bandwidth and fastest baud rate of any type of communications channel, but it is limited to short distances ranging from a few feet for the CPU and main memory link to about a thousand feet for the connection between a controller and a peripheral device.

A direct cable is the most efficient means of communication between computer systems that are located in the same building or adjacent buildings. The direct pathway between the computer components can be constructed with ordinary wire or special coaxial cable. Direct cables are used within a distributed processing network when all the computers in the configuration are located at the same site. This is a common situation in large-scale data processing installations. Direct cables are an excellent way to connect a dedicated computer to multiple graphics terminals that are spread out among user departments within an organization. It is advantageous for the cable from each graphics terminal to be connected directly into the bus structure as shown in Figure 4.2. Performance is diminished if incompatibility makes it necessary for the cable to be connected indirectly through the external communications controller. A

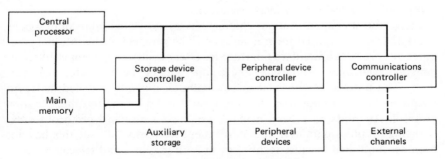

Figure 4.2.   Structure of computer bus.

long line driver device must be utilized to boost data transmission when cable length exceeds the limit for the controller to peripheral bus. A properly installed direct cable is an interactive communications channel.

Telephone lines are the most popular telecommunications channels. The two straightforward ways to utilize the telephone system are through dialed and leased lines. A dialed line can be used in conjunction with either an acoustic coupler or a modem and the computer system can provide automatic dialing under program control and automatic answering. The service and the cost are the same as for ordinary long distance telephone calls. A leased telephone line for exclusive 24-hour use by a computer system can be arranged at a set monthly cost. These transmission lines are generally of higher quality than those used for voice communications, so these lines can provide reliable data transfer at higher baud rates when used with a suitable modem.

The increasing demand from nongraphic computer applications for data transmission services has started a revolution in long-distance communications involving new ways to utilize telephone lines and plans for alternatives to the telephone system. A *value-added network* is one new option that is already available from several independent firms. These firms lease expensive long distance telephone lines and then arrange for its many subscribers to share the use of those lines through techniques that average the demand for service statistically and smooth out peaks in demand by temporary data storage. These sharing techniques make it possible for the firm to offer lower cost service to subscribers, pay the lease, and produce a profit on the value-added network. Another alternative that will be available in the future is a *private network* utilizing satellites and microwave stations on the ground. Several major companies in the computer industry have announced plans for private network services, but these computer companies will have competition from the leading firms in the telephone industry, who have also announced plans for specialized data communications networks using their existing transmission equipment. Similar activity is also occurring in countries other than the United States, with government involvement in most instances.

Every type of communications channel has an associated *protocol* to specify the data format required for transmission. The protocol of the internal computer bus provides a standard interface for attachment of any compatible components, even those supplied by the competitors of the computer manufacturer. The purpose of the modem in communications over dialed or leased telephone lines is to put data into the form defined by the telephone system protocol. Attempts have been made to establish a standard protocol for exchanging graphics data over communications networks [3], but this has not been accomplished because technology in both graphics and telecommunications is advancing so rapidly.

4.3. STORAGE

Interactive input methods make it easy for each graphics user to generate huge amounts of data as compared to the volume of data entered by users of noninteractive applications such as commercial record keeping and scientific calculations. This vast accumulation of graphics data presents the challenge of providing adequate storage facilities within the supporting computer system.

It would be ideal if all stored graphics data could be immediately accessible. However, practical economics have dictated a division of graphics system storage into three categories. The first category is *main memory*, or primary storage, which is directly available to the central processor. The second category is *auxiliary storage*, or local file memory, which provides indirect but interactive data availability. The third category is *archival memory*, or permanent storage, which holds computer data for long periods, generally outside the computer system with access through human intervention. ("Memory" and "storage" are synonyms in computer terminology.)

The reason for these three different levels of storage is that three distinct clusters are formed when storage equipment is evaluated with respect to access speed and unit cost. The high-cost, high-performance cluster is currently based on electronic semiconductor technology. The magnetic disk dominates the middle position of medium price and speed. The most prominent member of the low-cost cluster is magnetic tape, since it provides economical but slow access to large files on-line and provides extremely inexpensive off-line storage in a tape library. Figures 4.3 and 4.4 indicate the ranges for access time and for total data capacity of the members of these three performance clusters.

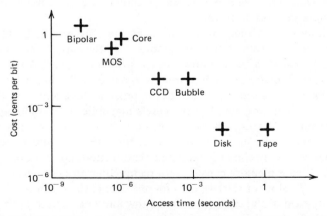

Figure 4.3. Storage equipment ranked according to access speed and unit cost.

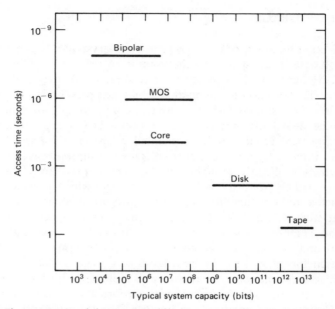

Figure 4.4.   Total data capacity for various types of storage equipment.

The three storage devices mentioned above as examples and all other important methods are covered in the following detailed explanation of storage
equipment. This section concludes with a discussion of main memory and of
techniques that have been developed to extend the effective capacity and
speed of main memory hardware.

Magnetic core technology was utilized as the only way of building main
memory for over 20 years after its development in the early 1950s, making the
term "core memory" a slang equivalent for primary storage. A *core* is a tiny
piece of magnetic material, such as iron, iron oxide, or ferrite. A bit of data is
stored by magnetizing the core in one of two possible directions. The data bit is
later retrieved by noting whether the core's magnetic state is changed by an
electric current that causes it to be magnetized in a known direction. If a
change is indicated by an induced voltage, then another current is immediately applied to restore the original magnetic direction representing the stored
bit of data. A core memory consists of a rectangular array of cores connected
by fine wires. To store or retrieve data for one core in the memory, two current
pulses are applied at the same time to one row and one column of the array so
that the only response is in the single core at the location where these two
pulses coincide.

Electronic semiconductor technology has replaced magnetic core memory in the more recent generations of computers. The first semiconductor memories were built with *bipolar transistors*. Each bipolar transistor acts as a flip-flop circuit with two branches that are connected so that only one branch can be on at any time. These bipolar devices provide extremely fast data access, but a relatively strong electric signal is required to operate them. Transistors of the *metal oxide semiconductor* (MOS) type were later developed. MOS devices operate with weaker electric signals but give somewhat slower data access. Both bipolar and MOS transistors are manufactured as dense interconnected arrays on small chips through *large-scale integration* (LSI) technology. This dramatically reduces the cost per bit of data capacity for memory hardware.

The *charge-coupled device* (CCD) and the *bubble memory* are two new developments in storage hardware that have not yet been widely utilized but have important potential for specialized equipment. A CCD operates by shifting packets of electrical charge through a line of MOS devices. A series of timed pulses are applied at the beginning of the line and charge is either introduced or not with each pulse to represent the "1" or "0" value of the stored bit. The packets of charge are continuously shifted down the line in sequence. At the end of the line, the pattern of charge or no charge is detected, amplified, and reapplied to form a closed loop. The advantage of a CCD over an array of independent MOS transistors is that each MOS device in the line is smaller and they are tightly packed so the same chip area can store four times as many bits. The disadvantage is longer access time because each stored bit can be manipulated only when it reaches the end of the line.

The operating concept of a bubble memory is similar to that of a CCD, but involves shifting magnetic bubbles rather than packets of charge. The bubbles are actually cylindrical regions magnetized in the direction opposite the direction of magnetization of the surrounding material and are created when a magnetic field of the proper strength is applied perpendicular to the surface of a suitable material. A bubble memory is a chip consisting of a synthetic garnet base, covered by a layer of garnet doped with iron, calcium, or germanium, and then topped with a pattern of conductors. A bubble memory chip is simpler to manufacture than a semiconductor chip although similar methods are employed. Several chips are put together in a standard package that also includes a permanent magnet to preserve the bubbles when power is shut off, coils to generate the magnetic fields that move the bubbles, and electronic circuits to control and detect the pattern of bubbles or no bubbles that represents the stored bits of data. Access time for a bubble memory is many times slower than for a CCD. The unique positive characteristic of a bubble memory is that it retains the stored data indefinitely without power, making it comparable to a magnetic disk or tape. A bubble memory is more expensive per bit of data than disk or tape, but it is a compact device that can operate reliably even when subjected to rough handling or a dirty environment, which disk drives and tape units cannot do.

Magnetic cores, bipolar and MOS transistors, charge-coupled devices, and bubble memories all store data through electronic or magnetic methods alone. In contrast, magnetic disk or tape involves data storage on a magnetic recording medium plus mechanical motion of that medium. This mechanical motion significantly reduces access speed and increases the likelihood of problems. However, the cost per bit of memory capacity provided by disk and tape is extremely low for on-line storage and is almost negligible for off-line storage. The economy of disk and tape storage is a particularly important consideration for most computer graphics applications since a large volume of data is required for active design work and since all completed designs must be maintained for future reference.

Like the nonmechanical storage devices, a disk provides direct, random access to any desired storage location, but its method of operation involves appreciably longer access times. Bits of data are stored sequentially along each of a number of concentric circular tracks on the surface of the disk. Access to the data is provided by a read/write mechanism, either a single head that moves to position itself over the appropriate track or a stationary configuration with one head per track. The delay involved in seeking a particular storage location is the sum of the time required for positioning the head (if any) and the time required for the spinning disk to bring the storage location under the head. A block of sequential data can be transferred very rapidly because the only delay is to seek the location of the first data item in the block.

Two distinct types of disk systems are available. Large-capacity, high-performance systems utilize *hard disks,* while systems designed to have a low purchase price and inexpensive, removable recording media are based on *flexible disks.* Flexible disks, also called floppy disks or diskettes, have a small storage capacity because of the smaller size of the disk (8- or 5.25-inch diameter) and because of a data density that is roughly 1000 times less than that of a hard disk. A removable hard disk must always stay mounted within a protective pack since slight physical damage could make the stored data irretrievable because of the exacting tolerance of the system. A flexible disk, on the other hand, is removed by itself and is then placed in a protective jacket like a phonograph record. Its flexibility makes it less susceptible to damage from accidents in handling, although it is affected slightly by changes in temperature and humidity.

A magnetic tape unit transfers long strings of sequential data at a satisfactory speed and reels of tape provide for permanent off-line storage of data in computer-readable form. Magnetic tape is actually a cheaper storage medium than printed paper since it is reusable. Magnetic tape provides only sequential data access; that is, to reach a storage location somewhere in the middle of a reel of tape it is necessary to go through all of the preceding data items at the tape unit's fixed processing speed. The processing speed is limited by the problem of moving the tape across the stationary read/write mechanism. The performance of a tape unit is measured by three characteristics—tape speed (inches per second), recording density (bytes per inch), and the resulting data rate (bytes per second). All standard tape systems fall within a narrow performance range, the highest data rate being about 200 times the lowest rate.

All the storage devices described in this section share a common trait—data are stored in bits. A single bit can constitute a data item, but a larger entity, either a byte or a computer word, is generally regarded as the data item for practical operations. A *byte* is a string of bits that is operated on as a unit by the computer. A byte is almost always 8 bits in length. A *computer word* is the number of bits that the computer can most comfortably handle at one time. Word length must be an even multiple of byte length. The typical word is 8 bits (1 byte) for a microcomputer, 16 bits (2 bytes) for a minicomputer, and 32 bits (4 bytes) for a large computer.

The computer places a data item in storage or retrieves it from storage by specifying where the data item is located. This is called *addressing*. Data stored on a disk or tape device are usually addressed in terms of the records, blocks, and files set up by the application program. In contrast, the rapid exchange of data between the processor and the main memory is based on a direct one-word address assigned to the storage location of each individual byte. The upper limit on the physical storage capacity that can be utilized within the main memory through direct addressing is set by the maximum number of unique locations that a one-word address can specify. Two distinct values can be generated by a single bit, so the number of unique addresses that can be represented with a string containing N bits is equal to the number 2 raised to the power N. The number of storage locations that can be specified by a single-word address using the three most common word lengths are given below:

8-bit	word:	2^8	=	256 (256-byte memory capacity)
16-bit	word:	2^{16}	=	65,536 (65-kilobyte memory capacity)
32-bit	word:	2^{32}	=	4,294,967,296 (4-gigabyte memory capacity)

The size of the main memory is important because at any given time it must contain all the instructions in the program being executed and all the data being directly operated on by those instructions. The traditional solution to the problem of running a complex, large graphics system on a computer with a relatively small main memory is to write the program in many small modules. An overall graphics application program then calls each functional module into the main memory as required in response to user actions at the terminal. This method of utilizing memory is called *overlaying* because new modules are transferred into main memory from disk storage by being written over previously called modules, thus replacing them.

Many modern computers incorporate in their operating systems a technique called *virtual memory* that automatically accomplishes the same result as overlaying, namely, fitting large programs and their data into a small main memory. The maximum capacity of main memory that can be installed in a minicomputer of simple design is limited by the number of different memory locations that can be given by using one computer word as the address. For example, a 16-bit word can specify 65K different locations. A virtual memory system for this same minicomputer could allow programs to utilize two-word addresses and thus create the illusion of a main memory with over four billion storage locations. The computer operating system converts virtual addresses to physical addresses during program execution and makes the instructions and data stored at those addresses available to the processor by continually swapping data between main memory and auxiliary disk storage. The most common swapping technique is *paging,* a process of handling data in fixed-size increments called pages that usually contain from 512 to 2000 bytes.

When the processor requests data located at a particular virtual address, the operating system converts that virtual address into a physical address in the form of the page number and the byte number within that page. The requested data are then supplied to the processor from main memory. If the operating system determines that the requested data do not reside in main memory at that time, then it suspends execution of the program, finds the needed data on the disk, brings a page containing the needed data into main memory, and then restarts program execution.

Virtual addressing and paging are automatic processes that occur rapidly. Simpler programs can be written when virtual memory is available, a significant advantage. A disadvantage is the danger that execution may be slowed down if the logical structure of the program conflicts with the arbitrary page assignments causing an excessive amount of swapping.

Cache memory is a technique for speeding up access to main memory, rather than extending its capacity. Speed is always important for an interactive application such as graphics. A cache memory is a small memory device installed between the processor and the main memory. Typically the main memory is built with MOS or magnetic core hardware, whereas the cache memory is built with much faster and more expensive bipolar hardware. The cache stores data in pairs consisting of a main memory address and a copy of the data stored at that address. When the processor requests data from an address in main memory, that address is first checked against the current contents of cache memory. If the address is found, the data half of the pair is passed to the processor utilizing the high-speed access of the cache. When the address is not found, the data are supplied to the processor from main memory in the normal way, but the address and its data content are moved into the cache at the same time. The new pair takes the place of some previously accessed pair. In addition, any data that are transferred from the processor into main memory are also stored or updated in the cache. These operations guarantee that the main memory contains a complete set of current data and that the cache contains an accurate copy of a selected subset of that data. An access that is completed from cache memory is termed a *hit*, while an access that must reference main memory is a *miss*. The percent of accesses that are hits depends on the characteristics of the program being executed and on the capacity of the cache. A cache memory in the size range of 2K to 8K bytes can be expected to provide about 90% hits.

PART TWO
Software

CHAPTER 5

Building the Computer Model

Interactive computer graphics is based on the concept of working with a *model* described by information stored in the computer. For a simple application such as drafting, the model includes only the information required to generate a picture of the physical object, such as the lines in a drawing or a detailed three-dimensional representation. The application areas of simulation or computer-aided design and analysis involve a more extensive model in which the graphic data are associated with additional facts or mathematical equations explaining nonvisual characteristics of the physical object [5]. An abstract entity such as a chemical process can be modeled by a graphic flow chart. The work with the computer model is of two types, the creation of the model through input by the user and the display of the resulting model by the computer. This chapter and the next deal with the programming and use of the data input functions that are required to build the model. Chapters 7 and 8 cover the data output functions used to generate views of the model. In this way, the software section is divided along the same lines as the hardware section, with separate chapters devoted to input and output.

The subject of interactive input encompasses more than just the way information is transferred from the input equipment to the graphics application program. In fact, the lowest level of input functions handle this transfer. It is the higher level functions that produce a satisfactory man–machine dialogue. This chapter begins with a discussion of the command language input functions to create and revise a drawing or model. Next, the requirements for an association between graphic and nongraphic data to fully describe a drawing or model are presented. This is followed by an explanation of the basic program structure that enables the graphics system to accept incoming communications and respond according to the predetermined rules of the command language. The chapter concludes with a presentation of the logical input device concept, a scheme for classifying all input operations according to their effect rather than by the type of equipment utilized.

5.1. COMMAND LANGUAGE

The *command language* is the set of rules by which the user and the computer carry on their conversation. The command language of each graphics system determines what type of input data is accepted and how these input data are utilized in building the model. The command language also provides for data entry that allows the user to select views of the model for display, as described in Chapter 7.

The graphics operator uses the input functions of the command language for three basic purposes: command selection, positioning, and pointing. *Command selection* means activating one of the graphic operations provided by the drafting system, such as the ability to create lines, circles, and rectangles. *Positioning* is used in conjunction with an input command to supply the necessary information about the location and size of the object being created. This is done by simply placing new points on the drawing. *Pointing* is the method of identifying existing objects on the screen to revise the drawing.

The information about the location and size of the graphic object required by each input command depends on the geometry of the object, but a graphics system usually offers a variety of different commands, each requiring different positioning information, so the operator can choose the most convenient input method for each particular design situation. For example, it is possible to have four different commands for circle input, categorized by the positioning information required as follows: (1) circle placement by center point and one circumference point; (2) circle placement by center point and the numeric length of the radius; (3) circle placement by the two endpoints of a diameter of the circle; (4) circle placement by any three points on the circumference of the circle. Because every circle in the data base is described in a standard format, it makes no difference which command was used to create a circle once it is part of a drawing. A typical format would contain the coordinates of the center point and the length of the radius. The four input commands access four different calculation routines within the graphics system that convert the position information entered by the vessel designer into the standard format for the data base.

One desirable characteristic of any input method is to minimize the number of actions required by the operator to achieve the desired result. For this reason, the graphics system uses the order in which the design points are entered to distinguish between the center point and the circumference point for command type 1. The alternative would be a requirement that each point be identified by a menu selection of either "center" or "circumference." The preferable method is point entry in a specific order, which requires two actions by the operator, rather than point entry with identification, which requires four actions. The two diameter endpoints or the three circumference points can be entered in any order when using commands type 3 and 4. The advantage of having the four different circle commands is that a single operator action identifies both the object to be created and the placement information to be entered.

The operator can short cut the time required to build a drawing from the basic objects (i.e., lines, circles, and rectangles) by utilizing a library of standard detailed symbols. The input command "place symbol" can copy a symbol from the library and place it on the drawing. Positioning a single point on the screen for the origin of the symbol determines the placement of the entire symbol. The *origin* is a designated alignment point predefined in the library at a convenient place somewhere inside or near the symbol. The operator must set up several input controls within the graphics system prior to placing a symbol. These input controls are the name of the symbol, the scale factor, and the placement angle. The *scale factor* is a number that is multiplied times each dimension of the standard symbol to determine the size on the drawing. The *placement angle* is an angle of rotation about the symbol origin that determines how the symbol is oriented on the drawing compared to its orientation in the library.

During the design process the operator frequently needs to delete a previously drawn object, move an object, or modify an object in some way. The input commands that the operator can use to accomplish these actions all involve interacting with the drawing that is already stored in the data base. This is a more complicated process than simply adding new data because it is first necessary to indicate to the computer which object must be revised. This operation is called pointing.

The operator can delete a circle by choosing the "delete" command and then positioning a point anywhere inside the circle or on the circumference. It is usually possible to clearly indicate which circle should be deleted by a suitable input point; however, doubtful situations can occur, such as an input point placed inside the smaller of two concentric circles. One method to resolve the uncertainty is to search the data base from the beginning, highlight each possible object on the screen, and allow the operator to accept or refuse that object. The search continues after each refusal until an object is accepted or until all candidates have been highlighted.

Input commands that revise the drawing can deal only with an object as a whole because all changes are made within the data base. An example of this is the "modify" command that can change a circle into an arc. The operator selects the command from the menu and then positions two input points on the circumference of the circle (Figure 5.1a). The portion of the circle between the points (Figure 5.1b) is omitted when the screen is erased and updated, so the remainder of the circle is displayed as an arc (Figure 5.1c). The visual effect is that the computer system has recognized the two points as locations on the circle and has removed the circular segment between those points, but the modification is not really accomplished this way. The computer system cannot recognize the two points as being on the circumference because a circle is not described in the data base by all the displayed points

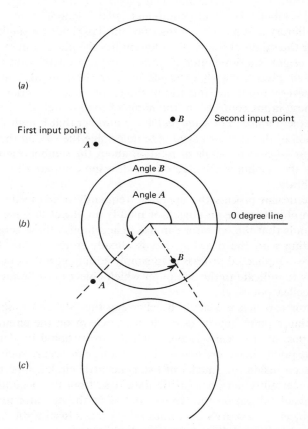

Figure 5.1. Process of modifying a circle. (a) Original circle. (b) Angles calculated by computer. (c) Arc displayed after screen update.

that make up the screen image. These points are the result of a hardware circle generator in the display device. Instead, the data base description is simplified to a format such as the center point coordinates plus the numeric length of the radius and the computer must calculate the modification using this description.

This modification is actually a process of removing the circle from the data base and replacing it with the arc. The graphics system creates a new data base description for the arc by copying the center point and radius length from the description of the circle and calculating the two angles that indicate where the arc begins and ends. The computer in effect extends imaginary lines from the center point to each of the input points and then measures the angle from the 0-degree axis to each of these lines (Figure 5.1b). This calculation can be carried out just as easily with input points that are inside or outside the circle as with points located exactly on the image. The modify command can change other objects in a similar manner, utilizing data base information such as the two endpoints for a line or the multiple vertex points for a polygon.

Another example of the manner in which the computer system revises graphic objects is the "move" command. The operator enters two input points. The first point identifies the object to be moved and establishes a reference point. The distance between the first and second points is calculated and is then applied to the coordinates of each point in the data base definition of the object. An image of the object quickly appears on the screen at the new location with the same size, shape, and orientation as before the move. In this example the drafting system minimizes the number of actions required by the designer in two ways. First, a single command initiates both the pointing operation and the subsequent revision to the object. Second, the same input point is used in the identification search and the distance calculation.

The operator can revise entire portions of the drawing through area commands. Instead of pointing to a single object on the screen, the operator chooses the command "define area" and places a series of points that are connected with lines to form a closed boundary. This boundary is held in temporary storage because it is not part of the drawing. All objects that are completely contained within this area are identified by the computer system. The designer can then make revisions with commands such as "delete area contents" or "move area contents."

The area boundary commands involve visual interaction with groups of objects on the screen. The designer can also associate objects in a nonvisual manner by assigning alphanumeric group codes as a permanent part of the data base descriptions. While the group code can be useful in revising drawings, it is more commonly used as an identification tag for processing non-graphic data associated with the drawing.

5.2. ASSOCIATION OF GRAPHIC AND NONGRAPHIC DATA

"Data" is not synonymous with "information"—information is produced through programmed procedures that utilize data. This section is concerned with the association of graphic and nongraphic data for maximum usefulness in generating information and the conditions imposed on data handling by the special characteristics of an interactive computer graphics system.

Graphic data alone are not useful for anything beyond generating pictures, but additional benefits are possible when graphic and nongraphic data are associated in an integrated data base. Throughout this book the phrase "data base" is used to mean the numbers and letters that are stored in the computer in some organized manner to describe the two-dimensional drawing or three-dimensional object that is created by the interactive computer graphics system. In this sense, every graphics system has a data base. However, the term "data base" has a more precise meaning when used in the sense of an integrated data base that is supervised through a data base management system (DBMS).

Software packages for data base management have existed since the early 1970s. However, all these packages were designed for strictly nongraphic applications. Applying the concept of data base management to graphic applications, and in particular to the task of associating graphic and nongraphic data, is a more formidable undertaking. Graphic applications have special characteristics and requirements.

First, there is an enormous volume of data involved in graphics. Many times more data items are added to the storage requirement by the detailed description of the computer model than are subtracted by the elimination of redundant items. The following example demonstrates this. A building foundation is represented by a single number for the required cubic feet of concrete in a stand-alone cost-estimating system. This number is the result of a separate manual calculation. The foundation is represented in an integrated graphics system by three coordinates (x, y, z) for each corner of its solid shape with information about how these corners are connected plus nongraphic information related to the concrete material. The cost-estimating system calculates the cubic feet of concrete from these raw data.

Second, the attractiveness of an interactive graphics system depends on its ability to respond almost instantly by visually displaying the result of each user action. Therefore, interactive computer graphics is totally incompatible with any data base system that would increase response time because of excessive complexity in its data storage and retrieval processes. The data handling method in a purely graphic system is optimized for fast response that far surpasses the speed of any existing nongraphic DBMS.

Third, the input technique must be simple and direct. It must rely on visual interaction as much as possible to promote a sense of naturalness in the man–machine dialogue. A combined system in which the entry of nongraphic data entailed a lot of typing would distract the terminal operator from the visual interaction with his creative design and thus would be unacceptable.

Fourth, there must be a true, intimate association of the graphic and nongraphic data. Input is simplified when the two types of data can be intermingled in any convenient entry sequence. Ideally, the operator can visually select an object on the screen to associate with a nongraphic data entry so no artificial object names have to be introduced. The operator can also use the same visual selection method to request retrieval and display of all nongraphic data currently stored for any graphic object.

The problems presented by the four special requirements listed above have been addressed in various ways. A proposed answer to the massive volume of data is to set up a temporary working storage area. The data directly concerned with a portion of the project are pulled out of the data base and placed in this area at the beginning of an interactive design session. The data in working storage are merged back into the integrated data base when the session is finished. Access to any item in the data base that is not in working storage would simply involve a longer response time. The major challenge in this proposed solution is to identify all the data related to a portion of the project, considering the interdependence of components.

One way to maintain fast response time is to keep graphic and nongraphic data in two completely separate files with an index to relate them. This solves the response problem during graphic design, but the input procedure for nongraphic data is more complicated. Also, a significant chance for inconsistency is introduced since the link is indirect. For instance, a graphic item can be deleted without also deleting its nongraphic attributes.

Many approaches that are touted as data base systems consist of nothing more than conventional techniques for manipulating data and have restricted usefulness. Developing an entirely satisfactory way of associating graphic and nongraphic data in computer storage is an unsolved problem. Work is underway on this problem in industry, in universities, and by the vendors of turnkey graphics systems. The great attention being given to this problem stems from a widespread recognition of the economic incentive behind its solution. A true breakthrough in this area will result in even faster acceptance of interactive computer graphics for practical applications.

5.3. PROGRAM STRUCTURE FOR INTERACTIVE INPUT

Interactive input is the communication from the user to the graphics system. The user communicates through the physical input devices at the graphics terminal, following the logic of the system's command functions. This section is concerned with the manner in which the graphics system is programmed to accept and understand the user's actions and how the system fulfills the command functions in response to the input. The major objectives of input processing are (1) to receive each user action, (2) to allow the computer to equitably service other terminals or background programs in a multiuser system while awaiting the next user action, and (3) to provide fast results for the user.

Each physical input device includes a small amount of temporary storage called a *buffer*. The buffer holds a device *flag* and one unit of input data. The flag is a sign to the computer that the user has acted. The flag is set to "1" when the user makes an entry and is reset to "0" by the computer after the data have been received. The type of input data in the buffer varies by device. For a keyboard data may consist of either one character or a string of characters terminated by the "enter" character. For a button data comprises the identification code for which button was pushed. The tablet and cursor are two devices interconnected so that the location of the cursor on the tablet is recorded at the moment a cursor button is pressed. The unit of data in this case is the point coordinates with the button code.

A modern computer includes *interrupt* hardware that causes the program in progress to be interrupted each time a device flag is set. A short program called an *interrupt handling routine* receives the input data from the device buffer and puts them in storage until the graphics system is ready to process them. After the data are received and stored, control of the computer is returned to the program that was in progress when the interrupt occurred. Interrupt priority determines which device gets the attention of the computer when two or more flags are set at the same time. The faster devices get higher priority. For example, a digitizer needs a higher priority than the keyboard because many points can be entered very quickly and must be recorded instantly, while typing a text string and terminating it with the "enter" key is a slower activity. The computer normally handles interrupts so rapidly that the user at the terminal is unaware of any delay.

The computer storage area for input data is called an *attention queue* or an *event queue*. The word "queue" was adapted for computer terminology from a British expression for waiting one's turn in line. The items waiting in line in this situation are requests from the user for attention by the computer, indicated by events that have occurred within the input devices. The data stored in the queue for each attention request include the terminal number (in a multiuser system), the device type, and the contents of the input data transferred from the device buffer. The interrupt priority is not stored. The attention queue is a first in, first out *circular buffer*, where the next attention, after the last space is filled, is stored in the first space. Reusing the storage area in this manner holds the amount of CPU that must be allocated for the queue within a reasonable limit. A graphics system with intelligent terminals could maintain individual attention queues at each terminal rather than bring all the input data into one shared file in the host computer.

A properly designed interactive system operates fast enough that the computer is usually waiting on the user, even in a multiterminal configuration. However, if the computer does get occupied with a lengthy calculation, the attention queue makes it possible for the user to keep working, with his input being stored until the computer can process it. The temporary lack of visual feedback is not a restriction in many situations. For example, the user may quickly place several vertices of a polygon before the system can display the line connecting the first pair of vertices. Because of this work-ahead effect, the experienced operator learns to wait a few seconds before assuming that his input was not received and reentering it. The system has built-in safeguards to stop the user when he gets too far ahead, because an overflow of this circular buffer would cause new input data added to the attention queue to destroy the previously stored data in the same space.

The input information is taken out of the attention queue one unit at a time by a portion of the graphics application program called the *task scheduler*. The purpose of the task scheduler is to route the input data to the appropriate *task* within the application program for further processing. Task is just another word for program. Each command for creating a graphic object has a related task that accepts the input data and puts them into a suitable format for addition to the data base. Figure 5.2 shows the overall program structure for interactive input, from the origin at the input devices to the conclusion at the data base. The system also includes tasks for setting input controls, for manipulating the displayed image, and for handling error conditions.

The task scheduler decides how to route the input data on the basis of three considerations: (1) which device originated the data, (2) the data content, and (3) the state of the graphics system.

The identity of the input device determines the method the task scheduler uses to examine the incoming data. For instance, a tablet with a four-button cursor acts as four separate devices. A point entered with the command button is translated into the corresponding menu command, whereas the same point entered with the design point button is converted into a location relative to the drawing displayed on the screen.

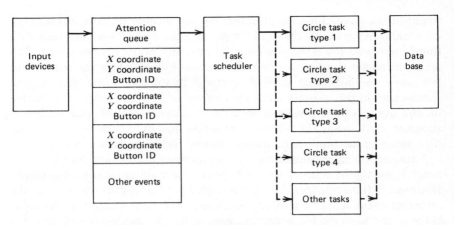

Figure 5.2.   Program structure for interactive input.

The data content also influences the operation of the task scheduler. One example is the fact that a command name entered from the keyboard is accepted by the graphics system while a slightly different name is routed to an error routine so a warning message can be displayed.

The *state* of the graphics system is the combined condition of all system variables at a given moment. The current values of the screen image parameters are a part of the state of the graphics system. Another part of the state of the graphics system is the active command sequence. For example, the sequence for the type 1 circle command involves two different states. After the menu command for circle type 1 is selected by the operator, the graphics system is ready to accept the center point. Call this state "1." After the operator enters the first input point, the system then waits to receive the circumference point. This is state "2." After the second point is entered, the sequence is completed and the circle is displayed. The graphics system is ready to begin again with another center point, which is state "1." The operator can alter the sequence at any time by entering a new command or by pressing the command reset button, causing the system to enter a different state. Other components of the state of the graphics system are the active settings of the input controls such as scale factor, placement angle, group code, and the various appearance attributes.

The task scheduler's method for routing input data to the appropriate task within the application program is complicated by the fact that the state of the graphics system must be considered, in addition to the input device type and the input data content. A rough measure of the number of possible distinct states during interactive input is the product of the number of different command functions times the average number of user data entries required for each command. The task scheduler must have a method for associating each user action with the proper computer reaction. One such method is a *table lookup* utilizing a separate table for each state. The task scheduler uses the current state to choose the proper table and then uses the input device type as a table index to locate the appropriate table item. The information stored in this table item is the name of the task that should process the input data and the setting for the next state, since each user action potentially changes the state of the system. This table method is based on simple logic, but it involves lengthy lookup operations and it fills a portion of the CPU with the multiple tables. An alternative to table lookup is procedure coding, a feature of some specialized high-level graphics programming languages that makes it possible to incorporate the decision-making process entirely within the program itself [6].

A strict separation of the input and output functions within the graphics system provides a neat modular program structure and guarantees that every object appearing on the screen is stored in the data base. The practical result of this modular programming is that the task that processes the input data and adds the new object to the data base does not automatically display the object. Instead, the task scheduler gives the user visual feedback by calling an output task as soon as the input sequence has been completed. The output task adds the new object to the display file of a system with a refresh screen or it directly draws the object on a storage tube without erasing the previous image.

A program structure for interactive input based on interrupt handling routines and an attention queue meets the three major objectives of input processing listed at the beginning of this section. A user action cannot be missed by the graphics system because the device flag activates the interrupt hardware in the computer. The computer can handle background programs and can provide fast results when the user does request attention by making an entry because no processing time is lost waiting between user actions. The task scheduler in the application program only needs to check one location (the CPU address of the current beginning of the attention queue) to determine if any user input is waiting for processing. Without interrupt hardware it is necessary for the graphics system to *poll* each input device on a regular schedule to determine if any data are waiting in the device buffer. Polling wastes computer time and can lead to loss of data if the user makes two or more entries on a single device during the time required for one polling cycle. Polling is seldom found in present day graphics systems.

The attention queue is a convenient interface between a standard graphics package (Section 9.3), which handles the basic input and output device services, and a customized application program, which handles the task scheduling and graphic object creation, because the standard package adds entries to the attention queue for the application program to remove and process.

5.4. LOGICAL INPUT DEVICES

Logical input devices are the abstract counterparts to the physical input devices discussed in Chapter 1. A synonymous term, *virtual input devices,* emphasizes that these devices exist in effect rather than in concrete form. A classification of the popular physical devices according to their simplest functions yields the definition of a set of logical input devices. A typical example is the set of logical devices supported by the ACM/SIGGRAPH Core System [7], which consists of PICK, KEYBOARD, BUTTON, LOCATOR, and VALUATOR. PICK is a pointing device capable of identifying an object within the displayed image. LOCATOR is a positioning device for the entry of point coordinates. Interactive input of alphanumeric text is accomplished through the KEYBOARD, but input of numeric values within a predefined range is done with a VALUATOR. The use of a BUTTON implies a choice among alternatives, for command selection or other purposes. These five logical device definitions are a selected group based on currently available equipment. One common physical input device that has no counterpart in the core system is the *switch*, a device that changes state between on and off. A switch is useful for controlling options such as the grid and axis placement constraints. Future developments in hardware design are likely to introduce functions that will require new logical device definitions.

A graphics application program that is written in terms of logical input devices is *device independent* because it does not receive data directly from the physical devices but instead receives data that have already been put into a standard form. The transfer of information from the input equipment to the application program is handled by a group of small, specialized programs called *device drivers,* which are written to be compatible with the specifications of the individual physical devices. Logical device simulation is accomplished through data manipulation by another group of specialized programs devoted to input functions. Figure 5.3 shows the program structure of a device-independent graphics system based on logical input devices.

Device-independent software can be moved from one installation to another that is equipped with different input hardware with a minimum of difficulty. The minor problems involved in switching from one device to a similar unit by another manufacturer are overcome by changing the device driver program. Device simulation is used to adjust for a different mix of hardware types. An example is the use of a number and letter menu to take the place of

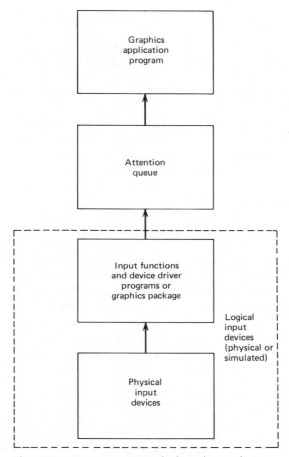

Figure 5.3.   Program structure for logical input devices.

a physical keyboard. Device simulation adjustments require that routines be added or removed from the input functions portion of the system, but the application program does not have to be changed in any way. A device-independent graphics system is also protected from obsolescence because improved input equipment can be substituted into the system with no major program changes. A current example is the introduction of a sixteen-button cursor to replace the original four-button model. The logical device concept makes it easy to switch frequently used command selections from menu squares (simulated BUTTONS) to actual cursor buttons.

The concept of logical input devices simplifies the work of the programmer of a graphics application. If the program structure shown in Figure 5.3 is used the programmer need not be concerned with the physical characteristics of the input devices and can concentrate on their functions instead. The programmer can utilize the logical devices that will be best suited for handling the information flow from the user to the computer required for his or her specific application and can omit the others.

The drawback with the logical device concept is that the program structure makes it impossible to take full advantage of all the unique features of each input device. In effect, device independence is system design based on the lowest common denominator among equipment. The fact that the best interactive response for the user can only be achieved with a graphics program tailored to suit the actual hardware is acknowledged by the designers of the ACM/SIGGRAPH Core System [7]. However, they decided to accept reduced interactive response to gain the advantages of device independence since the Core System is intended as a tool for a variety of users who have all different kinds of equipment. On the other hand, the designers of a commercial turnkey drafting system are preparing software to be marketed along with a selected set of hardware, so they can strive for top efficiency by writing their application program to suit the actual input devices.

Since the device definitions are derived from the simple functions of existing equipment, it is obvious that each logical device has one or more naturally corresponding physical devices. The natural device for the PICK function is a light pen working with a refresh screen. The KEYBOARD represents a typewriter-style keyboard. The BUTTON corresponds to any type of physical button or to a program function keyboard. The cursor and tablet combination is the device naturally suited for the LOCATOR function. Natural devices for the VALUATOR function include dials, trackballs, and joysticks. A physical device that is not directly applicable to a particular logical function can be adapted to that function through extra programming within the graphics system. A program-supported action by one device that is comparable to a simple action by some other device is considered to be a simulation. Many important input techniques depend on simulated input devices. The light pen used with a dense grid display or with a tracking cross hair for positioning is a simulated LOCATOR, and light pen selection of displayed light button options for system control is a simulated BUTTON.

Simulation of logical devices through program augmentation can be extended to the point where all interactive input for a graphics system is done with one physical device.

Single-device input based on the physical keyboard occurs in some older systems. In this case, there is a natural correspondence to the KEYBOARD function. The BUTTON is simulated by typing names of commands and symbols. A short alphanumeric label assigned to each object and each significant design point allows the PICK function to be simulated. The LOCATOR function is achieved by typing point coordinates, either as absolute coordinates or relative to some labeled design point. The VALUATOR simulation simply involves typed numeric characters that the computer accepts as a number.

The menu is such a flexible input technique that some graphics systems rely heavily on the tablet and cursor for single-device input. The most convenient use of the menu is to simulate the BUTTON function because it is possible to design the menu using pictures, descriptions, color, and a variety of area sizes to make the alternatives stand out. The menu is equivalent to a large set of program function keys. An area on the menu marked with letters and numbers can simulate a KEYBOARD, but entering characters with the cursor seems slow to a user capable of touch-typing on a physical keyboard. The VALUATOR logical device is simulated by menu squares assigned to frequently used values of controls such as placement angle and scale factor, with all other values entered through the simulated KEYBOARD. Highly interactive applications like rapid zoom and pan display manipulations cannot be handled by this simulated VALUATOR, so the menu must be supplemented by natural VALUATOR devices such as dials and joysticks for this purpose. System features such as the grid and axis placement constraints are controlled with menu squares that act as switches, alternating between on and off with each selection of that menu option. The pointing procedure involving assistance by the user to select the correct object (see Section 5.1) is a simulated PICK. This is not as elegant as the natural light pen pointing function, but a storage tube graphics system cannot implement anything except a simulated PICK. All these simulated logical devices are additions to the natural LOCATOR function of the cursor and tablet.

The preceding discussion of single-device systems is intended only as an example of simulation methods, not as a recommendation on system design. The result of the excessive device simulation required for single-device input is unnecessary program complexity and extra user effort. Maximum productivity is achieved with a mixture of input equipment matched to the application. The ACM/SIGGRAPH Core System [7] requires as a minimum set the following logical input devices: one PICK, one LOCATOR, one KEYBOARD, four VALUATORS, and eight BUTTONS. Which of these functions will be provided by physical devices and which by simulation is not specified. This is left to the discretion of the designer of a Core System graphics package.

All logical input devices fall into two broad categories, those that are *discrete, event-causing devices* and those that are *continuous, sampled devices*. A discrete device originates one unit of input data at a time. The system adds the unit of data to the attention queue in the form of an *event report*. An event report is the result of a user action such as pushing a button, entering a character string from the keyboard, or aiming a light pen at an image on the screen. In contrast, a continuous device, such as a cursor and tablet combination or a knob, generates values that vary smoothly as the device is moved from one position to another by the user. The computer samples the device by periodically recording the value generated. Three possible methods to control sampling are as follows: (1) rely on some timing mechanism within the input device to send values to the program at fixed intervals; (2) build a function into the program that will accept information from the device at defined periods; and (3) record the value from the continuous device at the time that an event is caused by an associated discrete device. The first and second methods both provide sampling at a fixed rate, but program control can better match the sampling rate to the requirements of the application. Sampling at regular intervals is occasionally employed for input techniques such as inking and digitizing. The third method is the most useful for interactive input because it allows the user to indicate when the value is meaningful. For instance, the positioning of two design points requires that the user move the LOCATOR through many intermediate points that are not intended as input data. However, the LOCATOR has an associated BUTTON that the user presses when the LOCATOR is aligned with the first design point and then presses again when it reaches the second design point. An event report containing the BUTTON input data with the associated LOCATOR point coordinates is added to the attention queue for each design point. In this way, only meaningful data are recorded.

CHAPTER 6

Interactive Input Techniques

A variety of input techniques have been innovated by many individuals over a period of years. The purpose of each technique has been to make the task of creating the computer model more natural and efficient for the user of the system. Each of the next eight sections discusses a group of related techniques that serve a specific function within the overall objective of simplifying the work of the user. These groups include menu alternatives, which are ways for the operator to indicate choices to the computer, macro commands that extend the capabilities of the command language, accuracy aids, sketching methods, digitizing, the input of text and dimensions, and a complete survey of techniques for three-dimensional input.

6.1. MENU AND MENU ALTERNATIVES

The graphics system menu presents the operator with all of his options for command selection, symbol placement, and so forth in much the same way that a restaurant menu presents the customer with meal selections. Alternatives to a menu for option selection are a program function keyboard, a sequence of light buttons, a tutorial, and a character recognition technique.

A *menu* is the paper overlay used in conjunction with a digitizer input device for the selection of commands and symbols (Figure 6.1). The menu is marked into precise rectangular areas and each command or symbol is shown within one of these areas, either by a brief description or by a picture of the graphic object to be created. Menu areas also may be reserved for a simulated keyboard with areas marked by the letters of the alphabet and the numbers 0 to 9. The graphics system is preset to recognize points within the assigned areas. The operator chooses an option from the menu by placing the

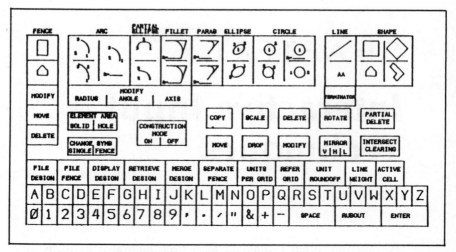

Figure 6.1. Portion of a tablet menu. Courtesy of M & S Computing, Inc.

digitizer's cursor within the area for the desired option and pressing a button.

A *program function keyboard* is a set of buttons, each of which is assigned to a special function within the graphics system, in contrast to the standard assignment of alphanumeric characters to the keys of a typewriter. The function of each button is indicated on an appropriately labeled paper or plastic overlay that fits over the base of the keyboard (Figure 6.2). The operator simply presses a button to select the command or graphic symbol represented by that button. A popular feature of program function keyboards is individually lighted buttons that are used by the computer to identify the currently active command. This is used as an alternative to writing a message on the display screen.

The attachment of meanings to the keys is analogous to the definition of menu squares, so the keyboard overlay can be user designed and interchanged for various applications in the same manner as the menu. The application program is set up to associate an event generated by a specific button with its predefined meaning. The function associated with each button is unique and does not change within the particular graphics system application.

The selection of program control options is the only role of the program function keyboard. Other input devices must be included in the system for the positioning and pointing operations. Whether this specialization is an advantage or disadvantage compared to the combination of all three operations

Figure 6.2. Program function keyboard. Reprinted with permission of Hewlett-Packard Company.

offered by the menu with tablet and cursor depends on the individual preference of the operator.

Option selection can also be accomplished through the use of *light buttons*, which are labeled areas on the display screen (Figure 6.3). Light buttons are in effect a menu that is displayed on the screen, utilizing the entire surface or limited to a reserved portion while the drawing is displayed on the remaining surface. The operator makes a selection from the screen by pointing a light pen at the desired option or by positioning a tablet and cursor input point within the light button area.

Light buttons have the advantage that the options presented can be rapidly changed by the application program to suit the design function that is currently in progress. This dynamic definition capability is in contrast to the static definition of the options presented by a tablet menu or a program function keyboard. Dynamic options could be used in the following manner. The system presents the operator with a menu of primitive graphic objects, such as point, line, rectangle, circle, and ellipse. The operator chooses to create a circle by pointing to the word "circle" on the screen menu. The system automatically brings up the next set of options, which are the four different types of placement information—center and circumference point, center and radius length, and so forth. The operator selects the first type. The light buttons disappear and a prompting message takes their place, instructing the operator about the required input. For the first type of circle, the messages are "enter center point of circle," followed by "enter any point on circumference of circle." The original selection of primitives returns to the screen when the input sequence is complete and the circle has been created. A sequence of screen menus and prompting messages such as this acts as a *tutorial* for the operator, with the computer in the role of the tutor. A tutorial involving the

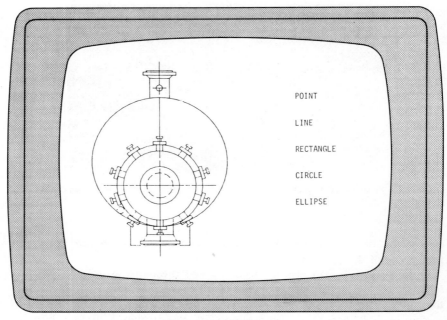

POINT

LINE

RECTANGLE

CIRCLE

ELLIPSE

Figure 6.3. Light buttons.

basic language commands could be used as a beginning course in graphics system operation. However, tutorials become cumbersome in the routine operation of a general-purpose drafting system because the operator grows familiar enough with the use of the system that he can generate input from a tablet menu faster than the computer can change screen options.

Light buttons have four advantages: (1) the operator is confronted with a smaller number of choices, limited to only those options that are valid for the current state of the graphics system; (2) prompting messages guide the user through the input sequence; (3) the operator's eyes remain on the screen at all times, both while selecting commands and positioning input points; and (4) the same physical device is used for both command selection and positioning. The main disadvantage is the program complexity required to provide the dynamic screen menu capability. Also, light buttons are best suited to a refresh system instead of a storage tube system because the screen display must be changed so frequently.

The advantages of allowing the operator to keep his eyes on the screen and to use the same input device for both commands and positioning also are found with an input technique known as *character recognition*. The operator

literally writes a letter, number, or simple symbol on the screen with any input device capable of entering a continuous trace, such as a light pen or
stylus and tablet combination. The application program accepts this
multitude of input points and analyzes them, but does not add them to the
drawing data base. The program includes a set of predefined character
shapes that it can recognize and then associate to a meaning. Some letters or
symbols can be assigned to identify commands. An impressive utilization of
character recognition is the ability of a graphics system to recognize a crude,
simplified version of a symbol drawn by the operator on the screen and
replace it with the precise symbol from the graphics library. The size, location, and orientation of the hand-drawn symbol can also determine the size,
location, and orientation of the standard symbol. Character recognition can
also convert hand lettering into computer characters for adding notes to the
drawing. A full discussion of the methods used in programming this process
of character recognition can be found in reference 1.

6.2. MACRO COMMANDS

Creating a drawing through the standard input commands is a step-by-step
procedure carried out by the operator at the graphics terminal. However, any
drafting task requiring repetition of the same steps each time can benefit
from the shortcut offered by a *macro command*, which is a single command
that stands for a sequence of operations. This computer terminology is consistent with the normal usage of "macro" as a modifier meaning large or
large scale. There are slight variations among graphics systems, but generally
a macro can utilize any standard feature of the graphics system, display
messages to the operator requesting input data, and wait until the operator
enters the data without interfering with other computer activities.

Any user who is knowledgeable in the operation of the graphics system can
quickly learn to set up macro commands. The user writes a series of
statements that follow the same logic as the interactive input sequence, using
short command names and other suitable notations. These statements are
stored in the computer. The designer uses the macro by selecting it from the
menu or by typing in its name. When the macro is selected, the computer interprets each statement in turn and performs the function called for by that
statement. A significant amount of computer time is required for inter-
preting the statements.

Macro commands are a valuable method of *extending* the command
language to provide specialized capabilities that are missing from the basic
graphics system. Another advantage is that several operators can develop
consistent working techniques by sharing the same macros. Macro com-

mands reduce the number of interactive actions that the user must perform to accomplish his drafting task. The total time consumed by a task is roughly the same whether it is handled interactively or through a macro because there is a trade-off between lags in response by the human operator and the delay caused by macro command statement interpretation by the computer. However, there may be a psychological effect from the inactivity of the operator while he waits for the macro to handle the task that makes the time required seem much longer to him.

Figure 6.4 shows how a macro command can be applied to the drafting of dimensions in engineering design to reduce the number of input steps required. The object shown is one end of a horizontal vessel. The dimension line runs parallel to the distance being measured with the numeric call-out centered above it. Witness lines extend to the object, perpendicular to the dimension line. The list on the left-hand side shows the steps the designer must perform to add this parallel dimension to the vessel drawing. The list on the right-hand side demonstrates that the number of data entries that the designer must make is reduced to a minimum through the use of the macro command shortcut since many of the previous steps can be replaced by predefined statements in a macro command.

6.3. ACCURACY

Computer drawings have a uniformly neat and precise appearance regardless of the individual style of the designer. Faults that might be overlooked on a typical hand-done drawing are exaggerated by the exactness of the computer plot. Lines that are almost but not quite parallel, corners that are not truly square, and corners where the lines do not meet or lap over would give a bad appearance to any computer drawing, even if it were intended as a preliminary sketch. Designers at a drafting board cannot afford to devote an excessive amount of time to making every drawing beautiful, but the computer-assisted designer has the means at his disposal to easily work with accuracy on every assignment.

The resolution of the screen is far less than the resolution of the final plot, so it is difficult to gauge the placement of input points by the eye alone. Therefore, the accuracy aids within the graphics system that are described in this section should be utilized routinely. These aids are essential for achieving high productivity on scaled drawings or any close tolerance work.

The ruled graph paper used for hand sketching has a counterpart in computer graphics, the *screen grid*. The grid appears on the screen as a series of regularly spaced lines or dots, with additional markers to divide the grid into multiples of the basic grid unit. The drawing can be displayed with or

(a) *NORMAL METHOD*		(b) *MACRO COMMAND SHORTCUT*	
Input steps	Description of input	Input steps	Description of input
1	Select command: create line	1	Select macro: parallel dimension
2 to 5	Enter design points *A*, *B*, *C*, *D*	2 to 4	Enter design points *A*, *B*, *C*
6	Select command: position symbol		Macro prompts user: Type dimension call-out
7	Select symbol name: arrow	5	Type: 3′ 3¼″
8	Enter design point *E* (same as *B*)		
9	Set placement angle: 180 degrees		
10	Enter design point *F* (same as *C*)		The macro sets point *D* to make the witness lines parallel and equal in length, places arrows on both ends of the dimension line, and centers the text above the dimension line.
11	Set placement angle: 0 degrees		
12	Select command: text, center-justified		
13	Type: 3′ 3¼″		
14	Enter design point *G*		

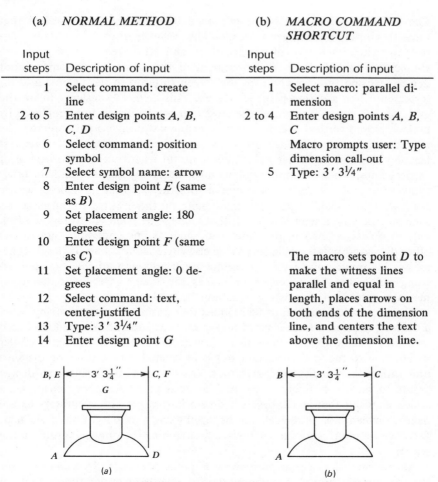

Figure 6.4. Comparison of parallel dimension input procedures.

without the grid. The advantage of the computer grid over graph paper is that the spacing of the grid units and the markers can be controlled interactively by the designer. Many systems are restricted to a rectangular grid, but it is helpful if the grid angle can be set for other commonly used drafting views, such as the isometric projection. The grid serves two main purposes, as a placement aid to create straight lines and as a measurement aid by the quick method of counting grid squares.

The grid alone is merely a guide for placing input by relying on the eye.

The graphics system can be programmed with automatic *constraints* that force the input into regular patterns. The designer utilizes interactive controls to switch each type of constraint on and off as required. A *grid constraint* acts as a lock on the movement of the system's positioning input device, causing the cross hair on the screen to jump to the nearest grid intersection when a design point is entered. This helps the designer follow the grid. An *axis constraint* causes the cross hair on the screen to be replaced by horizontal and vertical axes intersecting at the last design point entered. The next design point positioned anywhere on the screen jumps to the nearest location that lies on either axis. This is useful when drawing horizontal or vertical lines, when multiple symbols must be evenly aligned, and for other similar purposes. A *point constraint* assists the designer in making a new point exactly coincide with an existing point on the drawing for applications such as attaching a symbol to the end of a line. The point constraint can lock only to points defined in the data base, such as line endpoints, not to any other displayed points, including those elsewhere along a line. If the designer locates his input point within a certain small area around the intended existing point, the point constraint makes the match. Otherwise, an error message states that no existing point can be found.

There are additional input techniques that ensure accurate drafting when a drawing is created from a set of measurements, such as map making based on survey results. One of these methods is *distance roundoff*, which is similar in function to the grid constraint but is associated with a numeric distance unit rather than a displayed grid unit. Distance roundoff causes all design points to have coordinates measured in even increments. For example, a scaled drawing that must have all dimensions expressed accurately to the nearest sixteenth of an inch should be input using a roundoff unit of $\frac{1}{16}$ inch. Distance roundoff is useful when visually sketching the drawing layout on the screen.

An alternative to visual positioning is point placement by *numeric coordinates* entered through a keyboard device. The designer determines the unit of measure and the location of the origin point on the drawing. A new design point can be defined by a pair of absolute coordinates, which express a position relative to the origin, or by a pair of values for horizontal and vertical changes from the previous design point. The command language of the graphics system can include special commands for these two methods of accurate input. Additional commands can be programmed to check finished portions of the drawing for accuracy. The graphics system can perform precise measurements interactively and display results on the screen for purposes such as determining the coordinates of a point, the distance between two points, the degrees in an angle, and the area enclosed by a graphic object.

6.4. SKETCHING

This section deals with a variety of input techniques that offer the user flexibility in sketching a drawing by providing for tentative, trial positioning in contrast to the definitive, accurate type of positioning discussed in the preceding section. Equivalent input capabilities can be attained through two different approaches, one suitable only for systems with refresh displays having some microcomputer processing capability in the terminal, the other normally implemented on storage tube systems.

A refresh graphics system can be programmed using the techniques of *rubber band lines* and *dragging* to make it appear that the user can attach a graphic object to the positioning device and smoothly move it around on the screen. These two methods are similar in concept to the ordinary way a point is placed by moving the cursor cross hair around on the screen until it is located properly and then pressing a button to add the design point to the data base. A local microcomputer is required for trial positioning because the work of tracking the current location and generating the screen image is all done within the terminal. The definition of the graphic object is not added to the drawing data base until the rubber band or dragging procedure is terminated by the design point entry that fixes the location. A rubber band line is a straight line that has the appearance on the screen of a taut rubber band, secured to a pivot at one end. Moving the free end causes elastic stretching of the line to any length in any direction (Figure 6.5a). An effect similar to the rubber band line can be achieved for other simple graphic objects such as circles and rectangles (Figures 6.5b and 6.5c). For a circle, the center point is the fixed pivot and the positioning device controls only the overall size. For a rectangle, one corner is established by the first input point and the positioning device is attached to the diagonally opposite corner, making it possible to change both the size and the height-to-width ratio of the rectangle.

Dragging is the technique of symbol placement through trial positioning. A standard symbol, chosen from the graphics library and placed on the screen with a definite size and orientation, is attached to the positioning device at its placement point. The operator can move the symbol around on the screen until it reaches the proper location, using visual cues involving this symbol's relationship with other parts of the existing drawing. The purpose of dragging is to simplify the operator's work in situations where it would be difficult to determine in advance where the symbol's placement point should be located. Figure 6.6 shows this type of situation. The operator drags the star symbol on the left toward the one on the right until they touch, with no concern for the exact location of the placement point, which is the center of the star.

Figure 6.7 shows the advanced technique of *connectivity dragging*. The

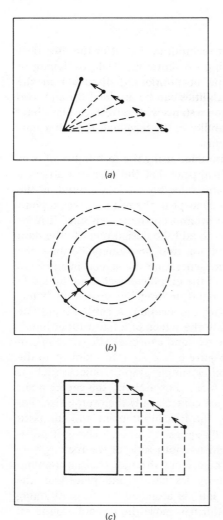

(a)

(b)

(c)

Figure 6.5. Rubber-band sketching techniques. (a) Lines. (b) Circles. (c) Rectangles.

operator indicates a new location for one symbol and then the graphics system calculates the adjustments required for all the other lines and symbols connected to the relocated symbol. This procedure requires a combination of the rubber band and dragging concepts with a sophisticated data base organized to keep track of the connectivity relationships among the graphic objects on the drawing. The calculations must be done in the main computer, not the terminal microcomputer, making interactive response very slow. Connectiv-

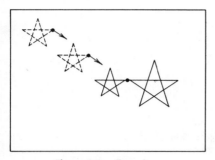

Figure 6.6. Dragging.

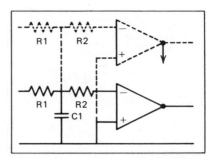

Figure 6.7. Connectivity dragging.

ity dragging can be an important aid in engineering design applications involving electrical circuits, piping systems, and other networks.

A storage tube graphics system utilizes the ability to modify and move graphic objects as a way of allowing the user to make adjustments after visually examining the results of his input. The *modify command* can be applied to a line that has just been created or to one that was previously stored to redefine that line's length or direction or both. The first input point identifies the line within the drawing and establishes which endpoint will be modified. The second input point is the new location for the line's endpoint. The new coordinates replace the previous information in the data base and the redefined line appears on the screen. This same modification procedure can be used to adjust the size and shape of other graphic objects by changing the definition of either end of the diagonal of a rectangle, the circumference end of a circle's radius line, the end of either the major or minor axis of a parabola, and so forth. The modify command can be programmed to allow a sequence of changes to the same object by using additional input points as subsequent new locations, or it can be limited to one revision.

The *move function* can be applied to any graphic object, whether it is a basic shape or a complex standard symbol. Also, the move function is not restricted to using the symbol placement point for the reference point as in dragging, but it can define the movement relative to any point on the object by calculating the distance between the first and second input points and then applying that same distance change to the data base coordinates of the symbol placement point. The size, shape, and orientation of the symbol do not change; just the location on the drawing is affected. The example shown in Figure 6.8 is a star symbol with the placement point defined at its center. The reference point is placed on one tip of the star, then the new location for the reference is placed on the tip of the adjacent star, resulting in a move that brings the star on the left into exact contact with the star on the right. The

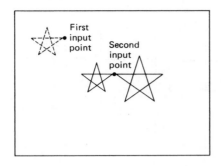

Figure 6.8. Move function for storage-tube system.

disadvantage with these storage tube techniques is that two separate input command sequences are required in every case, either to create a basic shape and modify it, or to place a symbol and move it, while rubber band lines and dragging accomplish both input and adjustment as a single operation.

Construction lines are another technique to assist the user in laying out and arranging the graphic shapes and symbols that comprise a drawing. Construction lines are a computer method equivalent to the use of the traditional mechanical drawing instruments such as a compass and a protractor. The purpose of construction lines is to allow the user to perform geometric construction using lines, circles, and other graphic objects that can be displayed on the screen upon request but that will never appear on any plotted output. The distinction between a construction element and a drawing element is simply an attribute value included in the data base description of the element.

6.5.   DIGITIZING

The term *digitizing* means to convert information from any source into numerical digits, normally as preparation for computer processing. In some of the early applications of computer graphics, input data were prepared through off-line digitizing. A picture or a physical object was marked to identify every significant point, usually by dividing the object into polygons and recording each polygon vertex point; then measurements were made to determine the coordinates of the input points and these coordinates were keypunched. Currently, digitizing is done interactively using equipment especially designed for this purpose. These input devices, which are fully described in Section 1.2, consist of a stylus or cursor pointing device held by the operator and a stationary mechanism for measuring coordinates such as a surface containing a grid of fine wires. A graphics system that incorporates a digitizing device into the user terminal can provide immediate visual results based on the digitized input. However, the operator only refers to the screen occasionally, keeping his attention focused on the task of moving the stylus from point to point on the drawing or the object being digitized.

Each point is recorded exactly as it is entered when the main objective is accurate data collection in applications like the study of medical X rays. In other applications involving the creation of a computer drawing from an existing manual drawing, the constraints described in Section 6.3 can be utilized to make slight corrections before the input points are recorded. These constraints give the drawing a better appearance and make the data easier to handle during later interactive editing. A special digitizer function in the command language allows the operator to align the horizontal and vertical axes of the computer system with those of the drawing (if it is placed on the digitizer surface in a reasonably straight manner) by entering two reference points. Another function enables the operator to set up the computer system to convert point coordinates on a scaled drawing to their equivalent real-world values by entering a scale factor and the true coordinates of one reference point.

The most accurate digitizing technique is for the operator to enter each individual data point by pressing down the stylus tip or pushing a cursor button. Closely spaced points must be entered to describe irregular curves. Regular geometric shapes such as lines and circles can be described by only two or three digitized points when the digitizing technique is used in association with the graphics system's normal input commands. A detailed shape that repeatedly appears on the original drawing or picture can be fully digitized one time and stored as a standard symbol. Then a single digitized point at the location of each occurrence of this shape is sufficient to place the symbol there. This point-by-point digitizing technique creates an orderly data base that occupies the minimum amount of computer memory.

Continuous digitizing is the process of obtaining data points by recording the position of the stylus or cursor at fixed time intervals under the control of either the digitizer device or the computer. The operator simply moves the stylus over the original drawing and the traced path appears on the screen. The technique is also known as *inking* because the operator appears to be writing on the screen with the stylus as if using a pen and ink. (Light pen tracking can also be called inking, but a light pen is never used for digitizing.) Input for character recognition (Section 6.1) is one application for inking, but it is based on free-hand writing rather than digitizing from a drawing or physical object. Continuous digitizing is a fast, convenient way to trace irregular curves, which is its only practical application because straight lines, circles, and other regular shapes cannot be traced smoothly with a hand-held positioning device. A slight hesitation during continuous digitizing causes multiple data points for the same location to be recorded, which results in unsightly bright spots along the trace on the screen unless the graphics program corrects the displayed data for this multiple recording. The main disadvantage of continuous digitizing as compared to the point-by-point data entry is the vastly greater number of input points that are generated and that must be stored in the drawing data base.

6.6. TEXT

There is usually a need to place written material on a drawing, whether it is an integral part of the design, such as measurements, or it is explanatory notes added by the designer. *Text* is defined as alphanumeric characters that are entered into the graphics system for the purpose of being shown on the screen display and the finished plot of the drawing. This distinguishes text from other alphanumeric input for system control purposes, such as names of commands or symbols and numeric values for scale factors or angles. Text can also be generated by the graphics system, such as automatically calculated dimensions.

To add a note to the drawing, the designer must enter the *content* and *position* of the text. Content is universally handled as a character string input through a keyboard, with the end of the string indicated by a special character such as the "enter" key. Position of text is a more complicated subject than content because the degree of control the user can exercise over the location, spacing, size, and appearance of the characters depends on the way the characters are generated for display and plotting. There are three general categories: (1) text generated by hardware in the display device or plotter; (2) text generated by standard software in the graphics system; and (3) text based on a user-defined alphabet stored in the computer. Hardware-generated characters give the user the least control, while there is wide variation between different graphics systems in the flexibility provided through standard or user-defined software-generated text.

The minimum control of text placement is for the user to specify the starting position of the first character of the string. Any calculations done to prepare various views of the drawing apply only to the coordinates of this starting point, defined in two or three dimensions. The system considers the entire text string as a box with its lower left corner located at the starting point. The box has a fixed height and width, determined by the character size and length of the string, and it is always presented upright and flat on the viewing surface. If any part of the box is outside the visible portion of the drawing for a particular view, the entire text string is eliminated from that view. The justification for this minimal text function is that the message will always be easy to read and that this method is the most efficient one for the computer.

The maximum flexibility in text positioning is for each small line that makes up each character to be considered as an independent graphic object. These lines are defined relative to the character string starting point, rather than by absolute coordinates, for ease in moving or deleting the entire string. However, output manipulations are applied to each separate line, so the text can be scaled, rotated in three-dimensional space, shown in perspective, or affected by any other viewing option that is available for graphic objects in general. Figure 6.9 is an example of flexible text positioning in three-dimensional space.

Some graphics systems have additional *text input functions* that are similar to the constraints described in Section 6.3. One type of constraint allows the operator to indicate a linear distance on the drawing and have the computer automatically left, right, or center justify the character string

Sorrento Valley

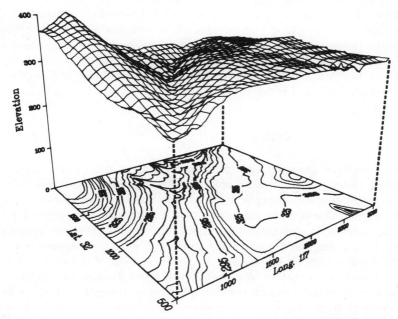

Figure 6.9. Text positioned in three-dimensional space. DISSPLA® is a proprietary software product of Integrated Software Systems Corporation, San Diego, California.

within that distance. Another one of these text input functions facilitates the addition of notes to the drawing through a rapid fill-in-the-blank method. This is accomplished through *text fields* that consist of predefined specifications for size, spacing, and justification. A text field can be positioned on a drawing in a direct manner, as for any graphic object. However, a more convenient method of placement is to include the required text fields in the standard symbol definitions stored in the graphics library so that the process of symbol placement will also include placement of the associated text fields. An empty text field does not appear on a plot, but it can be viewed on the screen as one dash for each potential character. The content of the note is entered by the operator pointing to a text field on the drawing and then typing the character string. An alternative method is for the computer to prompt the operator by highlighting each text field, following the sequence in which they were originally placed on the drawing, and then wait for the operator to type the content. The computer-assigned sequence numbers involved in this alternative method can also be referenced to merge data from an off-line text input facility with the drawing. The use of a simple keyboard terminal operated by a data entry clerk for off-line text input can increase the efficiency of the overall system in an application such as producing catalog pages that combine technical illustrations with extensive annotation.

There is a subspecialty of the computer graphics field devoted to page makeup and typesetting. These specialized systems feature an extensive range of functions for preparing two-dimensional text. They are gaining wide acceptance for advertising layout, newspaper page makeup, and design in book publishing. Further information on page makeup and typesetting systems can be found in reference 8.

6.7. DIMENSIONS

Dimensions are measurements that are written on a technical drawing to describe the physical size of an object or the geographic locations of objects. In a computer graphics application, dimensions are a specialized use of the text function that is discussed in Section 6.6. The role of dimensions in conveying information depends on the type of drawing. A computer-drawn electrical wiring diagram (Figure 6.10) shows the interconnections among the various wires, but not the lengths or specific routing of the wires. This is a *schematic drawing without dimensions*, which is a diagram that explains the arrangement or relationship between physical or conceptual items with no reference to size or location. The computer graphics vessel drawing shown in Figure 6.11 is a *schematic drawing with dimensions* because the vessel is roughly in proportion to its actual size and dimensions state the accurate ves-

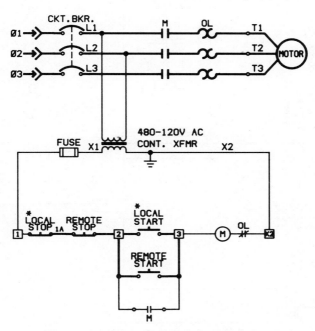

Figure 6.10. Schematic electrical wiring diagram.

sel measurements. Figure 6.12 is a *scaled drawing*. This manually drawn building plan is an exact reduced-scale representation, with the scale factor stated on the drawing. Almost all architectural drawings and maps, along with many engineering drawings, are scaled. The dimension notes can be omitted because they only repeat information that is inherent in the layout of the drawing itself.

Some innovative research has been done at the University of Cambridge in England by R. C. Hillyard and I. C. Braid [9] toward developing a systematic method of dimensioning and tolerancing as part of computer-assisted drafting. (A *tolerance* is the maximum acceptable deviation from the normal value of a dimension.) They define the desired result for their method of producing technical drawings in the following manner. The shape of the object and the arrangement of its parts is shown by the picture. The measurements for all lengths and all angles related to the object are stated explicitly on the drawing or can be derived from those that are stated. The dimensions stated are just sufficient to define all measurements with no repeated information. A computer system could find many different dimensioning schemes that would fulfill these conditions, each involving various combinations of stated

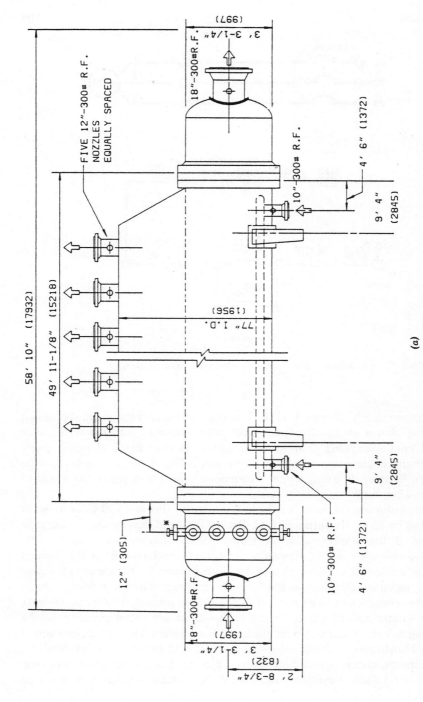

Figure 6.11. Vessel drawing. (a) Side elevation. (b) End elevation. Courtesy of Parsons Corporation.

(a)

FIVE 12"–300# R.F.
NOZZLES
EQUALLY SPACED

18"–300#R.F.

3' 3-1/4" (997)

10"–300# R.F.

4' 6" (1372)

9' 4" (2845)

77" I.D. (1956)

58' 10" (17932)

49' 11-1/8" (15218)

12" (305)

18"–300#R.F.

3' 3-1/4" (997)

2' 8-3/4" (832)

10"–300# R.F.

4' 6" (1372)

9' 4" (2845)

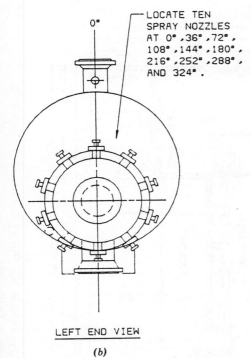

LOCATE TEN
SPRAY NOZZLES
AT 0° ,36° ,72° ,
108° ,144° ,180° ,
216° ,252° ,288° ,
AND 324° .

0°

LEFT END VIEW

(b)   **Figure 6.11.**   Continued

and derived lengths and angles. However, the optimal scheme is the one that explicitly states the dimensions that are the most meaningful for the design, manufacturing, or construction activity supported by the technical drawing. The researchers have concluded that the most practical strategy is to allow the human designer to indicate the important dimensions and then let the computer select the additional dimensions required to sufficiently define the object. In this way the computer helps the designer provide appropriately chosen dimensions that are neither incomplete nor redundant.

Hillyard and Braid have also investigated methods for programming the computer system to alter the shape of an object in response to designer-initiated changes in the dimensions and tolerances. The dimensions could then function as powerful design variables, not merely as notes on a finished drawing.

The dimensioning functions of the general-purpose drafting system in this chapter's highlight application are typical of those that are commonly available at the present time. The user must add dimensions as notes when a schematic drawing is being produced, following a procedure similar to the

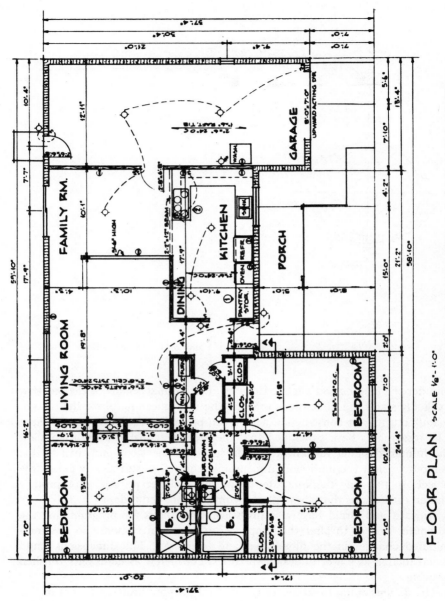

FLOOR PLAN SCALE ⅛" = 1'-0"

Figure 6.12. Scaled drawing. Reprinted, by permission, from Nelson L. Burbank and Herbert R. Pfister, *House Construction Details*, Simmons-Boardman, Omaha, 1968.

one described as an example of a macro command in Section 6.2. The computer system can generate dimensions for a scaled drawing from the information stored in the data base, which originated as input from digitizing a physical object or from interactive design. This dimensioning can be fully automatic for some simple applications. In more complex design situations, dimensioning is a semiautomatic process in which the computer supplies an accurate measurement for each significant length or angle identified by the designer and then positions the text at the location on the drawing indicated by the designer.

Dimensions consist of two-dimensional text that can be directly added to a two-dimensional computer drawing. A graphics system that builds a three-dimensional model cannot add the dimensions to the definition of the model, but instead adds them to a particular view that has been prepared for output as a final plot.

Measurements expressed in metric system units normally include decimal fractions. This is compatible with the way the computer deals with numbers internally. However, engineering drawings with dimensions in English units traditionally involve common fractions, rounded off to some limit such as the nearest sixteenth of an inch. It is necessary for the computer program used to generate English unit dimensions to be able to convert the measurements into common fractions and prepare an appropriate character string for the text.

There are several acceptable formats for presentation of the dimensions on the drawing, and the choice of format determines the type of user input that is required for dimension positioning. The style that is the easiest to provide with a fully automatic method is to simply place the measurement directly adjacent to the point, line, or angle that it describes. This style is utilized when interactive dimensioning is incorporated into the rubber band and dragging functions by displaying the current coordinates of the moving design point next to the cursor symbol on the screen.

The format known as *parallel dimensioning* (Figure 6.13) is the most popular mode of expressing dimensions for manual drafting. An interactive graphics system can accomplish this type of dimensioning only if the user supplies all of the positioning information. The user selects one of the four possible input functions for parallel dimensioning—interior, exterior, serial, or stacked. These options are shown in Figure 6.14. The user then indicates the beginning and end of each dimensioned distance and chooses a blank area nearby where the dimension and witness lines can be located without interfering with the rest of the drawing. Adherence to the conventions of manual drafting, such as placing a series of dimensions all on the same side of the object, is the responsibility of the user. Parallel dimensioning is desirable in many applications in spite of the great amount of user input re-

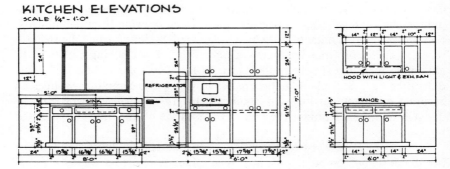

Figure 6.13. Example of parallel dimensioning. Reprinted, by permission, from Nelson L. Burbank and Herbert R. Pfister, *House Construction Details,* Simmons-Boardman, Omaha, 1968.

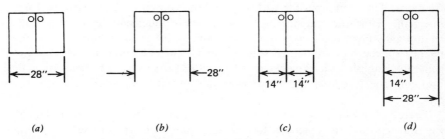

Figure 6.14. Types of parallel dimensioning. (a) Interior. (b) Exterior. (c) Serial. (d) Stacked.

quired because the limits of each linear distance are clearly indicated and because the users of technical drawings are most accustomed to reading dimensions presented in this format.

6.8.   THREE-DIMENSIONAL INPUT

Interactive graphics systems capable of building and displaying a three-dimensional model are rapidly gaining popularity in a wide variety of applications. However, the input methods utilized by these systems are not as well developed as the display methods. Many of the approaches to three-dimensional input that are currently being explored have the potential to improve the situation in the near future. However, it is unlikely that any single input technique will be suitable for all three-dimensional graphics systems.

The survey of currently available input methods presented in this section indicates how the techniques best suited to each application can be selected.

The explanations of the specific input techniques are easier to understand if some background information is covered in advance. This preparation provides a framework for organizing the survey of techniques in a logical manner rather than as a random list. The background information consists of three factors that strongly influence the choice of a suitable input method—the source of the data, the complexity of the object, and the modeling theory applied by the graphics system.

The first important factor in the selection of an input technique is the source of the data [10]. There are two possibilities: (1) data are generated directly or indirectly from an existing object to reproduce that object as a computer model and (2) data are created by the user to synthesize an object in the computer.

The second consideration related to data input is the complexity of the object that is being modeled [11]. This complexity can be evaluated in terms of three criteria: (1) An object that can be described by two-dimensional geometry is less complex than one that requires a full three-dimensional definition. For example, designing patterns for the clothing industry is a simpler application than designing molds for glass or plastic containers. (2) An object whose outline is made up of straight lines and flat surfaces is less complex than an object bounded by free-form curves and curved surfaces. Thus it is much easier to draw a plan for a concrete building foundation (rectangular shapes) than for a ship's hull (curved shapes). (3) An object of considerable complexity can be assembled from a multitude of components, each component being relatively simple in itself. An illustration of this type of complexity is a highway bridge, which is a complicated structure although it is built using structural steel members that are reasonably simple, such as I beams.

The third element of background information is not related to the characteristics of the object, as are the other two points, but instead involves the modeling theory that the graphics system utilizes to formulate a computer model of the object [12]. There are two basically different approaches to modeling in three-dimensional computer graphics: (1) A *surface* modeling technique describes an object by shaping a thin, flexible skin in three-dimensional space to represent the surface of the object (Figure 6.15). The surface can be defined in the computer data base as a set of three-dimensional surface points, as a network of polygon-shaped planes, or as a mesh of curved surface patches. This method (especially the mesh of curved patches) has been used extensively in engineering applications that involve free-form curves, such as automotive body design, and for artistic renderings of sculptured surfaces. (2) A *volume* modeling technique represents an object as a geometric solid. A complex object is defined as a composite of many

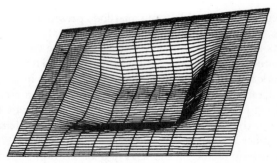

Figure 6.15. Surface model. Courtesy of David C. Anderson and John A. Brewer, Purdue University.

small solid elements, such as spheres, prisms, cylinders, cones, and simple polyhedra. A display of a volume model that shows all the edges of an object is called a *wire frame display* because the object appears to be only a hollow outline. Wire frame displays are often used as working tools so the computer can produce different views of the model quickly. In contrast, the computer must perform lengthy calculations to remove the hidden lines and produce a display that looks like an opaque solid object. The volume approach has been successful in creating mechanical models in engineering applications and construction prototypes in architectural design. The structure of the data base that represents a geometric solid allows the computer to do analysis and information retrieval such as calculating the volume and surface area of the object and generating cross-section drawings.

This survey of the currently available input methods begins with a technique that extends two-dimensional input data into a three-dimensional volume model. The *extrusion method* [13] requires a single two-dimensional data source, such as a plan drawing for a structural concrete foundation. The two-dimensional shapes are either digitized directly from existing engineering drawings or designed interactively at the graphics terminal. The operator uses the keyboard to enter a base elevation and top elevation for each polygon on the plan drawing. After the input is completed, the computer system generates a volume model using each two-dimensional polygon as both the base and top of a right prism and using the numeric elevations to determine the height of the prism. Similarly, any closed curve can be used as the two-dimensional shape to form the top and base of a cylinder. Figure 6.16 is an isometric view of the computer model of a structural concrete foundation that was created through the extrusion method [14].

The *multiple view method* constructs the three-dimensional volume model by combining input data from a set of two-dimensional views that lie in intersecting planes [13]. The actual data input task can be accomplished by us-

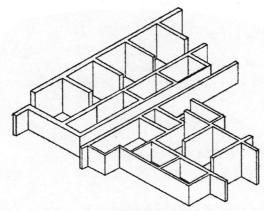

Figure 6.16. Structural concrete foundation (extrusion input method). This research was supported by Townsend and Bottum, Inc., Ann Arbor, Michigan; Ohio Edison Company, Akron, Ohio; and the Architectural Research Laboratory, The University of Michigan.

ing a pair of existing photographs or drawings placed on two digitizer tablets. A point such as the location of a nozzle on a vessel is entered by touching the nozzle on one drawing and then immediately touching the same nozzle on the other drawing. This enables the computer to determine all three coordinates (x, y, z) of that point. The programming is simpler if the source views are restricted to being in the planes formed by two coordinate axes, but the system is more flexible if arbitrary views may be used. A complex object usually requires input from more than two views. For instance, Figure 6.17 shows a three-dimensional mechanical design built from three orthogonal views.

Creative design requires that the graphics system display both views at once, either through a split-screen effect or, preferably, on two separate monitors. Two digitizer boards are again required, or, alternatively, a single board and the two input commands "position in xy plane" and "position in xz plane" can be used. The user interactively builds a pair of two-dimensional views of the object by placing a point at any desired location while looking at one screen and then immediately completing the input for that point by indicating its location on the second screen. The geometry of an object often makes it possible to utilize a programmed lock to fix the location in one view while a series of points are entered on the other view. For example, the xy coordinates for the corners of a concrete slab vessel foundation could all be entered quickly in the plan view using a common z value established for the top surface of the concrete by a single input in the elevation view. The multiple view method requires constraints or editing routines in the system to correct for slight inaccuracies in digitizing. For instance, if the

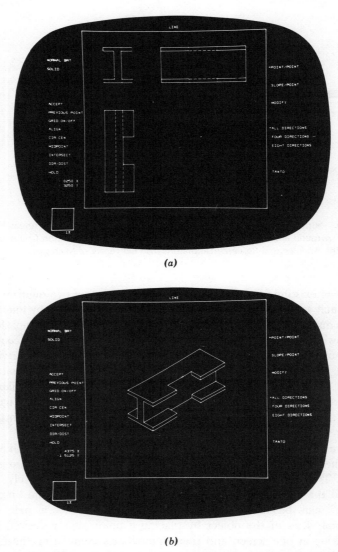

Figure 6.17. Mechanical design (multiple-view input method). (a) Three two-dimensional views. (b) Three-dimensional object. Courtesy of Information Displays Incorporated.

x coordinate of the input points from the plan view (xy plane) and the elevation view (xz plane) do not exactly match, the system should round off the values enough to show that the two entries actually define a single point.

The *serial sectioning method* [13] creates a three-dimensional solid shape by combining a series of cross-section outlines or contour lines. The cross sections are digitized as separate two-dimensional figures that lie in an evenly spaced stack of parallel planes. After the manual input is finished, a program completes the three-dimensional shape by joining the plane figures with lines that connect suitable data points on adjacent cross sections. Figure 6.18 shows these input steps. The serial sectioning method is frequently

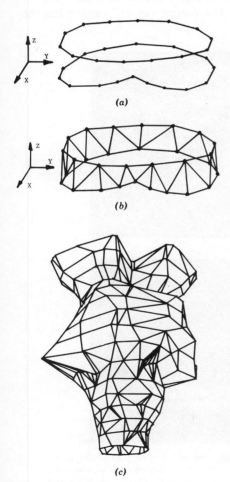

(a)

(b)

(c)

Figure 6.18. Human brain stem (serial sectioning input method). (a) Pair of two-dimensional cross sections. (b) Same pair of cross sections with suitable points connected. (c) Finished three-dimensional volume model. Reprinted, by permission, from H. N. Christiansen and T. W. Sederberg, "Conversion of Complex Contour Line Definitions into Polygonal Element Mosaics," *Computer Graphics*, **12**(3), 187–192 (1978).

utlilized to prepare structural engineering data for finite element analysis and to represent anatomical objects in medical research based on slices of specimens or X-ray tomographs.

The *volume element method* builds a complex solid object from a set of predefined primitive volume elements. Systems such as BUILD [9], PADL [15], and ANIMA II [10] use a variety of geometric forms such as spheres, prisms, cylinders, cones, and convex polyhedra with any number of faces. A command language enables the user to distort the primitive elements through warping and bending. The user can also scale, rotate, move, join, intersect, and cut the volume elements in the process of combining them to build the model. The sculpture of a whale in Figure 6.19*b* was made from the primitive objects shown in Figure 6.19*a*. The volume element method has the

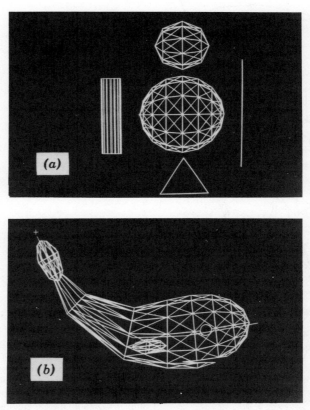

Figure 6.19. Volume element method. (*a*) Primitive objects. (*b*) Complex object, sculpture of a whale. Reprinted, by permission, from Richard E. Parent, "A System for Sculpting 3-D Data," *Computer Graphics,* **11**(2) (1977). Copyright 1977, Association for Computing Machinery, Inc.

advantages of requiring a minimal amount of data input and allowing the user to feel that he is working on the solid object directly.

Detailed information on input methods for surface models is beyond the scope of this book, but a brief introduction to three important approaches is worthwhile. The method developed by *Coons*, one of the earliest and best-known surface design techniques, requires that the user assign numeric values to control the shape of the surface. The methods introduced by *Bezier* and *Riesenfeld* allow interactive control through a network of control points, but these points do not lie on the surface itself. The most direct user interface is provided by the lesser-known *Overhauser* method, in which coordinate points on the surface are edited to design a free-form curved shape [16].

CHAPTER 7

Viewing the Computer Model

The most fascinating aspect of a live demonstration of interactive graphics is the power and flexibility of the viewing commands. Viewing commands provide the ability to view the model interactively throughout the process of building the data base and to present a single computer model in a variety of ways. Viewing techniques have reached a high level of development because much of the past research in computer graphics has concentrated on image display. Two chapters are devoted to the important subject of viewing techniques. The present chapter explains the operation of two-dimensional graphics systems and introduces all the basic concepts with simple mathematics. The next chapter presents these same concepts as they relate to three-dimensional viewing techniques.

This chapter deals with three major topics: (1) selecting a portion of the overall design for viewing through coordinate transformations, (2) changing the position of one object relative to the rest of the drawing by geometric transformations, and (3) defining graphic elements and using standard symbols to build complex drawings. The discussion of each topic covers the full range of currently applied techniques; no single system encompasses all the alternatives presented.

7.1. COORDINATE SYSTEM TRANSFORMATIONS

The view presentation of a drawing is the result of the way the graphics system converts each point's data base definition into its screen location. The graphics system uses the familiar Cartesian coordinate system to define each point by two numbers representing the location of that point compared to the origin, which is point (0, 0). The first coordinate is the distance along the x axis, with positive values increasing toward the right. The second coordinate is the measure along the y axis, with the positive direction oriented upward. The unit of measure along each axis can describe physical distance in terms such as feet and meters, or it can have an abstract meaning. The coordinates can be expressed as rational numbers involving decimal fractions if the computer can handle floating point arithmetic. Otherwise, the coordinates are restricted to integer values.

The operator at the graphics terminal defines the units of measure for his drawing to set up the *user coordinate system* (Figure 7.1). The drawing is stored in the computer data base in terms of user coordinates, so the operator can enter the data related to the drawing in the customary unit of measure for that application.

The graphics program prepares output data to suit the physical characteristics of the display device, especially the resolution. Resolution varies considerably among screens and among plotters, but every physical device has limited resolution compared to the possible range of point coordinates within the computer. For example, an addressable point grid of about 4000 × 4000 is associated with a highly accurate storage tube display. The *screen coordinate system* for this storage tube has its origin (0, 0) in the lower left corner of the screen and reaches its maximum range at the point (4000, 4000) in the upper right corner.

It would be convenient to have a standard of reference to avoid the confusion involving various physical devices with different screen coordinate systems. This standard is provided by the *normalized screen coordinate system* (Figure 7.2) where the endpoints of the screen diagonal are simply

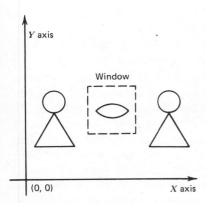

Figure 7.1. User coordinate system.

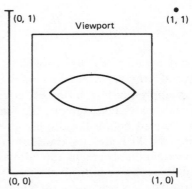

Figure 7.2. Normalized screen coordinate system.

(0, 0) and (1, 1). The coordinates of all other points are expressed as decimal fractions. A graphics system that prepares its output data based on the normalized screen coordinate system is *device independent*, since it has the potential to accommodate any display device without changes to the basic program. The basic program must be used with an auxiliary program called a *device driver* that completes the output data preparation in a way that is directly related to the specifications of the physical device.

Coordinate system transformations are used to convert a data base drawing that is defined in user coordinates into an image that is defined in normalized screen coordinates. The operator at the graphics terminal chooses both the part of the drawing to be displayed and the placement of the image on the screen. The rectangular boundary of the area of interest on the drawing is called the *window*. The size and location of the window are expressed in user coordinates because the window is specified in relation to the drawing. The portion of the screen that is used to display the image is known as the *viewport*. The dimensions and center point of the viewport are expressed in normalized screen coordinates. The coordinate system transformation from the window to the viewport is a mathematical operation given by the equations below. Let the data base point be (u_1, u_2) in user coordinates and (s_1, s_2) in screen coordinates. The window has center point (c_1, c_2) and dimensions d_1 (horizontal) and d_2 (vertical). The viewport has center point (c_3, c_4) and dimensions d_3 (horizontal) and d_4 (vertical). The equations for the coordinate system transformation are

$$s_1 = (u_1 - c_1)\,\frac{d_3}{d_1} + c_3$$

and

$$s_2 = (u_2 - c_2)\,\frac{d_4}{d_2} + c_4$$

The notation (u_1, u_2) designates a point in user coordinates and (s_1, s_2) identifies the same point in normalized screen coordinates. The computer must apply the transformation equations to each and every point stored in the data base. For example, the initial and final points of each line must be transformed before the display device can draw the line. The other points along the line are not transformed because they are created by the line generation hardware in the display device. In contrast, every data point would have to be individually transformed for an irregular curve. The values of the window and viewport parameters remain constant for the complete transformation of all image points. Some graphics systems do not provide viewport capability, but instead utilize the entire screen to display the contents of the window. This simplifies the mathematics by eliminating the variables c_3, c_4, d_3, and d_4 from the equations.

7.2. CLIPPING

The window selected by the operator usually does not include the entire drawing that is stored in the data base. If the graphics program does not check for visibility before sending the data to the display device, the coordinates of some points may be outside the range of the screen. For example, the display device can attempt to interpret a location such as (5000, 2000) to be equivalent to (1000, 2000) on a screen with a maximum point coordinate of (4000, 4000). This means that the image that should be off the screen on the right appears on the screen beginning at the left edge. The *wrap-around* effect is unacceptable because the part of the drawing inside the window is overlayed by the portion of the drawing that should be invisible. Many stroke-writing display devices avoid the wrap-around effect through built-in analog circuits that turn off the intensity while the beam traces points that have coordinates outside the screen area. This *scissoring* technique produces an uncluttered image, but it reduces the refresh rate for the visible image by wasting time on the invisible portion of the drawing.

Clipping is eliminating the parts of the drawing that are outside the window prior to sending display instructions to the screen. A point can be checked for visibility simply by comparing its coordinates to the high and low x-coordinate values and the high and low y-coordinate values for the corners of the window. Lines, circles, other curves, and text strings are much more difficult to check and classify as visible, partially visible, or invisible. For example, part of a line can be on the screen even though both endpoints of the line are outside the screen area.

An efficient method has been developed to identify lines that are either entirely on the screen or completely off the screen. Each endpoint of the line is assigned a computer code that indicates whether it is on the screen or above, below, to the right, or to the left of the screen area. The status of the line is determined by a logical comparison of the codes for its two endpoints. When both points are on the screen, the entire line is visible. When any position characteristic, such as "above," is shared by the points, the entire line is invisible. When one line endpoint is on the screen and the other is off the screen, the line is partially visible. The status of the line cannot be determined when both points are outside the screen area and do not have any matching position characteristic. This interpretation of the position code is verified by the sample lines on the coded grid shown in Figure 7.3. This clip-

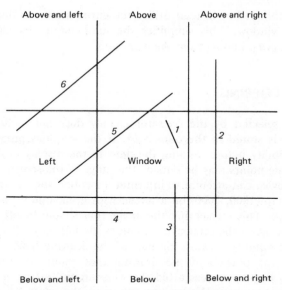

Figure 7.3. Clipping grid with sample lines.

ping method quickly determines which lines are entirely inside or outside the window, greatly reducing the volume of data that must be checked further. A line that is partially inside the window can always be divided into two or three segments that are each totally visible or invisible. The graphics program in the computer can directly calculate the points where each line in the image intersects the edges of the window. These points separate the visible and invisible line segments. Some high performance graphics systems do clipping in a special-purpose hardware unit rather than in the main computer. References 1, 6, and 17 give further information on clipping methods and the detailed mathematical processes associated with clipping.

7.3. GEOMETRIC TRANSFORMATIONS

When motion is displayed by an interactive computer graphics system, the smooth movement is actually composed of numerous small location changes. Each change in location is calculated using equations that are derived from the rules of geometry. The three basic geometric transformations are translation, scaling, and rotation.

Translation is defined as the uniform motion of an object along a straight line (Figure 7.4). Calculating a change in location due to translation is a sim-

Figure 7.4. Translation.

ple application of geometry. The typical interactive input sequence consists of any point on the object and the desired new location for that point. The computer calculates the x and y components of the distance between the first and second points. The calculated horizontal distance is added to the x coordinate of every point that describes the object. Similarly, the vertical distance is added to the y coordinate of every point. When the points are displayed according to the resulting coordinates, the object appears at the new location on the screen.

Let (p_1, p_2) be the original point and let (g_1, g_2) be the coordinates of the same point after translation by a distance of t_1 in the horizontal direction and t_2 in the vertical direction. The point coordinates and distance components are all expressed in the units of the user coordinate system. The equations for the geometric transformation of translation are

$$g_1 = p_1 + t_1 \quad \text{and} \quad g_2 = p_2 + t_2$$

Scaling increases or decreases the dimensions of an object. Equal scaling along the x axis and y axis changes the size, but not the shape of the object, while unequal scaling distorts the appearance of the object (Figure 7.5). The input to the interactive graphics system for scaling consists of the horizontal scaling factor, the vertical scaling factor, and the point about which the object is scaled. The graphics system must perform a translation to bring the scaling point to the origin of the coordinate system, calculate the scaling, and then perform another translation to return the scaling point to its original

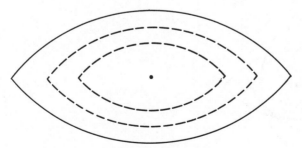

Figure 7.5. Scaling.

location. Scaling is calculated by multiplying the x-axis scaling factor times the x coordinate and the y-axis scaling factor times the y coordinate to find the new coordinates for the point. This calculation is repeated for each data base point associated with the object to yield the scaled image of the object.

Assume that (p_1, p_2) is a point defined for the original object and that scaling occurs about the origin $(0, 0)$. Let (g_1, g_2) represent the same point after scaling by a factor of s_1 in the horizontal direction and s_2 in the vertical direction. The point locations are expressed in user coordinates. The scaling factors are unitless numbers. The equations for scaling are

$$g_1 = p_1 s_1 \quad \text{and} \quad g_2 = p_2 s_2$$

The effect of this linear scaling is that a factor of 2 makes a line twice as long and a factor of 0.5 makes a line half as long. However, scaling both dimensions of a square by a factor of 10 results in a square with an area 100 times as large as the area of the original square.

Rotation means that each point on the object moves in a circular path around the center of rotation (Figure 7.6). The change in location is measured by the angle between a line from the center of rotation to the original point and the line from the center to the transformed point. Let the letter a represent this angle. Choose clockwise as the positive mathematical direction for this angle. The coordinates of the original point (p_1, p_2) are transformed into the coordinates of the new location (g_1, g_2) by the following equations:

$$g_1 = p_1 \cos a + p_2 \sin a$$

$$g_2 = -p_1 \sin a + p_2 \cos a$$

This calculation is valid only for rotation about the origin of the user coordinate system. If any other point is selected as the center of rotation, the transformation must be handled as a translation to the origin, the rotation, and a translation back to the selected center point.

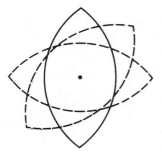

Figure 7.6. Rotation.

Actual applications of interactive computer graphics almost always require complex transformations rather than the simple geometric changes described by the preceding equations. Complex movement is the result of a series of simple transformations, so the new location for each point could be calculated by applying the simple equations in sequence. Fortunately, these equations can be replaced by an equivalent matrix method that provides a more convenient way to handle combined changes.

A *matrix* is a rectangular array of numbers that behaves according to the special rules of matrix algebra. Good summaries of matrix algebra can be found in the advanced textbooks on interactive computer graphics listed as references 1, 6, and 18. The three basic geometric transformations are expressed in matrix notation in the following way:

$$\text{Translation} \quad [g_1 \quad g_2 \quad 1] = [p_1 \quad p_2 \quad 1] \begin{bmatrix} 1 & 0 & 0 \\ 0 & 1 & 0 \\ t_1 & t_2 & 1 \end{bmatrix}$$

$$\text{Scaling} \quad [g_1 \quad g_2 \quad 1] = [p_1 \quad p_2 \quad 1] \begin{bmatrix} s_1 & 0 & 0 \\ 0 & s_2 & 0 \\ 0 & 0 & 1 \end{bmatrix}$$

$$\text{Rotation} \quad [g_1 \quad g_2 \quad 1] = [p_1 \quad p_2 \quad 1] \begin{bmatrix} \cos a & -\sin a & 0 \\ \sin a & \cos a & 0 \\ 0 & 0 & 1 \end{bmatrix}$$

The same variables appear whether the transformation is written in equations or in matrix notation. The coordinates of the point (x, y) can be written as the vector $[x \quad y \quad 1]$. A *vector* is a matrix that has only one row or column. Multiplying this vector times a transformation matrix results in a new vector containing the coordinates of that point in the translated, rotated, or scaled image. A complex transformation is made up of a series of simple transformations, so it can be calculated by a series of separate matrix multiplications for each point. However, a sequence of transformations can be *concatenated*, which means linked together in a series or chain. Concatenation is achieved by multiplying the simple transformation matrices together in the proper order to obtain a single matrix that represents the complex transformation. The vector for each point is then multiplied just once, utilizing the concatenated transformation. Minimizing the number of separate calculations makes the viewing operation more efficient.

Matrix multiplication is carried out as shown below for $A \times B = C$.

$$A = \begin{bmatrix} a_{11} & a_{12} \\ a_{21} & a_{22} \end{bmatrix} \qquad B = \begin{bmatrix} b_{11} & b_{12} \\ b_{21} & b_{22} \end{bmatrix}$$

$$C = \begin{bmatrix} a_{11}b_{11} + a_{12}b_{21} & a_{11}b_{12} + a_{12}b_{22} \\ a_{21}b_{11} + a_{22}b_{21} & a_{21}b_{12} + a_{22}b_{22} \end{bmatrix}$$

Each element in the first row of A is multiplied times the corresponding element in the first column of B; then the products are added together to form the first row, first column element of C. Then the first row of A and the second column of B are used similarly to form the first row, second column element of C, and so forth. The pattern of matrix multiplication requires that the number of rows in A be the same as the number of columns in B. Each geometric transformation is expressed as a square matrix so that the number of rows and columns are compatible for multiplication of any sequence of transformations. Performing matrix multiplication in the proper order is essential because $A \times B$ is not equal to $B \times A$. A matrix is not changed in any way as a result of multiplication with the matrix I, the identity matrix for multiplication.

$$I = \begin{bmatrix} 1 & 0 & 0 \\ 0 & 1 & 0 \\ 0 & 0 & 1 \end{bmatrix}$$

Notice that in each basic transformation matrix, all terms not directly related to translation, rotation, or scaling are equal to the corresponding terms in the identity matrix. Similarly, the third element in the point coordinate vector has the value of one. These extra elements serve to facilitate the mechanics of matrix multiplication without changing the results.

7.4. THE DISPLAY FILE

The operator works with the graphic entities that are provided by the application program, but the display device functions on a much simpler level. *Graphic primitives* are defined as the drawing elements that can be generated by the display hardware. Every display device can draw points and most can also draw lines, circles, and text characters. Complex graphic entities are made up of these graphic primitives.

An *attribute* is a quality that determines either the appearance or the status of a graphic primitive. Typical appearance attributes are line style, line width, display intensity, and color. Status attributes such as visibility, highlighting, and detectability can be used for control within the graphics system and for operator interface. The data base description of a graphic primitive includes a code for each attribute. The value of the code indicates the assigned appearance or status. For example, the line style codes could be 1 for solid, 2 for dashed, and 3 for dotted. Status attributes are coded as either on or off. Typically, status attributes can be changed at any time by either the operator or the program while appearance attributes are fixed when the primitive is added to the data base.

Graphic primitives are described by display instructions that drive the display hardware. A *display file* is a collection of these instructions. The way the instructions are arranged in the display file is similar to the way a nongraphic computer program is structured. A program is designed in modular form with a subroutine for each major operation. The subroutines can be called by name from the main program. This structure reduces the length of the program because a single set of statements can be called repeatedly to perform frequently used computations. Also, options within the main program can determine which subroutines to call for a particular calculation and which ones to omit. A similar structure within the display file helps the graphic system manipulate graphic entities and standard symbols. A named subroutine within the display file can contain all the display instructions for graphic primitives that form one graphic entity. This makes it possible for the graphics system to reference the graphic entity by name when specifying geometric transformations that apply to it. It also helps the system quickly find all the primitives that belong to the entity group for operations such as changing status attributes or deleting the entity. These subroutine names are automatically handled by the system. The operator at the graphics terminal refers to an entity by touching some point on its screen image.

An analogy between the use of a computer to produce numerical results and the use of an interactive graphics computer system can help explain how the display file is built and processed. The operations that convert the drawing stored in the data base into an image on the screen are listed next to the comparable programming steps in Figure 7.7. This viewing sequence example is typical of a simple refresh graphics display system. Graphics systems designed for storage tube displays or high performance graphics terminals use variations of this viewing sequence. These are discussed following the basic explanation.

The right-hand side of Figure 7.7 shows the steps in producing a numerical calculation. The user of the computer is an application programmer. He codes the *source program* by describing the calculation in some high level

Viewing sequence	Analogous function
Data base	Information
Operator enters the viewing commands	Programmer codes the source program
Graphic function calls	Source program
Graphic compiler	Compiler
Display file	Object program
Display file processing	Program execution
Image	Result

Figure 7.7. Simple refreshed graphics display system.

programming language such as FORTRAN or COBOL. This program obtains information from the data base. The program statements define computations and logical operations such as IF-THEN-ELSE. The user's source program is processed in the computer by a *compiler*, a special program that converts the high-level language statements into machine language codes (the *object program*). The machine language codes correspond to actual operations by the computer, such as LOAD REGISTER. Each logical operation is normally compiled as several machine instructions. The source program and the object program describe the same calculation in different terminology. The object program can be executed by the computer. The computer performs the indicated calculations and prints the numerical results.

The left-hand side of Figure 7.7 shows the sequence required to display an image. The user is the operator at the graphics terminal. The programming language is the set of interactive commands provided by the graphics system. The operator uses these commands to view the drawing in the data base. The system accepts these commands and generates the appropriate graphic function calls. A collection of the graphic function calls is a logical description of the image analogous to the source program. There is a component within the graphics system software that acts like a compiler. It applies the coordinate and geometric transformations to the graphic entities and converts the complex entities into graphic primitives. This compiler produces a set of display device instructions that is stored as a display file. The display file is analogous to the object program, but the display file instructions are not executed by a computer. Instead they are processed by the display device hardware, which includes the display controller, generators for lines, circles, and text characters, and the display screen. The result is an image on the screen.

In the preceding explanation, the viewing transformations are applied to the data in the graphic function calls and then the transformed data are converted into display device instructions. This is the proper sequence of operations for a simple refresh graphics system that handles transformations in the compiler software. The display file is built by a different sequence of operations for a high performance graphics system. The high performance terminal includes a microcomputer that makes the calculations required for matrix algebra, so the viewing transformations are handled by the terminal hardware. In this system, the compiler software converts the graphic function calls into display device instructions and then the transformations are applied to the data contained in the instructions.

The display file and the data base are essentially duplicate descriptions of the picture. Storing both descriptions is justified in a refresh graphics system since the display file is scanned during each refresh cycle to maintain the image on the screen. The process of applying transformations and converting the graphic data into display device instructions is done only when the screen image is changed. The graphics system may be designed to rebuild the entire display file for any change or to rebuild only the display file subroutines affected by the specific change. Either completely or partially rebuilding the display file for image changes is more efficient than maintaining a refreshed image directly from the data base without a stored display file.

A display file is not needed with a storage tube because the image is maintained by the screen phosphors. The operations of creating graphic function calls, applying transformations, and converting the data to display instructions can be performed by one section of the graphics system software. The display instructions generated by the software are sent directly to the display terminal. The display instructions must be completely regenerated following any change that requires erasing the screen, but additions to the image can be made by simply sending the new display instructions to the screen.

7.5. SYMBOLS

This section describes how standard symbols are created, how they are placed on drawings, and how display instructions are generated for them. When the graphics operator creates a new symbol, he must define the symbol's visible characteristics by entering attributes and graphic primitives. In addition, he must select a point within the symbol for reference as the placement point. The overall size of the symbol is defined by the smallest rectangle that can enclose its visible image. This rectangle may be drawn by the operator or it may be determined by the graphics system from the extreme values of the symbol's point coordinates. Finally, the operator enters the symbol by name in the library. The *master symbol* in the library is defined in the *master coordinate system*. It is often convenient for the master units to be the same as the units of the user coordinate system for the drawing, but this is not required.

The operator places the symbol on the drawing with an input command. He enters the symbol name and indicates the location by a point on the drawing. The symbol is added to the drawing by matching the predefined placement point with the input point. Additionally, the operator may apply a coordinate transformation to the symbol as it is converted from master coordinates to user coordinates. This operation is the same as the window to viewport transformation described in Section 7.1. Geometric transformations may also be applied to the symbol when it is placed, using the equations introduced in Section 7.3. Therefore, the *instance* of the master symbol on the drawing is defined by its name, its location point on the drawing, and any optional placement transformations.

There is a procedure called *boxing* that streamlines the clipping operation for symbol instances. Boxing utilizes the rectangle of overall size that is stored with each master symbol. The location point on the drawing and the placement transformations are applied to this rectangle to determine the area occupied by the instance. When the rectangle is entirely inside or outside the window, the instance is completely visible or invisible and no clipping is required. The visible instances are transformed and displayed. It is necessary to individually transform and clip each graphic primitive within the symbol instance only when the rectangle crosses the window boundary. Each visible symbol instance causes a display file subroutine to be generated.

CHAPTER 8

Three-Dimensional Viewing

A lifetime of experience in viewing three-dimensional objects gives a person certain expectations regarding the displayed image of a computer-produced model. These expectations serve as a standard against which the quality of the image is judged and as an aid in understanding the object represented by the image. The resemblence between state-of-the-art computer-generated images and photographs of real objects can be astonishing (Figure 8.1). However, this type of *photographic image* is created at great cost both in the computer resources required to make the necessary calculations for viewing and in the elaborate input required to build descriptions of the objects. Most of the practical uses for computer graphics in science and industry do not require photographic images. Therefore, the computer models of solid objects and the associated viewing techniques can be simplified to save time and money.

One simplification is to use a uniform color or shade of gray for every visible surface of a single object. Different objects can have various colors or gray shades, but special effects such as shadows and highlights are omitted. This type of image is known as a *shaded picture* and is reasonably easy to produce on a raster display device (Figure 8.2).

An *outline drawing* is a type of simplified image that is suitable for display on a line-drawing output device. It shows only the outlines of the visible surfaces and the lines of intersection between those surfaces (Figure 8.3).

The simplest type of image is a *wire-frame drawing* that shows the outlines of all surfaces. There is no attempt to simulate the way opaque objects make certain surfaces invisible (Figure 8.4). A wire-frame drawing is less pleasing visually, but it is considerably faster for the computer to produce. For this reason, the wire-frame viewing method is often chosen when rapid interaction with the data base is the most important consideration in an application.

Figure 8.1. Photograhpic image of simulated NASA Space Shuttle Orbiter. Courtesy of NASA.

This chapter focuses on the viewing techniques used to present a three-dimensional computer model as a wire-frame drawing, an outline drawing, a shaded picture, or a photographic image. Each computer-produced image represents one of many possible views that an imaginary observer can have relative to a scene. A *scene* is defined as any collection of three-dimensional graphic objects. Perspective projection, the method for viewing scenes as two-dimensional pictures, is described in detail in Section 8.2. The information conveyed by the third dimension is obviously lost when a scene is visualized as a flat image. A depth-cue technique partially restores the lost information so the user can infer the relative positions of the surfaces or outlines in the image. The various types of depth cues are surveyed in Section 8.3, then hidden-line and hidden-surface removal techniques are discussed further in Section 8.4, and illumination effects are explained in Section 8.5.

8.1. EXTENSION OF BASIC CONCEPTS

The two-dimensional viewing methods covered in Chapter 7 have straightforward extensions to support viewing of three-dimensional computer models. The data base to which these extended methods are applied contains additional entries. For instance, each point in the data base describing the model has three coordinates (x, y, z) instead of two (x, y), as with a flat drawing. Furthermore, a description of a three-dimensional scene must include information that tags points as polygon vertices and that identifies polygons as the

Figure 8.2. Shaded picture of a deformed cylinder, interior cutaway view. Reprinted, by permission, from J. H. Biffle, "Use of Graphics in Three Dimensional Structural Analysis of Solids," *Interactive Computer Graphics in Engineering,* American Society of Mechanical Engineers, New York, New York, 1977.

flat faces of solid polyhedrons. Figure 8.5 is a conceptual diagram illustrating the type of additional data base information that is required.

Each standard component in the model is added to the data base as an instance of a three-dimensional library symbol. Just as in the two-dimensional method, this addition is done through a computer-calculated transformation from the master coordinate system (used to express the symbol library description of the object) to the user coordinate system (used to describe the object as part of the model in the data base). This process is referred to as the instance transformation.

The viewing transformation creates the screen image of a selected portion of a two-dimensional data base. The points defining the image are derived from the points stored in the data base through a measurement unit conversion from the user coordinate system to the screen coordinate system. This viewing transformation must be extended to include an extra step when deal-

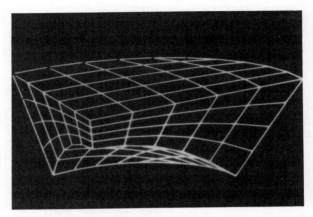

Figure 8.3. Outline drawing of three-dimensional solid object. Reprinted, by permission, from J. H. Biffle, "Use of Graphics in Three Dimensional Structural Analysis of Solids," *Interactive Computer Graphics in Engineering,* American Society of Mechanical Engineers, New York, New York, 1977.

ing with a three-dimensional data base. The user of a three-dimensional interactive graphics system chooses a hypothetical point of view; the image on the screen must reflect how the three-dimensional scene would appear from that point of view. A new frame of reference, the eye coordinate system, is used to express the position of the user's hypothetical eye relative to the model stored in the computer. Therefore, the extended viewing transformation is a conversion from the user coordinate system to the eye coordinate system, followed by a conversion from the eye coordinate system to the screen coordinate system. Perspective projection, the process of applying the viewing transformation to create a two-dimensional image from a three-dimensional scene, is explained throughly in Section 8.2.

The display instructions that drive the display hardware are generated in the same way, using graphic primitives and attributes, by both two- and three-dimensional graphics systems. The use of a display file with subroutines is essential when the graphics system features a refreshed display screen.

The simulated motion of plane or solid objects is displayed by an interactive graphics system through the application of three basic geometric transformations: translation, scaling, and rotation. The mathematical result of extending the concept of geometric transformations to three-dimensional graphics is to enlarge the notation for each transformation from a 3×3 matrix to a 4×4 matrix. Each point in three-dimensional space is correspondingly expressed as a four-element vector. The equations for the three

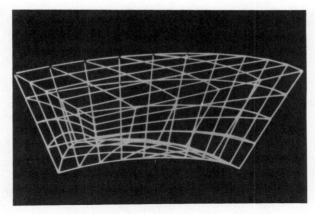

Figure 8.4. Wire-frame drawing of the object shown in Figure 8.3. Reprinted, by permission, from J. H. Biffle, "Use of Graphics in Three Dimensional Structural Analysis of Solids," *Interactive Computer Graphics in Engineering,* American Society of Mechanical Engineers, New York, New York, 1977.

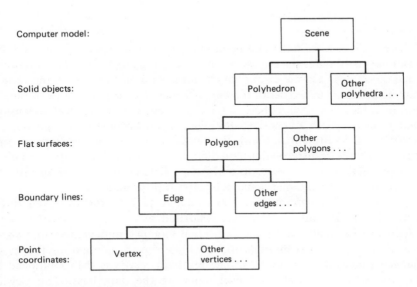

Relationships indicated by tree structure.

Figure 8.5. Conceptual diagram of data base description for a three-dimensional scene.

139

simple geometric transformations, which are extensions of equations in Chapter 7, are as follows:

$$Translation \quad [g_1 \ g_2 \ g_3 \ 1] = [p_1 \ p_2 \ p_3 \ 1] \begin{bmatrix} 1 & 0 & 0 & 0 \\ 0 & 1 & 0 & 0 \\ 0 & 0 & 1 & 0 \\ t_1 & t_2 & t_3 & 1 \end{bmatrix}$$

$$Scaling \quad [g_1 \ g_2 \ g_3 \ 1] = [p_1 \ p_2 \ p_3 \ 1] \begin{bmatrix} s_1 & 0 & 0 & 0 \\ 0 & s_2 & 0 & 0 \\ 0 & 0 & s_3 & 0 \\ 0 & 0 & 0 & 1 \end{bmatrix}$$

$$Rotation \quad [g_1 \ g_2 \ g_3 \ 1] = [p_1 \ p_2 \ p_3 \ 1] \begin{bmatrix} \cos a & -\sin a & 0 & 0 \\ \sin a & \cos a & 0 & 0 \\ 0 & 0 & 1 & 0 \\ 0 & 0 & 0 & 1 \end{bmatrix}$$

The original coordinates of a point in the data base are (p_1, p_2, p_3) and the resulting coordinates for the same point are (g_1, g_2, g_3). Translation moves a solid object over a distance of t_1 in the horizontal direction, t_2 in the vertical direction, and t_3 in the depth direction. Scaling changes the shape of the object by a factor of s_1 in its horizontal dimension, s_2 in its vertical dimension, and s_3 in its depth dimension. Rotation of a solid object through angle a about the z-coordinate axis with the center of rotation at the origin is computed with the transformation equation as shown. Similar simple equations handle rotation about the x axis and y axis. References 1 and 18 furnish full expositions on three-dimensional geometric transformations.

The rules of matrix algebra apply equally to both the two- and three-dimensional calculations. Complex simulated motion is calculated by concatenating the matrices for the individual motion components into a single matrix through matrix multiplication, taking care to maintain the proper sequence among the components. The resultant matrix is then multiplied by the vector of coordinates for each point in the data base. The viewing transformation and the instance transformation are also expressed in matrix notation. It is possible to concatenate the three types of transformations to form a single matrix and apply that matrix to the points that describe a graphic object. However, this approach is not suitable for a graphics system that performs any of these transformations in special-purpose hardware.

8.2. PERSPECTIVE PROJECTION

Perspective projection is the method used to create a two-dimensional screen image that simulates the way the human eye would see a real three-dimensional scene. The elaborate, artifically distorted projections used by artists and draftsmen to give emphasis to drawings of solid objects are generally not needed because of the great flexibility of an interactive graphics system in allowing the user to change his viewpoint. However, final output using a special projection such as isometric can be achieved through specialized programming within the application program.

Central projection, frequently used in computer graphics, imitates the view of an observer who looks at the scene from a reasonably close distance. The portion of the scene that is visible to this observer is contained within a *viewing pyramid*, as shown in Figure 8.6. The viewing pyramid is analogous to the two-dimensional window. The angle of vision and the distance of the observer from the scene act like the aperture setting on a camera to determine whether a wide-angle or narrow view of the scene is produced. Unless a deliberate distortion effect is desired, it is customary to set up the angle of vision so that the rectangular cross section of the viewing pyramid has the same shape (height to width ratio) as the display screen. Just as in two-dimensional viewing, the image does not have to occupy the entire screen. The user can specify a viewport as a portion of the screen, in which case the viewing pyramid's cross section has the shape of the viewport.

Three-dimensional viewing, like its two-dimensional counterpart, involves clipping the contents of the data base against the boundaries of the desired view to ensure that only visible portions of the design are transformed into instructions for the display device. In the three-dimensional case, the boundaries are the faces of the viewing pyramid. The user may wish to specify an unlimited view, so that the base of the viewing pyramid extends an infinite distance away from the observer. However, it is often more useful to specify a limited view volume. The user does this by placing the *front clipping plane* (also called *hither* or *near*) and the *back clipping plane* (also called *yon* or *far*) the distance from the eye required for the desired view. These planes are assumed to be perpendicular to the line of sight for simplicity. Suitable placement of the front and back clipping planes enables the user to create a cutaway view of the interior details of an object, to make a cross-sectional drawing, or to isolate regions of particular interest from the rest of the scene.

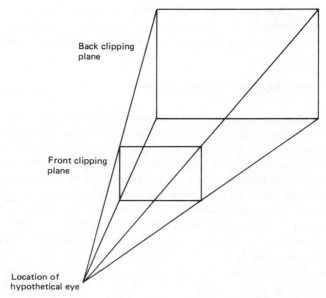

Back clipping
plane

Front clipping
plane

Location of
hypothetical eye

Figure 8.6. Viewing pyramid for central projection.

The image resulting from clipping between these planes can be equivalent to an image produced by hidden-line removal in some situations.

Two-dimensional clipping (presented in Section 7.2) is simply extended to provide for three-dimensional clipping, although the extended process is naturally more complicated to execute. For example, boxing is the shortcut for determining if an instance of a standard symbol is completely visible or invisible prior to detailed clipping. Boxing also applies to three-dimensional viewing, but the rectangular box is extended to become a rectangular volume enclosing the range of maximum to minimum x, y, z coordinates for the symbol instance (Figure 8.7).

The viewing pyramid is specified in a Cartesian coordinate system that is centered at the location of the hypothetical eye, with a z axis that extends with increasing z value in the direction of view. The x and y axes are oriented in the familiar manner, with x values increasing to the right and y values increasing to the top. This frame of reference is called the *image* or *eye coordinate system*. The direction of the z axis in both the eye and the screen coordinate systems (z axis points into screen) makes them left-handed, whereas the user coordinate system is defined to be right-handed.

The eye coordinate system moves with the hypothetical viewpoint as the user looks at the computer-produced scene from different angles and distances, so it is not aligned with the user coordinate system in which the

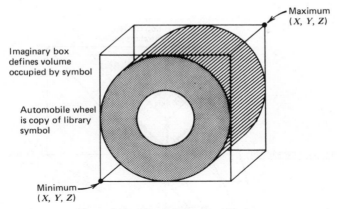

Maximum
(X, Y, Z)

Imaginary box
defines volume
occupied by symbol

Automobile wheel
is copy of library
symbol

Minimum
(X, Y, Z)

Figure 8.7.   Three-dimensional boxing.

solid objects are defined. Figure 8.8 shows a situation in which the eye and user systems are not aligned. The cube inside the viewing pyramid is an object defined in the data base. This cube has one corner at the origin and edges that fall along the three axes of the user coordinate system. This allows for clarity in the illustration and for simplicity in later discussion of this example.

Perspective projection requires three major computer operations. The first step in producing a perspective projection of a three-dimensional scene is to perform a coordinate transformation from the user system to the eye system on each point in the data base. The coordinate transformation can be formulated as a series of geometric transformations—a rotation in space that aligns the cube's axes with the viewing pyramid's axes and then translations that bring the corner of the cube to coincide with the eye position. Finally, the switch from the right-handed user system to the left-handed eye system is made by reversing the plus or minus sign of each z coordinate by applying the following transformation matrix:

$$\begin{bmatrix} 1 & 0 & 0 & 0 \\ 0 & 1 & 0 & 0 \\ 0 & 0 & -1 & 0 \\ 0 & 0 & 0 & 1 \end{bmatrix}$$

The matrices for rotation, translations, and sign reversal can be concatenated into a single matrix for multiplication of each data base point

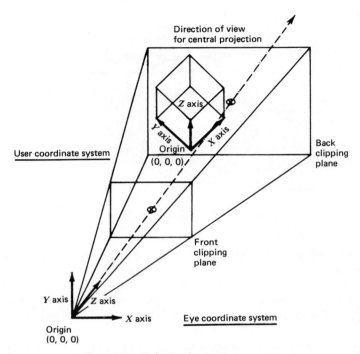

Figure 8.8. Cube inside viewing pyramid.

defining the cube. When the data base defines a collection of objects rather than a single cube, the same matrix is applied to every object. The purpose of this entire operation is to change from one coordinate system to another, not to use geometric transformations in their other role of simulating motion by objects.

The second step in the process of perspective projection is clipping. Clipping is performed in the most straightforward manner when the points defining the solid objects are expressed in the eye coordinate system because the viewing pyramid along with the front and back clipping planes are also specified in the eye coordinate system.

The final step required to create a perspective projection is the actual casting of the three-dimensional scene as a two-dimensional picture. The perspective projection is generated through a transformation from the eye coordinate system to the screen coordinate system, an operation that consists of dividing by the depth of each point. Let (e_1, e_2, e_3) be the eye system coordinates of a point and let (s_1, s_2, s_3) be the screen system coordinates of the same point. The perspective projection equations are then as follows:

$$s_1 = \frac{e_1}{e_3} \qquad s_2 = \frac{e_2}{e_3}$$

The screen image that includes the two-dimensional point (s_1, s_2) shows the appropriate perspective distortion effect as a result of this calculation. Although the screen depth s_3 is not needed to draw the image, it is calculated for possible use in controlling depth cues, including hidden-line and hidden-surface determinations. It is calculated using the equation

$$s_3 = c_1 + \frac{c_2}{e_3}$$

where c_1 and c_2 are constants that can be chosen to give the most satisfactory depth precision depending on the eventual application.

In addition to the calculation given above, the values of s_1 and s_2 must be adjusted to fit properly on the physical display device through multiplication by the ratio of the distance that the user will sit from the screen divided by the distance from the center to edge on the screen surface. This is a dimensionless ratio. If the user does not sit exactly where planned, the adverse effect on his or her view of the screen is negligible.

Up to this point all of the discussion dealing with perspective projection is in reference to a central projection. The central projection simulates the realistic effect of depth perception, but the requirement that each point's coordinates must be divided by the point's depth causes a great deal of work for the computer. Division is the most difficult of the elementary arithmetic operations for the computer to handle.

The most common projection in computer graphics is the simpler *parallel* or *orthographic projection*. The distinguishing characteristic of the orthographic projection is that the viewpoint is assumed to be located an infinite distance away from the scene. This means that the rays from the eye are parallel and the visible portion of the scene is enclosed by a viewing volume that is not a pyramid, but is in the form of a rectangular *viewbox* (Figure 8.9). Because no adjustment to the shape of objects is required in going from the three-dimensional scene to the two-dimensional image, the depth value is simply ignored and the equations for the projection from eye coordinates to screen coordinates become

$$s_1 = e_1 \qquad s_2 = e_2$$

The orthographic projection is quite satisfactory for the majority of practical applications of computer graphics where the equivalent real objects, such as automobiles, would not show much perspective distortion. Only in special-

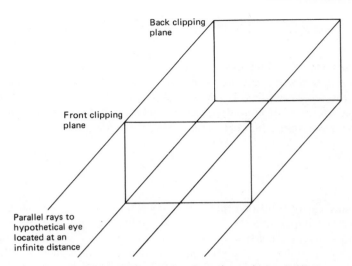

Figure 8.9. Rectangular viewbox for orthographic projection.

ized applications such as aircraft flight simulation and architectural renderings is the realistic perspective effect worth the extra computational cost.

Further information on the mathematics of perspective projection is
available in references 1 and 18.

8.3. REALISTIC-LOOKING IMAGES

The operator seated at a graphics terminal gets no more feeling of three-
dimensional definition from a single image on the screen than he would from
a drawing on paper. It is not practical to produce a realistic-looking picture
on a stroke-writing screen because fancy touches, such as cross-hatching to
emphasize areas, consume too much time, as the display must stroke each
line separately. However, the operator can better visualize the three-
dimensional object when he sees features in the picture that indicate depth,
even if it is indicated in an artificial way. Features added to the image for this
purpose form a broad category known as *depth cues*.

Objects in the distance seem to fade away in a view of a real scene. The
graphics system operator gets this same impression from the screen image if
object boundary lines get gradually dimmer for portions of the computer
scene that are further away from the hypothetical viewpoint. This type of
depth cue takes advantage of the built-in third dimension of a refresh CRT,
the beam intensity control.

The impression that objects fade away in the distance can also be created by a computer-generated picture that utilizes true perspective projection or that exaggerates the deformation in the shape of objects caused by the apparent convergence of parallel lines in the distance. Exaggerated perspective conveys depth information in some applications, but it is more likely to confuse the user instead.

A computer graphics system can give depth cues that cannot be matched with paper drawings. Motion simulated through a series of rapidly changing images can overcome the lack of depth in a single screen image. The operator recognizes the three-dimensional character of the computer design while watching it in motion by unconsciously applying real-life experiences to the interpretation of what he or she is seeing on the screen. A graphics system user can gather full information about the appearance of a solid object by examining it from all sides and by simulating different types of motion.

Interaction between the two eyes in a human being is responsible for the natural depth perception that is essential for sports activities such as catching a baseball. This interaction occurs because the two eyes are set slightly apart in the head, giving each eye a unique line of sight and making each eye's view of a real object slightly different from the other eye's view. A computer graphics system that generates *stereoscopic views* uses this natural interaction as a depth cue [1,5,18]. Stereoscopic viewing requires a graphics terminal equipped with one of several types of special apparatus for presenting a computer image to one eye and a slightly different image to the other eye. The user's natural vision combines these two images to give the illusion of a physical, three-dimensional wire-frame model instead of drawings. The disadvantage of using stereoscopic views as a depth cue is the unusual equipment that the user must learn to tolerate and the visual strain that may occur while merging the images.

The user can absorb the most information about a three-dimensional object in the least time if the displayed image contains only a simple presentation of the essential details, with no extraneous material that must be consciously ignored. *Hidden-line removal* is a depth cue technique that gives the graphics user a line drawing that has an important quality that is usually seen in real life—opaque surfaces hide everything behind them from view. When the hypothetical view is changed, new portions of the object or the scene become visible and some previously seen portions become invisible. This depth cue is especially desirable for a final plotted output because draftsmen omit hidden lines from conventional drawings. Hidden-line removal in three-dimensional viewing is so important that a separate description is given in Section 8.4.

Photographic images of a computer model produced on a raster screen or plotter can be far more realistic than line drawings. Raster technology is distinguished by its ability to display areas filled with gray shades or colors, and these areas are ideal for showing the surfaces on three-dimensional objects. In contrast, a line-drawing display device must represent a surface by showing its boundary lines.

Raster images suffer from the same flatness as line drawings and, like them, must be augmented with depth cues to give the appearance of solid objects. The depth cues used with raster images are designed to imitate the appearance of real scenes. Naturally, the graphics system user expects to see only surfaces that face toward his or her hypothetical point of view because a solid object hides its own rear faces and it also blocks from sight any other objects or portions of objects located behind it. The user is able to interpret a line drawing that includes all boundary lines, whether they should be hidden or not, by accepting the drawing as a wire-frame representation. However, a shaded picture including all surfaces is never utilized because it would be an impossible mess. A raster graphics system has hidden-surface elimination as an integral part of the programming that prepares the video signal.

A person looking at a computer-generated image will accept the displayed areas as the surfaces of solid objects much more readily if the computer system simulates the effects of lighting on a three-dimensional scene. The observer expects surfaces that are closer to the light source to cast shadows on the surfaces that are further away. Shadow calculation methods utilize the path of light rays from the light source into the scene in a manner analogous to the way the line of sight from the hypothetical eye position toward the scene is used to identify hidden surfaces. Computer simulation of lighting effects can convince the observer that various object surfaces in the scene are shiny, dull, patterned, or wrinkled. Translucent objects, which diminish but do not block the visibility of other objects behind them, can also be imitated.

The impressive realism that can be achieved in computer-generated images is clearly demonstrated by Figure 8.1. However, the calculations required to produce this realism slow the display process down so much that photographic images cannot be used for an interactive dialogue. Also, extremely detailed input information is necessary to build a data base suitable for generating realistic images, especially when patterned or textured surfaces are simulated [19].

8.4. HIDDEN-LINE AND HIDDEN-SURFACE REMOVAL

This section is a general introduction to the techniques for hidden-line and hidden-surface removal, not a comprehensive explanation of specific programs. A dozen or more different computer algorithms designed for the purpose of hidden-line or hidden-surface removal exist at the present time. (An *algorithm* is a rule of procedure for solving a recurrent mathematical problem.) Details concerning many of these algorithms are available in references 1,6, and 20. The existence of such a large number of different approaches is due to the specialized nature of each algorithm, determined by the following factors:

1. There is a major division among programs based on whether their goal is the hidden-line removal for a boundary drawing on a stroke-writing display or the hidden-surface removal for an area-filling image on a raster screen. This section is divided into two parts focusing on these categories since line drawings are calculated from the *geometric relationships* among the three-dimensional objects and raster images are created by determining the *pixel contents* at each location on the screen during scan conversion.
2. A few algorithms are well-suited to implementation in special-purpose processor hardware, while the rest can only be programmed to run on a general-purpose computer. Generation of images for dynamically changing views at an interactive rate such as thirty frames per second requires specially designed, dedicated processor units.
3. Each algorithm is designed to handle a narrowly defined type of three-dimensional entity. For instance, an algorithm that handles objects defined as approximations using plane-faced polyhedra cannot handle mathematically defined objects such as spheres and cylinders (Figure 8.10).
4. The efficiency of performance of every algorithm decreases as the complexity of the three-dimensional scene increases. However, the essential

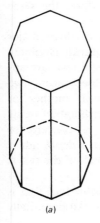

(a)   (b)

Figure 8.10. Three-dimensional entities. (a) Cylinder approximated as a polyhedron. (b) Mathematically defined cylinder.

factor affecting performance of an algorithm based on geometric relationships is the complexity of the entire scene as described in the data base. In contrast, the greatest influence on the efficiency of a pixel-contents algorithm is the complexity of the finished visible image. The concept of complexity itself is hard to express in meaningful quantitative terms since it could be a simple count of graphic objects, surfaces, or edges, or a percent of overlapping polygons, or some other measure.

The combined influence of all four factors means that no fair benchmark test can be devised to prove which of the dozen or more algorithms is superior. Instead, each fulfills a specialized role. Development of improved hidden-line and hidden-surface removal procedures is continuing at the present time.

8.4.1. Geometric Relationships

Geometric relationships are the basis for hidden-line removal techniques designed to operate on the three-dimensional representation of objects. These objects are defined as polyhedral solids, with each face being a flat surface having a polygon boundary. The polygon's edges are straight lines. The polygon's vertices, which are the endpoints of the edge lines, are described in the data base as x, y, z coordinates in the eye coordinate system. It is assumed that after hidden-line removal is accomplished, the resulting boundaries of visible surfaces and lines of intersection between visible surfaces will be processed by an orthogonal projection to obtain an image for display. If these geometric techniques and the projection are applied before any clipping is done, then the resulting data describe all the lines in the entire scene that are visible from a particular angle of vision, and these data can be clipped repeatedly to generate various close-up or wide-angle images from the same angle of vision.

The geometric method for hidden-line removal consists of three major steps. First, a *visibility test* is applied to each solid object to quickly eliminate the totally hidden back faces of that object. Second, a series of tests are applied to the scene to determine the *relationships* among the object faces—two polygons that intersect, one polygon that completely surrounds another, or two polygons that do not overlap at all. The relationship determination treats the faces of the polyhedral solids as separate polygons with no concern for their relative distances from the hypothetical viewpoint. Third, a *depth test* is applied to any pairs of overlapping polygons to determine which of the two is visible.

The *visibility test* is designed to identify only a totally invisible face that is hidden by the volume of the solid object to which it belongs. All potentially visible faces must be subjected to further analysis. This visibility test involves a comparison between a line of sight drawn from the eye position to a point on the object's polygon face and the *surface normal vector* at that point. A surface normal vector is defined as an outward-pointing vector perpendicular to the plane containing the polygon (Figure 8.11). When the angle between these two lines is greater than 90 degrees, the surface is invisible and it is eliminated from the set of surfaces that make up the displayed image.

The next step in geometric hidden-line removal is to determine the relationships among all the potentially visible faces of all the objects in the scene. The most efficient approach is to apply the quickest tests first and leave the more elaborate test calculations for the situations that cannot be resolved any other way. Therefore, the first relationship test is a type of prescreening called the *minimax test*, shown in Figure 8.12. The calculation requires that all vertices of polygon A be examined to find the highest and lowest x coordinate and the highest and lowest y coordinate, and that polygon B be examined in the same way. These maximum and minimum coordinate values are then

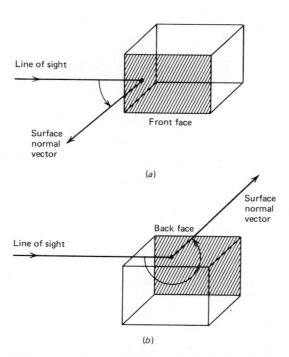

Figure 8.11. Visibility test based on angle between line of sight and surface normal vector. (a) Less than 90 degrees. (b) Greater than 90 degrees.

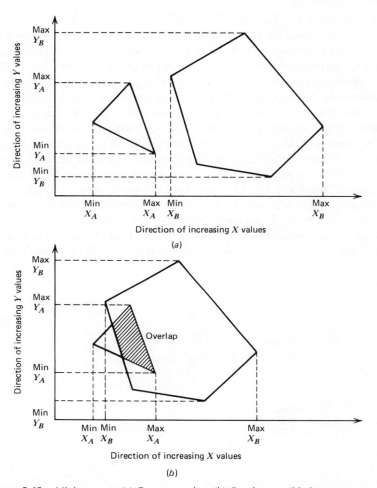

Figure 8.12. Minimax test. (a) Cannot overlap. (b) Overlap possible but not proven.

compared. If *at least one* of the following statements is true, then polygons A and B *cannot* possibly overlap.

1. Max x_A is less than min x_B.
2. Max x_B is less than min x_A.
3. Max y_A is less than min y_B.
4. Max y_B is less than min y_A.

When the minimax test cannot rule out the possibility that the two poly-gons overlap, the two polygons must be tested further to determine if their edges intersect or if one is completely surrounded by the other. The test for an intersection is less complex so it is done first. Each line segment that is an edge of polygon A must be checked to see if it intersects any of the line seg-ments that are edges of polygon B.

When there is no intersection between two polygons, either one polygon completely surrounds the other or they do not overlap at all. Two alternative procedures are commonly used for testing if one polygon surrounds another.

One surrounding-polygon algorithm involves calculating the sum of the angles from a vertex point of polygon A along imaginary lines drawn to every vertex of polygon B (Figure 8.13). The total is always either 360 or 0 degrees when the proper arithmetic sign for each angle is utilized. If the sum is 360 degrees, the point is inside. If the sum is 0 degrees, the point is outside. The operation is repeated for each vertex point. A surrounds B when every vertex of A is inside B. The result is inconclusive when every vertex of A is outside B because polygon A may surround polygon B or they may not overlap, so the entire procedure must be done again with the roles of A and B reversed to de-termine the relationship between the two polygons.

The other surrounding-polygon algorithm involves drawing an imaginary line starting at a vertex of polygon A and continuing all the way through poly-gon B, avoiding any vertex of B (Figure 8.14). If this line intersects the boundary of polygon B an *odd* number of times, the vertex of A is inside B. If it intersects an *even* number of times, the vertex is outside. For polygon B to surround polygon A, all vertices of A must be inside B. This test must be done independently for each possible relationship—A surrounds B or B sur-rounds A.

The result of all the preceding relationship tests is to identify pairs of over-

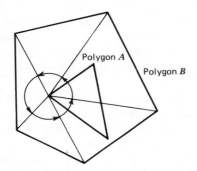

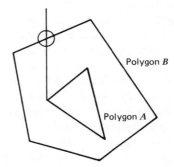

Figure 8.13. Sum of angles equal to 360 degrees indicates that vertex of A is inside B.

Figure 8.14. One intersection (odd num-ber) indicates that vertex of A is inside B.

lapping polygons. The pairing is not simple because one polygon may overlap several others and itself may be overlapped by one or more polygons. Also, a line of intersection between two polygons not only has the potential to become a displayed graphic element in an outline drawing, but it breaks each of the intersecting polygons into two parts that must be examined separately. Each pair of overlapping polygons must undergo a *depth test* to determine which polygon is visible and which is obscured from a particular point of view. The discussion below covers two methods for calculating relative depth called the *piercing test* and the *priority test*. These two depth-calculation methods are compatible with geometric hidden-line removal.

The piercing test is designed to determine whether a specific point is visible or obstructed. A test point on the vertex, edge, or surface of a polygon is chosen and then an imaginary line is drawn from the test point to the location of the hypothetical eye. If this line does not pierce any of the polygons that overlap the polygon containing the test point, then the point is visible. Any polygon through which this line passes obviously hides the test point from the observer. In addition to the qualitative visible verses hidden decision, this method can also yield a quantitative depth value for the distance from the observer to the test point and from the observer to any polygon pierced by the line (Figure 8.15). The piercing test is suitable when a central projection will subsequently finish creation of the two-dimensional image because central projection assumes that the eye is a finite distance from the three-dimensional scene.

The *priority test* can be used only in conjunction with an orthographic projection because it assumes that the viewpoint is located at an infinite distance. The aim of the priority test is to sort all the polygons in a scene based on their depth.

Figure 8.16 shows the *direct way* to calculate priority. To find a point of visual interference between two polygons, it is necessary to make orthographic projections of both. Once any visual interference point has been found, the three-dimensional representation of the polygons is utilized to find the depth of this point on each respective polygon. It is then a simple chore to compare these two z-coordinate values to decide which polygon is closer to the observer and thus visible. The most difficult aspect of this direct method is finding a point of visual interference.

The *sorting method* is another way to implement the priority test that avoids the need to find interference points. The initial sort puts the polygons into priority order based on the greatest depth value for any point on each polygon. Figure 8.17 shows where the greatest z-coordinate value occurs on polygons A and B. As a result of the initial sort, polygon A has a lower priority than polygon B. However, the initial sort is followed by a scanning of the entire polygon list in reverse order to discover any cases where two or more

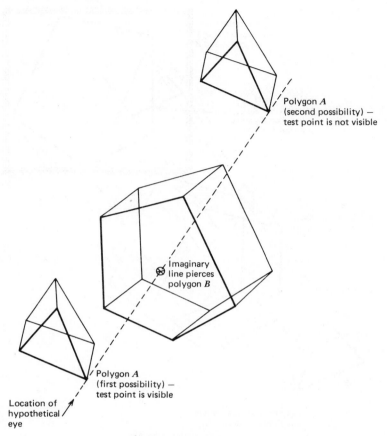

Polygon A
(second possibility) –
test point is not visible

Imaginary
line pierces
polygon B

Polygon A
(first possibility) –
test point is visible

Location of
hypothetical
eye

Figure 8.15. Piercing test.

polygons overlap in depth. If more detailed calculations determine that a polygon of lower priority actually obscures some part of a polygon preceding it in the list, then the priority assignments must be corrected. This is the case in Figure 8.17, because A actually hides a portion of B. However, in many cases the initial order will prove to be accurate and the proportion of detailed calculations required will be limited.

8.4.2. Pixel Contents

The characteristics of raster display devices are the basis for a group of hidden-surface removal techniques designed to determine the pixel intensity for

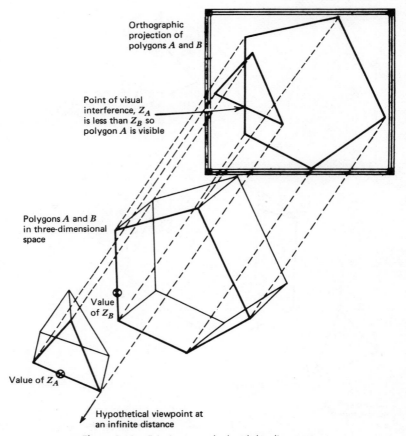

Figure 8.16. Priority test calculated the direct way.

visible surfaces only. The techniques are actually intermingled with scan conversion, which is the transition from the geometric data base description of objects into the scan format required by a raster display. The hidden-surface techniques produce one specific image, so they are applied after the other image preparation steps of clipping and orthographic projection. This reduces the portion of the scene that must be examined during hidden-surface removal, thus improving performance.

The concept of a frame buffer (bit map) is introduced earlier in Section 2.4. The minimal frame buffer consists of 1 bit of stored data per image pixel and it is capable of holding a single black-and-white frame. For hidden-surface removal, this concept is extended to become a *depth buffer* consisting of

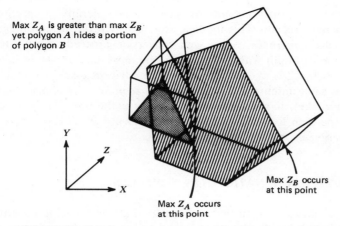

Max Z_A is greater than max Z_B yet polygon A hides a portion of polygon B

Y

Z

X

Max Z_B occurs at this point

Max Z_A occurs at this point

Figure 8.17. Priority test implemented with the sorting method.

two arrays in storage. One array contains several bits per pixel to store the intensity, and possibly the color, to be displayed on the screen. The second array contains several bits per pixel to store the depth (z coordinate) of the object that is visible in the image at that pixel location. The depth buffer's two arrays occupy a great deal of storage space.

Data are obtained for the depth buffer in a straightforward manner. First, both arrays are initialized by storing in every pixel location the background intensity value (displayed where no surface exists in the scene) and a nominal depth value. Second, a polygon is chosen essentially at random to be put through the scan conversion process. Intensity and depth values are calculated for every pixel location in the image that falls within the area of this polygon. Third, a depth comparison is made. The new intensity and depth values are substituted into the buffer for each pixel where the calculated depth is less than the value already stored in memory because this means that the observer is closer to the current polygon than to any previously processed surface. The contents of the buffer are not changed for any pixel where the new depth is greater than the stored value because the polygon is hidden by another surface at that location within the image. The second and third steps, scan conversion and depth comparison, are repeated until all polygons in the three-dimensional scene have been processed. The contents of the intensity array are then transferred from the buffer to the display device. The resulting image shows only the surfaces that are visible from the hypothetical viewpoint.

The efficiency of hidden-surface removal is improved by exploiting the observation that a pixel is likely to share the same intensity as nearby pixels because a single surface tends to occupy a considerable proportion of the screen in most scenes. This tendency for nearby pixels to be similar in content is called *coherence*. Since scan conversion proceeds along a horizontal line from left to right within the image, the most natural way to take advantage of coherence is to expect sequences of adjacent pixels within a scan line to be the same intensity. The property is *scan-line coherence*. Similarly, a pixel is also likely to share the same intensity as the pixels in the nearby locations in the scan lines above and below its own line. This property is called *area coherence*.

8.5. ILLUMINATION ON SURFACES

Figure 8.1 shows the realistic raster image that can be achieved through the combination of two depth-cue techniques—hidden-surface removal and simulated illumination. This section is an introduction to the methods used to calculate illumination effects; a more detailed treatment of this topic is found in reference 1.

The lighting on scenes in the real world usually consists of diffuse illumination combined with light from one or more single sources. Diffuse illumination is the result of light being repeatedly reflected from all the surrounding surfaces so it reaches the three-dimensional objects with equal intensity from all directions. The term "single source" indicates light from a definite source such as an electric light bulb, direct outdoor sunlight, or sunlight coming through a window. The intensity of light from a single source is concentrated along the line from the source to the surface of the object. Visual distinction among objects in a real scene is possible because different surfaces reflect different proportions of the incoming light.

A *gray-scale image* is similar to the picture on a black-and-white television set. It represents the various intensities of reflected light as shades of gray along a predefined scale from white for maximum intensity to black for minimum intensity. The graphics system creates the gray shades in the displayed image through the beam intensity controls within the CRT. The appearance of each object in a gray-scale picture depends on an attribute indicating the object's reflectance. This attribute is assigned by the user and it is entered as part of the object's description in the graphics system data base. *Reflectance* is a measure of the proportion of the light falling on a surface that is reflected. The remaining light is absorbed. This property is expressed as a reflectance coefficient having a fractional value between zero and one.

For diffuse illumination, the intensity I_D of the reflected light depends only on the energy L_D of the diffuse light reaching the surface and the reflectance coefficient R. The equation is $I_D = RL_D$.

For single-source illumination, the intensity of the light falling on the surface also depends on the cosine of the angle of incidence of the light. This is known as Lambert's law. Single-source illumination causes two types of reflection, *diffuse reflection* in which the surface material scatters the light equally in all directions, and *mirrorlike reflection* (highlights) in which the light is principally returned with an angle of reflection equal to the angle of incidence. Figures 8.18 and 8.19 are diagrams of these two phenomena.

The equation relating the intensity L_S of the light from a single source and the intensity I_S of the diffusely reflected light is $I_S = (\cos A)RL_S$. Angle A is the angle of incidence between the path of the incoming light from the single

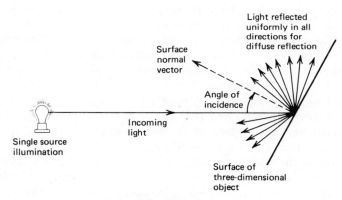

Figure 8.18. Diffuse reflection.

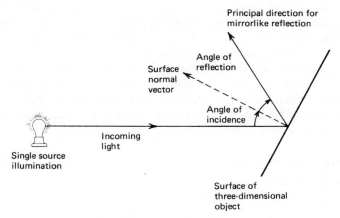

Figure 8.19. Mirrorlike reflection.

source and the surface normal vector. A *surface normal vector* is a line perpendicular to a flat surface or perpendicular to the tangent at a point on a curved surface. The direction of the normal, rather than the orientation of the surface plane, is used in computer graphics calculations because it is mathematically convenient, especially for curved surfaces and at intersections between planes. The highest proportion of reflection occurs for incoming light traveling along a path in the same direction as the normal vector. (The cosine of 0 degrees is 1.) The brightness of the reflected light is reduced as the light source is moved to the side until the incoming light misses the surface entirely at angles of 90 degrees or more between the light path and the normal vector. (The cosine of 90 degrees is 0.)

In mirrorlike reflection, the position of the observer in relation to the principal direction of the reflected light is important in determining how bright the highlight on the surface appears to the observer. Each surface is assigned another reflectance coefficient H to indicate whether the surface should appear to be shiny or dull. Unlike the constant coefficient R, the coefficient H has a value that varies with the angle of incidence of the light, increasing as that angle approaches 90 degrees. The intensity I_H of the highlight can be approximated using the equation $I_H = H (\cos C)^n I_S$. The exponent n is an arbitrary number between 1 and 10 that adjusts the apparent gloss of the surface. This equation is not based on the laws of optics, but instead is an artificial computer method for creating satisfactory visual effects.

To determine the display intensity for a surface, it is necessary to calculate I_D for the entire surface and to make separate calculations to find the I_S and I_H values attributable to each single light source for each portion of the surface. The display intensity for that portion is the sum of all these individual intensity values.

These methods for calculating illumination effects in a gray-scale picture are easily adapted to producing a full-color picture. The typical display device for color raster images is a CRT with separate intensity control circuits for the three primary colors—red, blue, and green. A real object's color is due to its reflection of various wavelengths of light in different proportions. Therefore, color is simulated by assigning separate reflectance coefficients for the three primary colors. Then the equation for diffuse illumination and the equation for diffuse reflection of light from a single source each become a set of three equations:

Diffuse Illumination

$$I_{D(\text{RED})} = R_{(\text{RED})} L_D$$

$$I_{D(\text{BLUE})} = R_{(\text{BLUE})} L_D$$

$$I_{D(\text{GREEN})} = R_{(\text{GREEN})} L_D$$

Diffuse Reflection from a Single Source

$$I_{S(RED)} = (\cos A)R_{(RED)}L_S$$
$$I_{S(BLUE)} = (\cos A)R_{(BLUE)}L_S$$
$$I_{S(GREEN)} = (\cos A)R_{(GREEN)}L_S$$

The equation for mirrorlike reflection of light from a single source is unchanged. The visible highlights are always the same color as the incoming light regardless of the properties of the surface. This phenomenon can be observed in real scenes where white light from sunlight or electrical lighting always produces white highlights.

CHAPTER 9

Application Programs

This chapter deals with the most important and most difficult problem concerning interactive computer graphics, how to actually use it. The fundamental goal, beneficial application programs, must not be lost amid all the details concerning individual pieces of equipment and specific programming techniques.

The easiest way to apply graphics to productive work is through a *turnkey system,* a complete package of hardware and software purchased from a single vendor. Section 9.1 explores the capabilities of a typical turnkey system for general-purpose drafting. Another relatively easy way to put graphics to work is through the acquisition of just software in a proven *application product* with extensive specialized capability for a particular task. Three examples of application products for computer-aided design and computer-aided manufacturing (CAD/CAM) are studied in Section 9.2. In practice, there is little distinction between these two approaches because turnkey vendors improve the market for their systems by offering optional software packages for specific applications, and application product developers offer complete systems to prospective users by entering into licensing agreements with major hardware vendors. When considering either a turnkey graphics system or a graphics application product, the term "user" means a person who would otherwise perform the task through conventional methods. The user receives a completely operational system that requires no additional programming.

In contrast, a *graphics package* is generalized software that supplies only the most fundamental operations. The user of a graphics package is a computer programmer who treats it as a stepping-stone for incorporating interactive graphics into existing or newly developed application programs. The advantage of custom programming with a graphics package is a virtually limitless range of possible uses. Section 9.3 deals with the characteristics of the graphics package itself and examines how it acts in conjunction with the *operating system* (a program that supervises the way the computer handles all other programs) and a specific application program to result in a functional system.

9.1. TURNKEY GRAPHICS SYSTEMS

This section discusses the software capabilities that are provided, and the way in which these capabilities are implemented, for a typical turnkey system. A turnkey system is an interactive computer graphics system consisting of hardware and software furnished together by a single vendor in fully operational condition as a general-purpose drafting tool. Applicon introduced the first turnkey interactive graphics processing system in 1970. The vendor list at the end of this chapter shows the large number of popular systems that now fall into the turnkey system category under this definition. The typical system described in this section is a composite of all the products mentioned in the vendor list. Each individual system has a few unique features that may be significant for a specific application, but the products of the different vendors are remarkably similar in their general capabilities. Turnkey systems are oriented toward producing high-quality technical drawings because they originated as two-dimensional drafting tools, although most have been extended to offer three-dimensional graphics utilizing the multiple-view input technique and producing a static wire-frame image.

The hardware in a turnkey graphics system generally consists of multiple user stations supported by a minicomputer with tape and disk storage units, a hardcopy unit, and an electromechanical pen plotter. Each user station is always equipped with at least one graphics screen, normally a storage tube. This may be the sole display device or it may be augmented by a second graphics screen, an alphanumeric screen, or a small alphanumeric LED display. The input equipment at a user station normally consists of a keyboard and a tablet with cursor combination. A set of program function keys may also be included. Joysticks and control knobs are less common, while light pens are rare. Figure 9.1 shows the equipment in a four-station turnkey graphics system.

The capabilities of the turnkey system are discussed with respect to features dedicated to (1) building the computer model, (2) viewing the computer model, and (3) data handling. The term "model" here means the content definition of either a two-dimensional drawing or a three-dimensional scene formed by a collection of two-dimensional elements placed at any orientation.

9.1.1. Features Dedicated to Building the Model

Each model-building feature of a turnkey system addresses one of three operational needs—creating the model, revising the model, or adding annotation for a finished drawing or view of a three-dimensional scene.

The model is built through *commands* that create and revise *drawing elements*, both primitive geometric elements and predefined symbol elements.

Figure 9.1. Equipment offered as a four-station turnkey graphics system. Photograph courtesy of Applicon Incorporated.

A set of *primitive geometric elements* is provided by the turnkey system for general-purpose drafting. The simplest drawing element is the *point*. Elements in the set that are based on the *straight line* include a single segment, an open string of connected line segments, a rectangle, and a polygon. A *polygon* is any closed figure with straight sides. It may have any number of sides and may be irregular with sides of different lengths. There are two types of curved lines. The *conic section* is a mathematically defined curve. Conic section drawing elements include circles (arcs), ellipses, parabolas, and hyperbolas as either complete or partial figures. The *free-form curve* is generated by the graphics system according to an algorithm to fit a series of points entered by the user. The free-form curve is a closed figure if the first and last input points coincide. Otherwise, it is said to be open. Straight and curved lines can be combined into a single entity. A *complex string* is an open figure formed by connected straight line segments and curved lines. A *complex shape* is a closed figure with both straight and curved sides.

The *symbol* feature of a turnkey system enables the user to interactively define additional drawing elements, each consisting of one or more primitive elements, assign symbol names to the new elements, and store them in a computer library for future use in model building. Symbol name is the link between the master design in the library and every instance of that symbol in models. Alteration of the master design is reflected in all subsequent displays or plots of any model containing that symbol.

One or more previously defined symbols can be incorporated in the construction of a new symbol, thus producing *nested symbols*. This process can be compounded to result in multiple-level nesting. The turnkey system also has the capability to *drop symbol identity*, which eliminates the symbol name link to the library for a particular symbol instance and coverts its data base description into a collection of primitive elements. The appearance of the drawing element, which does not change during this operation, is then also protected from change due to revisions in the library. The drop-symbol-identity operation dismantles the structure of a nested symbol in reverse order, so that the symbol that is defined last is the first to be broken into its constituent parts.

Drawing elements are the material from which the model is built, but interactive commands are the tools that enable the user to create and revise these drawing elements. The typical turnkey system has over 200 primitive commands. This extensive set of standard operations means that even complicated drafting functions are easy for the user to perform. However, a subset of about twenty-five commands is sufficient for most basic drafting tasks and it is this subset that normally appears on a menu or on program function keys. The remainder are requested by typing the command's name. A method for setting up user-defined macro commands provides the turnkey system with the potential for an unlimited number of complex, customized operations.

There are several distinctive types among the primitive commands dedicated to building the model. The *parameter declaration command* explicitly sets the value of a parameter that either controls the manner of operation of the system itself or influences the effect of drawing element placement and manipulation commands. A typical turnkey system has about fifty different parameter declaration commands. A value that is set by any of these commands remains as the controlling value until it is deliberately reset. This property is sometimes referred to as *modal operation*.

Parameter declaration commands to control the functioning of the system normally include facilities through which the user permanently sets the origin point and the measurement units of the user coordinate system for each model. For a house plan, the origin could be on the property boundary and the units could be feet and inches, while for a gear wheel, the origin could be at its center and the measurement units could be millimeters. The user also sets the accuracy to which the system rounds off incoming data. Typical round-off values would be $1/16$ inch or 1 mm for coordinates of an input point, 1 degree for the magnitude of an angle, and the nearest whole number for a scaling factor. Parameter declaration commands allow the user to set the spacing of grid lines and grid division markers, control whether or not the grid is displayed, and turn on or off certain drafting aids, such as the horizontal, vertical, and grid constraints and round-off functions. When interactive user assignment of commands to menu squares or program function keys is available, it also operates through parameter declaration commands.

Parameters that affect the creation of primitive geometric elements consist of line thickness, line type, line symbology, and class. Primary class is an element that is part of the stored model, whereas construction class is an element used as a temporary drafting aid. The placement of symbols is controlled by declaration commands that set the current symbol name, angle, and scale. Declared parameter values for scale factor, placement angle, and so forth determine the result of specialized drafting techniques such as area-filling patterns, the automatic attachment of a terminator symbol to the ends of line segments, and the automatic repetition of a symbol in a row and column arrangement. Logical relationships within the data base for both primitive elements and symbols are assigned through parameters such as overlay number, user-defined association, and designation of a closed figure as representing either a solid object or a hole in an object.

Another type of primitive command dedicated to building the model is the *data collection command*. This type encompasses all commands that generate original entries in the data base describing the model. A major portion of these commands are related to drawing elements. There must be at least one input command for each primitive geometric element. However, the typical turnkey system provides a variety of input commands for many of the frequently used primitive geometric elements. Each of these commands requires a slightly different set of information from the user to specify the size, shape, and placement of the element. An example of multiple input commands for a single element is the eight different methods for creating a simple straight line segment as shown by Figure 9.2. The attributes of the individual element added to the model as a result of an input command are determined by a combination of the data entered by the user and the system parameters in control at the time.

There is a single input command that adds to the model an instance of any symbol in the system's library. The appearance of the drawing element created by this operation depends on the basic design stored in the library and on modifications to that design controlled by the system parameters related to symbol placement.

A complete turnkey system must also have methods for entering nongraphic information into the data base and associating the nongraphic data items to specific elements within the graphic model. The user normally enters the nongraphic data through the keyboard and then indicates the associated graphic element on the screen through a pick operation.

The data base created through data collection commands can subsequently be revised by means of *data editing commands*, another type of primitive operation. Each editing operation consists of two parts. First, the user specifies what portion of the model is to be included in the operation. Second, the user chooses how that portion is to be manipulated.

The portion of the model affected by a data editing command can consist of a single primitive geometric element or a single instance of a library symbol. The user indicates the selection of a single item of either kind with a pick

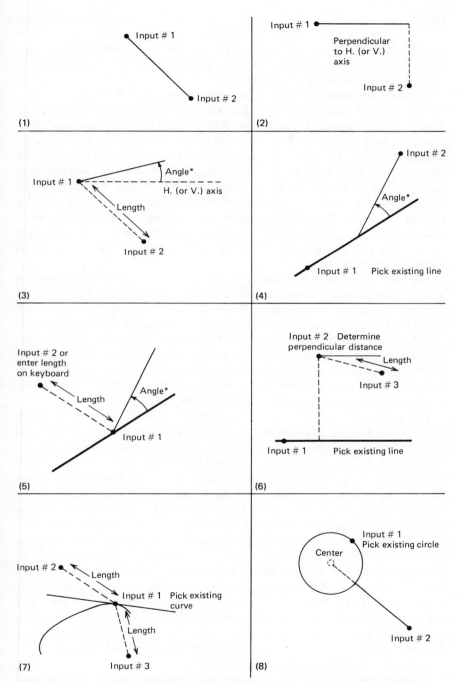

Figure 9.2. Input commands for creating a straight line segment. (*1*) Between points. (*2*) Through a point with horizontal (or vertical) constraint. (*3*) Through a point at an angle. (*4*) Through a point intersecting another line. (*5*) From a point on another line. (*6*) Parallel to another line. (*7*) Tangent to a curve. (*8*) Radial line to arc or circle. Angle marked by an asterisk is a system control parameter.

167

operation. Alternatively, a command to revise the model can be applied to a collection of graphic entities, with the collection specified either through a *spatial grouping* or a *logical relationship*.

A spatial grouping is a defined area or volume, set up with a temporary boundary that the user superimposes on a display of the model. This boundary is often called a *fence*. A graphic manipulation affects all the graphic items, primitives and symbol instances alike, that are contained by the fence. By definition, an exclusive fence contains only those elements that are totally inside the closed boundary, whereas an inclusive fence contains all items that are even partially located within it. An example of fence usage is a drawing that must be revised to bring a mounting bracket 1 inch closer to the end of a mechanical device. This bracket consists of two bolts, two nuts, and a metal strap. The user can draw a fence around the bracket and move it as a whole rather than individually move each of the lines and circles that make up the bolts, nuts, and strap.

The user can temporarily isolate a portion of the model's data base for graphic manipulation by indicating logical values to define the desired items. The typical turnkey system offers the possibility of using criteria based on a data hierarchy with four ranks such as drawing name (model name), overlay number, user-assigned association, and drawing element type. The user identifies the portion of the model that he wishes to revise by selecting values for one or more of these ranks. For example, the user can delete all drawing element types for part number 253 (a user-assigned association) that are on overlays 4, 5, and 6 of drawing name DESIGN.

The portion of the model that is identified as a single element, a spatial grouping, or a logical relationship can be manipulated in a variety of ways. For a particular graphic operation such as deletion, the typical turnkey system has three different data editing commands so the user can choose the type of revision and the mode of identification with a single action. Therefore, the command menu or program function keys show three deletion commands—Delete Element, Delete Area, and Delete Relationship. The typical turnkey system provides the following graphic manipulation functions: delete, duplicate, move, scale, rotate, mirror, partial delete, and modify geometry. The effect of each of these revision operations is shown in Figure 9.3. Partial delete is an editing operation that removes the part of a primitive geometric element that is between two points. For example, the user can shorten a line segment from either end or change it into two separate segments by eliminating a portion in the middle. Modify geometry is an operation that has a specific meaning for each primitive element, but generally it alters the data base information that determines size and shape. For instance, the user can modify a polygon by changing the location of one vertex.

The complete set of primitive data editing commands provides the user with ways to change anything that the primitive data collection commands allow the user to enter. Therefore, in addition to the graphic manipulation commands just described, the typical turnkey system also provides commands for altering the assignment of values for the overlay and user-defined association ranks in the data hierarchy. The nongraphic data stored by the system in association with the graphic model are accessible for modification through a special editing command that is similar in operation to the nongraphic data input command.

The preceding discussion of primitive model-building commands covers three distinct types—parameter declaration commands, data collection commands, and data editing commands. A single command of any type performs a relatively simple operation, but the typical turnkey system allows the user to define complex operations and store them within the system as macro commands. Unfortunately, macro command definition is not an interactive function like symbol definition. The user cannot simply perform a sequence of commands from the terminal and have the system capture and hold the sequence as a new macro command. Instead, macro commands are written using a programming language that includes statements corresponding to the primitive commands. This language includes additional capabilities such as iterative loops that repeat a subset of operations a desired number of times and variables that are replaced with input data from the terminal each time the macro is used. Constant data can be programmed into the macro itself to avoid unnecessary input. The most convenient way for the user to enter the program statements for a new macro is through the on-line text-editor system that accompanies most minicomputers.

This concludes the list of capabilities necessary for the creation of a three-dimensional model within the graphics system. However, the final output, whether it is a view of a three-dimensional model or a technical drawing with a two-dimensional data base, requires annotation because annotation is two-dimensional and is not suitable to be part of a three-dimensional model. Annotation includes text of all kinds plus labels, dimensions, and tolerances composed of text and simple graphics. The typical turnkey graphics system has an elaborate set of annotation features since the system is oriented toward high-quality technical drafting.

The features for annotation consist of primitive elements and commands, so they are analogous to the features for building the model itself. However, the primitive elements for annotation are simple and limited in number. The basic element is the *text string*, which is just a series of alphanumeric characters handled as a unit. The *text node* and *text field* are place holders for a text string to be entered subsequently. The text node is a predefined placement point for a text string. The size, spacing, and other properties of the text are determined at the time the actual characters are entered by the system

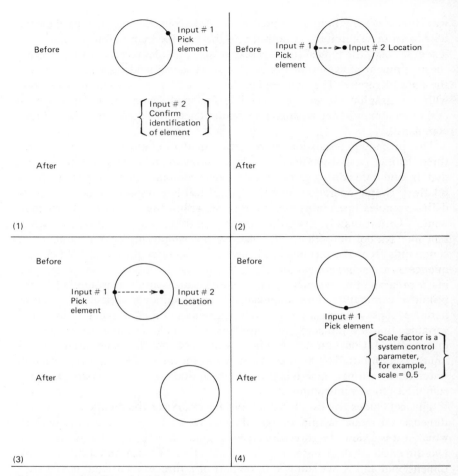

Figure 9.3. The effect of graphic manipulation functions. (*1*) Delete. (*2*) Duplicate, (*3*) Move. (*4*) Scale. (*5*) Rotate. (*6*) Mirror. (*7*) Partial delete. (*8*) Modify geometry.

parameters controlling text. The text field is a complete definition of both the placement point and the properties of a text string. Only the content of the string remains undetermined until the characters are entered. An example of a text field in use is a standard note with a blank space for a purchase order number to be filled in on each customer's copy of the basic drawing.

The label and the dimension are actually just combinations of ordinary two-dimensional graphic elements with text, but the combination is handled as a unit by the system and is segregated in the data base. The primitive element

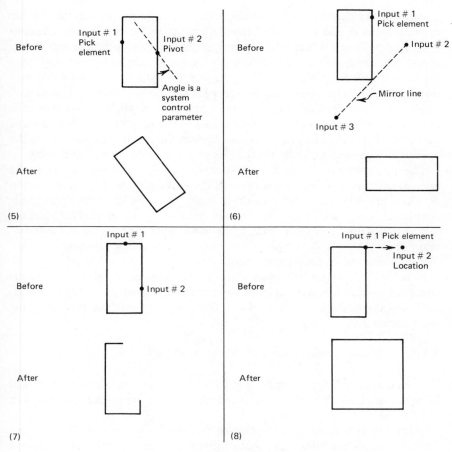

Figure 9.3. Continued

for a label is a text string accompanied by a leader line with an arrowhead pointing toward part of the model. The primitive element for a dimension is a line parallel to the part of the model being measured. At each end of this line there is an arrowhead and a perpendicular witness line reaching toward the model. The dimension call-out is a text string located along the dimension line that states the measurement, unit of measure, and optionally the tolerance of that measurement. The typical turnkey system offers a multitude of dimension variations.

Annotation is generated through the same three types of primitive commands that are involved in building the model. The parameter declaration commands are particularly important since system parameters control all the characteristics of text except the placement point on the drawing and the content. Text parameters that exist in a typical turnkey system include font, slant, aspect ratio, and size for characters; angle for line of text; line length and spacing for multiple lines of text; left, right, or center justification for string in a text field; and above or below placement for text parallel to a straight line. A single set of parameters controls the appearance of all text, whether it is entered by an input command, changed by an editing command, or created as part of a label or dimension. Parameter declaration commands also enable the user to choose among the optional styles of dimensioning and tolerancing.

The data collection function for text simply requires that the user enter the content as a string of characters through the keyboard and indicate a location on a two-dimensional model view or drawing. Three different text placement commands are provided for entering text at a new placement point, placing text at an existing text node, and filling in an existing text field. Other commands provide the ability to place a text node or a text field, elements that are always created in an empty condition.

Annotation is revised through data editing commands that alter single characters within a text string or replace the entire content. All types of text, including the characters in a label or a dimension call-out, are revised by the same commands.

9.1.2. Features Dedicated to Viewing the Model

This section describes the methods available to the user for viewing the model he or she has built. Visible output is generated on an interactive screen or as a finished plot.

A turnkey system for general-purpose drafting is not capable of generating the dynamically changing views that produce simulated motion. The system is not equipped with the software and hardware to perform geometric transformations and calculate display instructions quickly enough. Also, the storage tube (the most common interactive output device) cannot produce continuously and rapidly changing images. However, the transformations described in Chapters 7 and 8 are available in a typical turnkey system for producing individual views of either a two-dimensional drawing or a three-dimensional model.

The system has *three-dimensional viewing commands* that enable the user to select a particular view of the model by defining a viewing cube for parallel projection or a viewing pyramid for perspective projection. Unfortunately, the user is not able to find the optimum view interactively, as could be possible if rapidly generated images from changing viewpoints were available. Instead, the user is required to describe the hypothetical eye position and the other viewing parameters numerically in terms of angles and distances. In some systems a graphic representation of the viewing cube or pyramid helps the user derive these angles and distances. If the resulting image is not satisfactory, the user modifies the numeric description and generates another view. Image generation is prompt because it is done on-line rather than in batch mode, but it is not fast enough to be considered an interactive function.

In addition to parallel and perspective projection, many systems also have viewing commands devoted to specialized drafting techniques such as isometric projection. Sectioning is a drafting technique that presents the image resulting from the intersection of the three-dimensional model and a plane. A turnkey system automatically generates a cross-sectional view when the user sets up the viewing cube or pyramid with front and back clipping planes that coincide. Viewing operations can be included in macro commands along with any other primitive commands to create even more specialized techniques.

The data that correspond to the two-dimensional image are held separately from the three-dimensional model from which they were derived. The user can save a satisfactory view by storing it in the computer under a unique drawing name. The data describing a stored view are in the same format as the data base created for an original two-dimensional drawing, so the user can apply all capabilities for input and editing to the task of touching up a computer-generated view prior to final plotting. Annotation can also be added at this stage. Modifications and additions to a stored view do not affect the model at all and, likewise, changes to the model do not reach previously generated views held in storage.

Hidden-line removal is not generally available in turnkey graphics system, so a wire-frame image is the only kind of view that can be produced from a three-dimensional model. The typical turnkey system offers semiautomatic hidden-line removal, which means that the user must identify the lines that would be obscured by a solid object and delete them from the image using the normal graphic manipulation commands. Descriptions of a turnkey system sometimes use the term "semiautomatic" in situations where it would be more accurate to say that the user must do the larger share of the work to accomplish a task and the computer does the smaller share.

Two-dimensional viewing commands are also provided. These commands allow the user to display or plot a selected portion of a drawing or a stored view by specifying a spatial grouping (area), a logical relationship, or both. The concept of selective viewing is similar to the concept of selective modification with data editing commands, but the mechanics are different.

The window is the spatial grouping mechanism for interactive display. The window area is enclosed by a rectangular boundary that has the same proportions as the screen or the same proportions as a viewport in systems with split-screen capability. Commands for window control allow the user to choose the location and size of the window. A location for the window's center is indicated interactively by placing a point on the drawing or by typing coordinates. Size is chosen by one of several interactive methods. The direct way to select window size is to place two points that indicate the diagonal corners of the rectangular boundary. Alternatively, the user can fence a portion of the drawing and allow the system to fit the smallest possible window that includes all the fenced elements. Similarly, the user can enter the desired magnification factor and allow the system to supply the window of correct size to produce the desired view. The user can also choose a new window size by enlarging or reducing the existing window. Some turnkey systems do not support windows of arbitrary size, but instead approximate the user's choice by supplying one of a sequence of predetermined windows. The largest preset window is a display of the entire data base; the smaller sizes are derived through successive reductions of one-half the length of the window diagonal.

Many turnkey systems have split-screen capability, so two, four, or as many as sixteen different images can appear on different parts of the screen. Methods for handling multiple windows and multiple viewports are essential for adequate visual feedback to the operator while he or she is using the multiple-view input method to build the three-dimensional model. Split-screen capability is also a convenient and effective way to present the finished model from various eye positions or through different types of projections.

The spatial grouping mechanism for plotting is a set of *plot coordinates* defining the diagonal corners of the chosen area. The plotted area must be a rectangle, but it does not have to have the same shape as the screen. Unfortunately, the user cannot visually select the rectangle's corners, but must describe them through numeric values on a plot request. The plot request may be a tutorial display provided by the graphics system or it may be input data for a separate plot program that runs in batch mode. The turnkey system's interactive measurement functions can help the user determine the plot coordinates.

The logical relationships that are used for selective viewing are the same as those for data editing. A display or plot can consist of only that portion of the data base identified by the logical criteria or it can include all of the data base except the specified portion. Drawing name, the uppermost rank in the data heirarchy, is more important for viewing than for editing because it is often desirable to have one or more stored drawings superimposed over the display or plot of the current drawing.

The viewing functions described above are basic graphic operations that would be included in a turnkey system's capabilities regardless of the type of display hardware involved. The typical turnkey system also includes a number of viewing control commands that mainly serve to improve response time for updating the storage tube display, although they also allow the user to limit the display to the required level of detail, thus eliminating clutter. These controls are available at two levels. The *selective display controls* eliminate some of the more elaborate display effects, such as variable line thickness, specially programmed line symbology, and area-filling patterns. The *fast display controls* reduce the display to a bare minimum. This entails showing a symbol instance as only an empty rectangle indicating its size and showing free-form curves as straight line segments connecting the curve's input points. Text is shown in the plain text font produced by the display device's character generator instead of the more attractive programmed lettering style. Text can be reduced even more drastically, if the user desires, by setting a system control to replace each text string with a line segment of the appropriate length and orientation. Both the selective display controls and the fast display controls can be turned on and off by the user as desired. They are only shortcuts for generating faster display updates and do not affect the drawing stored in the data base.

Response time with a storage tube display is improved by reducing the frequency of time-consuming screen updates. When the system is operating in automatic update mode, the image is erased and completely redrawn after each graphic operation that moves or deletes elements. When the automatic update mode is turned off, the system immediately displays the results of operations that add elements to the image, but operations that move or delete elements are only acknowleged by a notation on the screen. The system provides a command that allows the user to request an updated image whenever it is needed.

9.1.3. Features Dedicated to Handling Nongraphic Data

The typical turnkey drafting system makes provision for handling nongraphic data to a limited extent. The capabilities include measurement of graphic features, extraction of data concerning drawing elements, and retrieval of previously stored nongraphic data.

All types of measurements from the model or drawing can be produced interactively with the accuracy of the data base. These measurements include the coordinates of a point, the length of a line, an angle, and the area of a closed figure. The resulting quantities can be displayed, used as input data for simple calculations performed by the system, or incorporated into reports along with other nongraphic data.

Extraction of nongraphic information from the graphic data base utilizes the same kind of spatial groupings and logical relationships as mentioned earlier in the discussion of graphic manipulation and view selection. Appearance attributes such as hardware-generated line types, user-defined line symbology, and area-filling patterns are *not* available as criteria for computer-aided data extraction, although they play an important role in visual recognition. This is a severe limitation on the way similar graphic elements can be distinguished from each other for information extraction. For example, a design for a mechanical device includes both steel and plastic components that are differentiated by area-filling patterns. The computer system cannot use those patterns as a key to calculate the volume of steel and the volume of plastic in the device.

Symbol name is an important key for extraction of nongraphic data from computer-stored drawings. This makes it worthwhile to carefully plan a symbol library so that each graphic entity to be identified during data extraction is represented by a symbol with a unique name. A separate symbol for each entity is necessary even in the case of similar designs that could be created more efficiently by placing and modifying a generalized symbol. The symbol name should be meaningful so it can serve as a description on the reports yielded by the data extraction operation.

Information originally entered as a nongraphic data item can be retrieved by two keys—the characteristics of its associated graphic element and its own item name. Each of the nongraphic data items associated with a particular graphic element must have a unique variable name, but items having the same name may be associated with many graphic elements. For instance, the symbol GEAR has nongraphic data items PART, SIZE, and WEIGHT associated with it. In addition, all other symbols for mechanical components in the same drawing also have part number, volume, and weight information stored in the data base. The data extraction facility of a turnkey system is well suited to producing a bill of material by listing all the symbol names that appear on the drawing along with the number of instances of each symbol. However, the data handling features can be used in many other applications if the user puts suitable advance planning into the way the drawing or model is built. The typical turnkey system provides a modest *report generator* that is capable of organizing data and printing legible reports.

9.2. GRAPHICS APPLICATION PRODUCTS

A graphics application product is software that represents a complete application system for a specific field. The main differences between a graphics application product and a turnkey graphics system concern the origin and emphasis of the software. Graphics application products generally have been developed by independent firms whose businesses are in the application fields. The developer leases the software alone, not in combination with hardware. A major portion (or even the predominate share) of the software is devoted to nongraphic data processing, which the graphics capabilities support or enhance. The discussion in this section is based on three roughly comparable CAD/CAM systems. These are *AD-2000*, developed by Patrick J. Hanratty, Ph.D., president of Manufacturing and Consulting Services, Inc., *CADAM*, a product of the Lockheed-California Company, and *UNIGRAPHICS*, offered by United Computing Corporation, a subsidiary of McDonnell Douglas Corporation. These systems are capable of carrying a mechanical component all the way from initial design through actual production on a numerically controlled (N/C) machine tool.

A software product is never an ideal system because compromises during development are inevitable and the working procedures of an outside user are not identical to those of the developer. However, a graphics application product has definite advantages. First, the benefits of a large investment by the developer are available for a reasonable monthly fee. Second, the product's performance can be determined through demonstrations, benchmarks, and the results achieved by the developer and by other users over a period of years. Third, the system reaches full productivity in a short time because the developer assists in installing the software on the user's hardware and in testing its performance, the developer offers an organized training course for new operators, and the developer furnishes an operator's guide and other documentation. Fourth, maintenance of the software is a service that is included in the monthly fee. There should not be many program faults in a mature, proven product, which means that maintenance consists mostly of enhancing the system and keeping it compatible with hardware and operating system changes initiated by the computer manufacturer.

A graphics application product is even more strongly user-oriented than a turnkey system because it is designed to cater to a narrower range of needs. The terminology peculiar to the application is adopted for screen tutorials that prompt the user, for descriptions that appear on the menu or program function keys, and for all documentation. Therefore, it is not necessary for the user to customize these items. A product incorporates default values, predefined symbol libraries, and the like to comply with all formal or informal industry standards for terminology, symbology, data format for interface to other programs, and output format. Therefore, the user does not have to devote an initial period to priming the system with these standards.

Most of the basic operations for building and viewing the model of a mechanical component and for producing high-quality production drawings that are found in a general-purpose turnkey system are also offered by a CAD/CAM product. However, the fact that a product is intended for a single field exerts a dominate influence on the selection of features to be included or excluded. For instance, a special input command for monuments is a turnkey system feature, useful for drawing maps, that is omitted from a CAD/CAM product. Conversely, preprogrammed calculations for center of gravity, moment of inertia, and so on, are CAD/CAM features that do not exist in a turnkey system.

Most graphics application products duplicate conventional working procedures as much as possible and developers rarely seek breakthroughs in computer-assisted work methods because a system patterned after accepted business practices in its field has many practical advantages. The user can learn to use this type of system easily and rapidly. The conventional approach minimizes the need for changes in related business procedures to accommodate the computer-aided work method. Also, since graphics techniques themselves are unfamiliar to most potential customers of the software, the retention of other familiar concepts increases the product's sales potential.

The typical graphics application product is designed to be run on a large computer (not a minicomputer like the turnkey system) so graphics input and output functions and nongraphic data processing can be handled by a single computer. Therefore, the cost of computer time is a significant portion of the total operating cost for the graphics application product. However, full utilization of the large computer can lower this cost in two ways. First, the same computer that supports the application product can be used for running other work at a lower priority. Commercial or scientific batch processing is an especially suitable use for the extra computer capacity. Second, a large computer can normally support many terminals, so full utilization of the system lowers the unit cost of computer assistance.

Some systems such as AD-2000 are designed to be computer- and terminal-independent, so the software can easily be adapted to operate on suitable equipment of any brand; however, most products are written with characteristics that limit their operation to a particular computer and operating system combination and to a specific type of interactive terminal. Lockheed's CADAM is an example of this since it is designed for an IBM 360 or 370 computer or an equivalent and for IBM 2250 graphic display units or plug-compatible display devices from alternative suppliers such as Adage. The popularity of CADAM is actually responsible for creating a large share of the market for this type of terminal equipment.

The primitive elements and primitive commands for building and viewing a graphic model that exist in a typical graphics application product are similar to those described for a turnkey system. Complex operations that the user would have to set up as macro commands in a general-purpose turnkey system are included as standard features in software for a specific application. For example, the basic and extended geometry options of AD-2000 have seventeen different ways to input the definition of a design point.

AD-2000 utilizes several of the three-dimensional input methods that are presented in Section 6.8. In the multiple view input method, every primitive element is a figure in a plane. The extrusion method is utilized through a PROJECTED ENTITY command that duplicates any two-dimensional figure at a specified depth and generates connecting lines between the matching end points on the two identical figures. The volume element method is available through the creation of mathematically defined shapes such as spheres, cylinders, and cones. A surface model is built with a primitive element known as the CURVE MESH SURFACE. In all, the AD-2000 system provides ways to model curves, surfaces, solids, and shells.

An example of a complex viewing operation that is preprogrammed in a CAD/CAM system is a dynamic display showing exactly how the part will be machined. Figure 9.4 is a composite of the complete tool path for machining the part shown in the outline drawing.

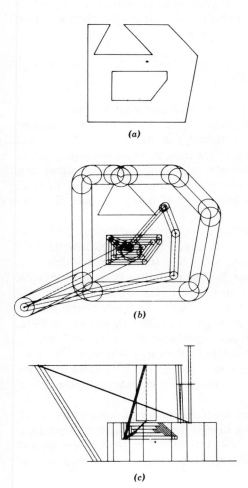

(a)

(b)

(c)

Figure 9.4. Display of tool path for manufacturing a part on an N/C machine tool. (a) Part, top view. (b) Tool path, top view. (c) Tool path, side view. McDonnell Douglas Automation Company.

Nongraphic data are treated in a strictly neutral manner by a general-purpose turnkey system, making it the responsibility of the user to identify each nongraphic item by assigning a name and a data type (numeric, character string, and so forth). A CAD/CAM product has a similar generalized data handling capability that is useful for optional entries such as notes on production drawings. However, the CAD/CAM software specifies a group of mandatory data items that must be entered during design because they are an integral part of the manufacturing information. The system also adopts accepted machining practices by providing default values that the user can override. The user enters data for the mandatory nongraphic items through a modal operation in which the value of each item is set once and remains valid until it is reset. The current values automatically become part of the data base description of each graphic element added to the model.

9.3.   GRAPHICS PACKAGES

A *graphics package* is a software system consisting of a set of subroutines or functions used by an application program to generate images on an interactive display device or plotter and (optionally) to receive data from input devices. A graphics package frees the application programmer from concern about the details of functions directly related to interactive graphics. Therefore, an application system can be completed in less time and it can be written by individuals with limited knowledge of interactive graphics programming.

The CalComp plotter software package, developed in the early 1960s, was the first commercial graphics package. It served as a de facto standard for computer graphics for many years and today it is still the most widely used software package. Its capabilities are limited to output of two-dimensional graphics on a pen plotter or an equivalent device [21].

The Tektronix Terminal Control System (TCS), the fundamental module in the Tektronix PLOT-10 software package, was originally released in 1971. It is currently installed at over 2000 sites worldwide as support software for Tektronix storage tube terminals. It is effectively a standard for a CRT software package since it is the most common system for interactive graphics. TCS provides a comprehensive set of operations for input and display of two-dimensional graphics [21].

The CalComp, Tektronix, and other early graphics packages were developed by the manufacturers of graphic display devices to make their products easier to use and therefore easier to sell. Equipment manufacturers are still one of the most important sources of graphics packages, but universities and independent organizations have also developed a number of graphics packages, including DISSPLA, GCS, GINO-F, and GPGS-F. The source of each of these packages is shown in the vendor list at the end of this chapter. These nonmanufacturer systems were designed with emphasis on computer and device independence, so that application programs based on these packages could be shared by users having many different kinds of equipment. This goal of program portability is the chief motivation behind an effort aimed at establishing standards for graphics packages that is currently in progress under the sponsorship of ACM/SIGGRAPH and others. This effort has generated a study comparing a number of popular existing graphics software packages [21] and a proposal identifying a set of graphics functions as a standard core graphics system [7]. The scope of this core system is defined as fundamental functions for two- and three-dimensional line drawings with text and viewing transformations for both passive (output only) and interactive (input and output) graphics. The ACM/SIGGRAPH proposal is the reference for this section's discussion concerning the typical functions of a graphics package.

The division of work in a business office is analogous to the separation of functions among the application program, the graphics package, and the computer's operating system. In a normal office, the supervisor makes all significant decisions and determines what actions will be taken. To some extent, his work is based on information supplied by incoming mail and phone calls, and his results are transmitted through outgoing mail and phone calls. The secretary is responsible for organizing and managing the supervisor's communications. Incoming mail is opened, sorted, and later filed. Outgoing mail is typed and addressed, and copies are filed. The secretary answers and screens incoming calls and places outgoing calls. The actual communications channels are provided by an infrastructure that consists of the post office, the telephone company, and other organizations that provide similar essential services.

The functional separation within an interactive computer graphics system is diagrammed in Figure 9.5. All significant activity is originated by the application program, which has the role of the office supervisor. The graphics package works directly with the application program to handle graphic input and output functions at a high level, just as the secretary works closely with the supervisor to handle meaningful items of communication. The computer's operating system is the infrastructure for a graphics application since it provides neutral supporting services.

An *operating system* is software that controls the execution of computer programs and that may provide scheduling, debugging, input/output control, accounting, compilation, storage assignment, data management, and related services [22]. The operating system is normally furnished by the com-

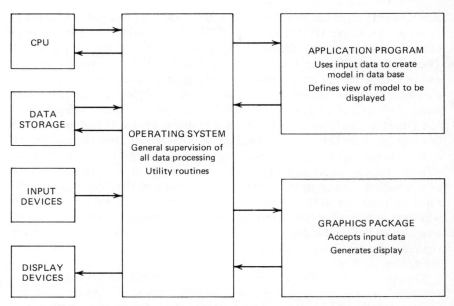

Figure 9.5. Component functions within an interactive graphics system.

puter manufacturer. In the overall scheme of a complete graphics application, the operating system is intended to provide services for the graphics
package and the application program, not to provide services directly to the
user. For this reason, the application program should be immediately
available when a graphics terminal is turned on, so the user does not have to
deal with the operating system, even to simply request the application program. The user should never come in contact with the computer's operating
system for several reasons. One objection to such contact is the bad interactive technique involved in expecting the graphics user to type complicated,
cryptic instructions that are really intended for use by only a programmer or
computer operator. A more serious objection is the danger of accidental or
deliberate destruction of data files or programs in disk storage by a graphics
user with access to the operating system's powerful functions.

The purpose of the graphics package within a complete application system
is to produce a picture on a screen or a plotter. An auxiliary role of the
graphics package is to transfer data from interactive input devices to the application program. The functions of a graphics package are said to be on a
much *lower level* than the functions of a turnkey system because the graphics
package functions are more closely related to hardware operations whereas
the turnkey system's functions are similar to the user's work activities. The

low-level nature of a graphics package is distinctly apparent in a comparison of the turnkey system functions outlined in Section 9.1 with the examples given in the next few paragraphs. These examples of typical graphics package features are based on the ACM/SIGGRAPH graphics package proposal [7].

The graphics package's primitive functions for output consist of the ability to move the CRT beam to a specified location, draw a single line segment, draw a series of connected line segments, mark the position of a point, and display text. A set of attribute values associated with each primitive output function determines general display characteristics such as color, intensity, line width, and line style.

The graphics package provides a full range of two- and three-dimensional viewing transformations, including window selection, viewport assignment, and clipping. However, it does not adopt the method of the three-dimensional view specification involving hypothetical eye position and angle of vision that is presented in Chapter 8. Instead, the user describes the desired view in terms of the graphic object itself. For instance, he chooses a point on the object where he wishes to focus his attention, called the *view reference point*. He also defines a surface on the object as the *view plane* onto which he wishes to project the image.

The primitive functions for input are based on a set of logical input devices consisting of PICK, KEYBOARD, BUTTON, LOCATOR, and VALUATOR. There are additional functions for graphics package control operations such as setting default values for the display attributes and for inquiry about a number of status indicators, such as the current viewing transformation matrix.

The functional specification of the ACM/SIGGRAPH graphics package calls for two special interfaces between the graphics package and the application program. A kind of interface called a *hook* makes it possible for an application program to access information or procedures that exist within the graphics package but are not reachable through standard operations. One proposed hook is the capability to concatenate a matrix supplied by the application program with the viewing transformation matrix calculated by the graphics package. This would be an efficient way to apply geometric transformations involving the model. Many turnkey systems are also designed with hooks that allow the user to add custom features without disturbing the vendor's software. The second type of special interface is an *escape mechanism* that allows for special display functions such as generating curves in hardware. The display function's name and its associated parameters are passed from the application program to the display device driver, going through the graphics package by means of the escape mechanism.

All creative operations are the responsibility of the application program, since the graphics package and the operating system only do housekeeping chores for the interactive graphics system. The creative activities of the application program include: (1) processing the data entered by the user at the terminal to build the model and to select views of the model, (2) determining both the structure and the contents of an application-specific data base, and (3) supplying the graphics package with a definition of each object to be displayed. This definition is either retrieved from the data base or passed directly from computations by the application program.

VENDOR LIST

Information provided by these companies was used in the preparation of Chapter 9. This is not intended to be a complete list of all suppliers.

TURNKEY GRAPHICS SYSTEMS

Adage, Inc., 1079 Commonwealth Avenue, Boston, MA 02215 (617) 783-1100 (GS/300—software is at graphics package level)

Applicon, Inc., 154 Middlesex Turnpike, Burlington, MA 01803 (617) 272-7070 (IMAGE)

Auto-trol Corporation, 5650 North Pecos Street, Denver, CO 80221 (303) 458-5900 (AD/380)

California Computer Products, Inc. (CalComp), 2411 W. La Palma, Anaheim, CA 92801 (714) 821-2011 (IGS-500)

CALMA, 527 Lakeside Drive, Sunnyvale, CA 94086 (408) 245-7522 (CADEC)

Computervision Corporation, 201 Burlington Road, Bedford, MA 01730 (617) 275-1800 (The Designer)

Evans and Sutherland Computer Corporation, 580 Arapeen Drive, Salt Lake City, UT 84108 (801) 582-5847 (Picture System 2—sophisticated hardware, software is at graphics package level)

General Turtle Corporation, 120 boul. Industriel, Boucherville, Quebec J4B 2X2, Canada (TT2500)

Gerber Scientific Instrument Company, 83 Gerber Road, South Windsor, CT 06074 (203) 644-1551 (IDS)

Information Displays Inc., 150 Clearbrook Road, Elmsford NY 10523 (914) 592-2025 (System 150)

M & S Computing, Inc., P.O. Box 5183, Huntsville, AL 35805 (205) 772-3411 (IGDS)

Project Software & Development, Inc., 14 Story Street, Cambridge, MA 02138 (617) 661-1444 (GRAPHITI software and PSDI Graphic Workstation hardware)

Scientific Process & Research, Inc., 400 Cleveland Avenue, Highland Park, NJ 08904 (201) 846-3477 (SPAR/GRAPHICS)

Synercom Technology, Inc., P.O. Box 27, Sugar Land, TX 77478 (713) 491-5000 (IN-FODRAFT)

Tektronix, Inc., Information Display Group, P.O. Box 500, Beaverton, OR 97077 (503) 638-3411 (4081 and 4051—software is at graphics package level)

GRAPHICS APPLICATION PRODUCTS

Central Institute for Industrial Research, Forskningsv. 1, P.O.B. 350 Blindern, Oslo 3, Norway, Telephone (02) 69 58 80 (AUTOKON and others)

Computer Aided Design Centre, Madingley Road, Cambridge CB3, OHB, England, Telephone 0223 63125 (Pipework Design Management System and others)

Lockheed-California Company, Burbank, CA 91520 (CADAM)

Manufacturing and Consulting Services, Inc., 3195A Airport Loop Drive, Costa Mesa, CA 92626 (714) 540-3921 (AD-2000)

United Computing Corporation, 22500 S. Avalon Blvd., Carson, CA 90745 (213) 830-7720 (UNIGRAPHICS)

GRAPHICS PACKAGES (List of packages reviewed in reference 21.)

Adage, Inc., 1079 Commonwealth Avenue, Boston, MA 02215 (617) 783-1100

California Computer Products, Inc. (CalComp), 2411 W. La Palma, Anaheim, CA 92801 (714) 821-2011

DISSPLA—Integrated Software Systems Corporation, 4186 Sorrento Valley Blvd., Suite N, San Diego, CA 92121 (714) 565-8098

GCS, "Graphics Compatibility System"—U.S. Army Corps of Engineers, Waterways Experiment Station, Vicksburg, MS

GINO-F—Computer Aided Design Centre, Madingley Road, Cambridge CB3 0HB, England, Telephone 0223 63125

GPGS-F, "General Purpose Graphic System in Fortran"—Computing Centre, University of Trondheim, N-7034 Trondheim—NTH, Norway

IG, "Integrated Graphics"—Computing Center, University of Michigan, Ann Arbor, MI

Tektronix, Inc., P.O. Box 500, Beaverton, OR 97077 (503) 638-3411

PART THREE
A Practical Tool

CHAPTER 10

Management Concerns

Successful production with interactive computer graphics results from properly identifying one or more tasks to be accomplished, selecting the appropriate graphics system for these tasks, providing the people and work routines to operate the system, and using objective criteria to predict and later judge the benefits. This chapter provides suggestions for handling each of these management responsibilities. Further information is available from sources given in Section 10.5 and the chapter appendix.

10.1. APPLICATION CHARACTERISTICS

According to expert opinion, "a nearly paperless computer-graphic work environment" could be built with the existing technology [23]. A system based on a computerized model would provide the means to perform all tasks involved in a complex project such as the design of a chemical plant. However, total commitment to a new technology involves a risk that most enterprises are unwilling to take, so almost all existing applications include only particular aspects of an overall project. Therefore, the popular approach to identifying an application is to isolate a small part of the job that can be done cheaper, faster, or better using interactive computer graphics.

Effective selection of a potential application requires two kinds of knowledge—information concerning graphics techniques, which this book seeks to provide, and familiarity with the prospective user. An understanding of how the user does the work manually is a prerequisite for determining if the task has the characteristics of a successful graphics application. Insight into why the user does something in a particular manner is necessary for evaluating work-method changes that can make the use of graphics more efficient.

Common features of successful existing applications are listed below under two classifications, drafting and design. *Drafting* is the documentation of a finished design through drawings. *Design* is the creative process of developing an idea. This list of characteristics is intended to be an aid in identifying profitable new uses for interactive graphics. Although one significant improvement in the way a task is done is often enough to justify a graphics system, the applications that benefit the most from computer assistance have several of these characteristics. For example, map drafting is an application that requires lettering, accuracy, symbols, updates, and attractive appearance.

10.1.1. Drafting Characteristics

1. Many similar drawings with slight differences.
2. Drawings that undergo many revisions.
3. Drawings with a large amount of lettering.
4. Drawings that must be accurate.
5. Drawings with information that is currently extracted by hand and entered into a computer for other purposes.
6. Drawings prepared for several alternative proposals.
7. Complex drawings with several types of information that may be presented separately or together.
8. Drawings that present several different views of the same object.
9. Drawings formed of standard symbols.
10. Drawings that must be done quickly, even at a cost premium, because they are prerequisites for other work.
11. A work environment where shortages of qualified drafting manpower exist or where the cost of labor is unusually high.
12. Drawings that require periodic update with consistent technique over a long span of time.
13. Drawings where attractive appearance is important, such as catalog illustrations.
14. Drawings that currently are done using cut-and-paste or overlay techniques with mylar or butter paper.
15. Pictures derived from numerical origin, such as charts and graphs for business management.
16. Large amounts of visual information that must be organized, such as aerial surveys in mapping.
17. Data that can be presented graphically for better understanding and quicker recognition.

10.1.2. Design Characteristics

1. Abstract ideas that are most easily expressed graphically.
2. Models that are constructed from standard components, using a computer library of submodels.
3. Work that can benefit from access to an archive of past designs.
4. Models that require extensive labeling.
5. A computer model that is interactively fitted to data collected from the real world.
6. A computer model that can be built from digitized data, through three-dimensional techniques or from multiple two-dimensional sources.
7. A mathematical model that is the result of multiple trials using different values for the variables.
8. Models involving the family-of-parts concept, where parameter values define variations in size or shape within a group of similar items.
9. The design of two-dimensional visual patterns.
10. Work that can take advantage of automatic design programs for diagramming, pipe routing, electronic circuit layout, or other tasks.
11. A design founded primarily on practical considerations that must also be tested for visual effect, such as an architectural design.
12. A model that makes it possible to study the movement of components during operation.
13. A model that makes it possible to check for interference among components.
14. A combined model that makes it possible for designs by various disciplines to be viewed together or for each contribution to be displayed separately.
15. A model that makes it possible to examine hidden internal components, such as fittings inside a ship's hull.
16. A model that represents a process rather than an object.
17. A complex object that would be difficult to build using physical modeling materials or an object for which the accuracy required would make the cost of a physical model unreasonable.
18. A design that must be documented with technical drawings and listings of nongraphic data.
19. A design that leads to production with automated manufacturing techniques.
20. A model that must be described numerically for nongraphic simulation calculations.
21. A design that must be checked for a proper relationship to a human figure.

22. A design that must be illustrated by photographic-quality images, such as those produced by a television like raster display.

10.2. TURNKEY SYSTEM SELECTION

The normal purchasing cycle required for a company to buy a turnkey graphics system is about 1 year. It begins when the company meets with several vendors to get a general idea about capabilities and to estimate the cost of an appropriate system. The company puts the estimated amount of money into the next year's capital budget and the budget is approved. The company then has lengthy consultations with several selected vendors, chooses a system, and places an order. A shorter purchasing cycle sometimes occurs when the company has money available that must be invested before the end of the fiscal year.

The recommended selection process is to focus on one primary application and then write a functional specification. A *functional specification* is a document that describes the expected results rather than the hardware or software. A functional specification listing major features by name only is adequate when the choice is among general-purpose turnkey systems with vendor-supplied application packages. However, the functional specification must be more detailed when the application has unusual requirements. The best practice in this case is to write a user's manual for the proposed system in which the required input and the expected outcome of every single operation are described in words that a typical user can understand. This functional specification should be approved by the potential users. The selection process is then a matter of obtaining a real system that performs like the fictitious sytem suggested by the user's manual.

The system capability check list (given below) is an example of a functional specification for a mapping application at the level of detail suitable for evaluating turnkey graphics systems.

10.2.1. System Capability Check List

1. CONVERSATIONAL MODE. The user must be able to do his work while thinking in his normal manner, without undue awareness of the computer system.
2. INTERACTIVE RESPONSE. The system must handle any routine graphics operation in less than 1 second.
3. CONCURRENT USE OF ALL FEATURES. All normal functions must be able to operate simultaneously so one user cannot prevent another user from working.

4. SIMPLICITY OF OPERATION. The normal user must be able to turn the system on and off and accomplish all routine functions without the assistance of specialized personnel. Basic operator training under the guidance of a competent instructor should not require more than 40 working hours.

5. DOCUMENTATION. The user's instruction book should be complete, accurate, and easy to understand.

6. TERMINALS. The system must support multiple terminals, each consisting of interactive input and output devices. The equipment and arrangement of the work station must be comfortable to use for long periods of time by both right- and left-handed individuals.

7. EXPANDABLE. The only practical restriction on the number of work stations that can be added to the system must be the inevitable increase in response time as a result of sharing the computer among more users. When the number of added work stations exceeds the capacity of the original computer, it should be possible to connect another computer within the system.

8. EXTENSIBLE. The design of the system must allow for the addition of more features and applications in the future.

9. UPWARD COMPATIBILITY. Any future changes in hardware or software must not interfere with the system's ability to deal with existing drawings.

10. RELIABILITY. The system must be available for operation 95% of the time during normal business hours. Occasions when the system is considered as not available include equipment breakdowns, program problems, planned maintenance, and deliberate stoppages for any purpose.

11. PRECISION. The system must define a graphic point by three coordinates such as (x, y, z) or (North, East, Elevation). Each coordinate must be held in computer storage as (at least) a 32-bit binary number to provide approximately four billion units of resolution along each axis of the design space. For example, this is equivalent to a square area 4000 miles long on each side mapped to an accuracy of $\frac{1}{16}$ inch.

12. USER-DEFINED UNITS. The user must be able to set up any desired system of measurement units for input and output data by reference to the units of resolution of the design space.

13. USER-DEFINED SCALE. The user must be able to define the correspondence between the design space and the physical output medium, so he can set the scale of each plot and interactively control the scale of the screen image.

14. GEOMETRIC ELEMENTS. The system must provide a wide variety of basic shapes to be used in the construction of drawings.

15. GRAPHIC CONSTRUCTION. The system must provide a set of commands capable of manipulating geometric elements and symbols to create a drawing.

16. GRAPHIC EDITING. The system must provide a set of commands to make geometric changes affecting individual items or groups of items. The power and scope of the graphic editing commands should equal that of the drawing construction commands.

17. DATA ENTRY. The user must be able to construct the drawing while working interchangeably in either plan or elevation view. The ability to enter data while working in any arbitrary view is desirable.

18. BATCH DATA ENTRY. The system must provide a method for accepting batches of computer data prepared ahead of time and for merging this input into the graphic data base. A typical application is the entry of field survey data.

19. DIGITIZER INTERFACE. The system must be capable of supporting a large digitizer board as optional equipment at each user terminal.

20. USER-DEFINED SYMBOLS. The user must be able to create his own symbols and store them in a computer library. These symbols may include both primitive geometric elements and other previously stored symbols. The number of symbols in the library must be limited only by the amount of available on-line storage space. It must be possible to isolate and revise an individual symbol appearing on a drawing.

21. USER-DEFINED COMMANDS. The user must be able to create procedures made up of several simple commands, name them, and store them in a computer library.

22. USER-DEFINED MENU. The user must be able to decide which of the commands and symbols will appear on the menu and their locations. The only limit on the size of the menu or the number of menu items must be the area of the digitizer surface and provision for reasonably large selection boxes.

23. LETTERING. The text features that add lettering to a drawing should include interactive selection of style, size, and spacing for the characters, temporary storage so that an entire text string can be entered, and the location of prespecified slots for text on a drawing.

24. DIMENSIONING. The system must provide a semiautomatic method for adding dimension call-outs to a drawing.

25. STORAGE MANAGEMENT. The system must keep track of the data files in storage and must be able to automatically locate the latest version of each drawing whether it is on disk or tape. The system must provide separate storage for large amounts of information that are held for long periods of time and smaller volumes of information that are involved in current work. A temporary storage area must be assigned to

each terminal to hold the active drawing while a backup copy of the same drawing remains in interactive storage.

26. DATA PROTECTION. It must be possible to access all stored drawings from all terminals, but the availability of information must be restricted to authorized users through a system of protective passwords.

27. DATA ORGANIZATION. The geometric and alphanumeric information in storage for a drawing must be organized in a logical way so that specific items can be accessed.

28. ASSOCIATIVE GEOMETRIC DATA. The geometric description must be structured so that meaningful nongraphic information can be derived from it for calculations and reports.

29. REPORTING. The system must be capable of producing simple alphanumeric reports on the screen or on paper containing information from the data base presented in a user-defined format.

30. DISPLAY. The system must be capable of displaying a two-dimensional plan, elevation, or arbitrary view of the three-dimensional geometric construction. Perspective projection, giving the illusion of depth, is a desirable display option.

31. PLOTTING. The system must be able to produce a high-quality plot of any view that can be displayed. Operation of the plotter must not interfere with other work functions taking place at the same time.

32. HARD COPY. Equipment to produce a quick paper copy of the image on the screen must be located in the terminal work area.

10.2.2. Vendor Support Services

Most vendors of complete hardware/software packages for interactive graphics adopt as their marketing strategy the turnkey approach, in which a single supplier furnishes the user with everything he needs. In addition to a well-balanced set of equipment and a proven application program, the turnkey vendor furnishes installation, warranty, maintenance, documentation, and training. Installation services encompass location planning, testing of hardware before shipment, unpacking and setting up of equipment at the user's site, and performing an acceptance test of hardware and software. A comprehensive warranty covers the system for a short period, normally 90 days. After this period, a service contract provides both preventative maintenance and the parts and labor for repairs at a fixed monthly charge, as well as a software update service that maintains the graphics program at par with the most recent version. The primary documentation requirement is a user's guide to the operation of the graphics system, written by the vendor. A copy of the user's guide should be issued to the supervisor and to each full-time operator. In addition, a complete set of manufacturer's operating and service manuals for the computer, the computer's standard software, and all other pieces of equipment should be kept at the user's installation. A copy of the graphics system's source program is a valuable safeguard against vendor default on software maintenance. Most vendors, however, refuse to release the source program since weak copyright laws make it difficult for them to protect their rights. Training, another turnkey support service, is described in Section 10.3.2.

Buying a turnkey graphics system is equivalent to taking the vendor as a business partner because he is responsible for all initial and continuing support. Therefore, the buyer should analyze the stability and reputation of the supplier. The following questions suggest points to check:

1. Is the company's financial position solid? Is the company growing?
2. What proportion of the company's sales is in interactive graphics compared to other products or interests? Will the company continue to be active in graphics in future years?
3. Where is the nearest field service office, how many people are assigned to it, and how much territory does it cover?
4. How many people are working on software maintenance and enhancement?
5. Does the vendor have a policy of keeping new versions of the program compatible with existing graphics data files? What is the cost of a major software revision for established users? Does the vendor offer special terms to help users upgrade the equipment in previously installed systems when new products are introduced?
6. Does the company use a standard price list and standard contract terms for all customers?
7. What are the supplier's future development plans for the graphics system? Are current users informed of these plans?
8. Is there an active users' group that shares experiences and ideas? Does it publish a newsletter and have regular meetings? Does the vendor provide financial or staff assistance? Does the vendor respond to suggestions and complaints from the users' group?

The support services provided by a turnkey vendor make implementation of a graphics application much simpler. The user is then able to concentrate solely on the application, which is his or her field of expertise.

10.2.3. Choosing the System

The selection is typically made by a committee composed of one or more people from the department with the primary application and representatives from other departments with additional uses. Price is usually not a consideration in choosing among competitive turnkey systems. Vendors report that the sales decision is usually based on emotional factors, such as with which sales representative the client feels most comfortable. It is possible to try to put the selection on a scientific basis by listing desirable features, assigning a weight to each feature, evaluating each system according to the list, and computing a numeric value for the relative merit of each system. This approach is not recommended because it is virtually impossible to assign the weighting factors in a statistically valid way. It is difficult enough to produce a complete list of necessary features, without weights, for the functional specification.

A *benchmark* is a problem used to evaluate the performance of hardware or software or both [22]. It is extremely difficult to set up a helpful benchmark for interactive computer graphics systems. The reproduction of an existing drawing is not meaningful because most systems are capable of drawing almost anything; instead, it is efficiency that must be tested. A well-designed benchmark must include all aspects of the prospective application, such as multiple views of the three-dimensional model for an industrial product or a construction drawing and its associated bill of material. The results of a benchmark are highly dependent on human factors, such as the skill and speed of the vendor's operator and his ability to assess client preferences.

The customer has a valid need to see his own type of work being done with graphics. However, it is unreasonable for a client with no first-hand experience in graphics to expect to design a proper benchmark. The best alternative to performing a benchmark is to visit a satisfied user who is in the same business, watch him work, and ask about his results.

10.3. PERSONNEL AND PROCEDURES

This section deals with the management of an interactive computer graphics installation. The discussion assumes that the application is predominately drafting and that the user company has purchased a turnkey graphics system. The topics that are covered include the selection and training of terminal operators, supervision, facility planning, and production procedures.

10.3.1. Operator Selection

There are two opposing points of view regarding the kind of employee who should be chosen as a graphics operator—the best versus the cheapest. The argument is often put forward that the assistance of a computer system makes up for the deficiencies of an inexperienced worker, so savings are achieved not only through the high productivity ratio of graphics, but also through a lower average wage. This is a dangerous fallacy. The purpose of a graphics system is to multiply the effectiveness of a company's most skilled and experienced workers, not to enable a learner to make mistakes on a larger scale. It takes a company years to develop a skilled worker. Implementing a graphics system immediately multiplies the equivalent number of skilled workers. Therefore, a properly selected group of graphics operators should generally be paid more than their counterparts who are still assigned to the drafting board.

The personal qualities that are desirable in an individual selected for training as a graphics operator are as follows:

1. Willingness to accept challenge.
2. Ability to understand and follow instructions.
3. Cooperative team spirit.
4. Tolerance for a reasonable amount of frustration.
5. Curiousity about cause and effect.
6. Initiative to find efficient procedures.

A turnkey graphics system is designed so that it can be competently utilized by an operator with no prior exposure to computer technology. It is much more important for a graphics operator to have extensive knowledge in the application field.

10.3.2. Training

A 1-week training course conducted by the vendor is normally included in the purchase price of a turnkey graphics system. This course should be attended by the designated graphics supervisor and as many of the initial group of graphics operators as possible. The purpose of the course is to teach beginning operators the system functions, the input for those functions, and the corresponding computer response. The operator's class normally consists of lectures and plenty of hands-on practice. A well-composed user's guide for the system makes an adequate textbook for this training.

This course can be conducted at the vendor's plant or the user's site. Training operators at the factory prior to the system's delivery shortens the typical three-month start-up period by several weeks. The vendor's course should be preceded and followed by planning sessions conducted by the users themselves to set up procedures and standards. The advantage of gaining a head start must be weighed against the employees' travel expense. At least one vendor (Computervision) has set up several regional training centers in conjunction with existing district sales offices to reduce the distance that a client's employees must travel. A few vendors conduct follow-up or review sessions at the user's site about a month after installation and most vendors will consult with users over the phone at no cost throughout the life of the system.

From time to time, subsequent training will be needed to replace operators who are transferred or terminated and to provide new operators when the system is expanded. The user organization should provide this training for two reasons. First, an in-house class is less expensive than paying for a visit by a vendor representative and it allows for more flexibility in scheduling. Second, the user company can incorporate its own procedures and standards into the graphics training. A graphics operator with at least 6 months experience is a suitable teacher for this in-house class.

One of the significant advantages of interactive computer graphics is that the symbol and macro-command libraries represent accumulated experience that the company retains when an employee leaves, so a replacement operator can effectively take up where his predecessor left off after a short learning period. Ownership of a computer graphics system can actually reduce the total amount spent on training for a company that regularly hires entry-level draftsmen. This is because the company will need fewer employees to handle a given amount of work and because the employee turnover rate will probably be reduced.

10.3.3. Supervision and Staffing

Senior management must clearly define the role of the graphics supervisor and must make a deliberate choice among several different staffing plans. Confusion over the supervisor's responsibility and the employees' assignments is a common cause of unsatisfactory results.

The graphics supervisor must know that the size of his next pay raise depends solely on how well the graphics system performs. He must have full and exclusive authority over the graphics operators, the equipment, and the working procedures. The supervisor should also be responsible for the following operations: estimates of cost and completion date for new drafting work, work priorities, operator and terminal time schedules, quality control, security, in-house training, and turnkey vendor support services. He may handle these tasks himself or delegate them to the operators. Comprehensive supervision may be difficult to arrange if the supervisor of a small system has other duties or if the operators for a large system belong to several departments. Nevertheless, a single point of responsibility and control is essential for a robust, coordinated graphics effort.

The discussion below examines three alternative staffing plans—the internal service bureau (a group of operator specialists), the resource center (graphics integrated into the duties of each design draftsman), and a moderate approach involving dual-role operators.

An internal service bureau is a pool of operators who spend their entire working day at a graphics terminal. Drafting work is submitted to the pool in a complete but rough form, ready for polished drafting. This staffing approach is satisfactory if the application consists mainly of formal drafting. In a large company with a small graphics installation, it is advisable to rotate operators out of the pool after about a year. This operator rotation helps an individual's career by allowing him to get varied experience and it allows a larger number of employees to be exposed to graphics in preparation for the time when this technology becomes the norm.

Another way to manage a graphics system is to regard it as a resource center (similar to a reference library) that is available to various departments and employees whenever their work requires it. Blocks of terminal time, say 1-hour intervals, are available to a large group of casual users through advance reservations. This approach produces poor results because consistent supervision of working procedures is impossible. Also, the graphics system tends to be left standing idle too much of the time. Inertia being a part of human nature, people often prefer to continue doing their work the familiar way rather than pursuing improved computerized methods. Also, it is easier to stay at the home-base desk, where all books, notes, and drawings are laid out, than to gather up all the working material and carry it to an impersonal graphics terminal. The mechanics of accepting reservations, reconciling conflicting demands for access, scheduling plotter priorities, and so forth are a source of constant trouble. Even an enthusiastic user who is enjoying beneficial results can become quickly discouraged when he cannot get adequate time on the system. This resource center plan is the worst staffing alternative.

A compromise staffing plan is to have a number of people regularly assigned as graphics operators, each of whom divides his working day between a desk and a graphics terminal. The engineering department at a major refinery successfully uses a graphics system this way to make drawings for revamping the plant. Each design technician is scheduled to spend either the morning or the afternoon on the graphics system doing drafting and the other half of the day in the refinery checking information or at a desk preparing for the next drafting session. This plan is beneficial whenever the application involves both drafting and nondrafting duties. The variety of activity during the day prevents boredom and increases motivation, a benefit that more than offsets the inconvenience experienced from time to time when an operator needs a little more or a little less than 4 hours to handle his daily drafting.

A company that has a simple 8-hour working day may need to keep its graphics system in production 16 hours a day to generate an adequate return on the capital investment in equipment. For this company, the most satisfactory arrangement for two-shift work is a plan of overlapping hours. Assuming that normal business hours are 8 AM to 5 PM, the first graphics shift should work from 3:30 AM to 12:30 PM and the second shift should follow from 12:30 PM to 9:30 PM. The hours can be compressed by eliminating the mealtime hour and allowing the graphics operators to bring food to eat at their desks during a short break. The significant advantage of overlapping hours is that the operators on both shifts have half a day in which to consult with their co-workers concerning drawings, if necessary, and half a day of uninterrupted terminal work.

10.3.4. Working Conditions

The basic physical requirements, in addition to the graphics work station itself, are a comfortable chair for the operator and an adequately large working surface for spreading out papers. Distractions are minimized by setting aside a private area for the graphics installation.

Bell Laboratories has made a practical study on establishing a suitable environment for a graphics operation in their own production unit that designs printed circuit boards [24]. Their study recommends placing the support equipment in a separate room adjacent to the work-station area. Support equipment includes the computer, the disk drives, the plotter, and other similar items. This separation reduces the noise level experienced by the terminal operators and allows for independent control of the air conditioning in the two areas. The study recommends that the terminals be grouped together, separated only by low partitions. Figure 10.1 is a sample arrangement for a six-terminal installation. The partitions are arranged to give a feeling of privacy around the display screen while providing an opening around the operator. This opening allows an individual to see and talk with the other operators so he or she does not feel isolated. This chance for relaxed talk between workers is particularly important for people working on the night shift since the remainder of the building outside the graphics area is dark and silent. Each work station should have its own telephone extension.

Good lighting is important. The glass face of a graphics screen reflects background images that annoy the operator. Poorly designed lighting can make this problem worse. The Bell Laboratories study identified three types of required lighting: screen, document, and maintenance.

Screen lighting is subdued. Storage tubes have dim green images that demand viewing in a darkened room. Refreshed display screens have fairly bright images, but operators find it more comfortable to view them in reduced light. Screen lighting can be provided by indirect lights mounted on

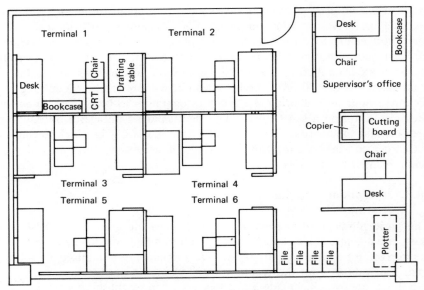

Figure 10.1. Room layout for six-terminal installation.

the wall behind the screen. A dimmer switch is desirable to allow an operator to adjust the light in his own area. Incandescent lighting is best because fluorescent lights tend to flicker when dimmed to low intensities.

Document lighting is a brighter light for reading papers. It can be provided by a directional desk or wall lamp with adjustable position. Adequate light is mandatory for accurate digitizing because the operator must pinpoint thin lines on existing drawings.

Maintenance lighting is the normal office lighting that must be available when the equipment is being serviced. This is easily provided by normal ceiling fixtures.

The performance of the graphics system has a psychological influence on the operator. Satisfaction is derived from a productive man–machine joint effort, but boredom, panic, frustration, and confusion are potential reactions to disturbances within the man–machine conversation. James Foley and Victor Wallace [25] suggest that a properly designed interactive system can avoid these negative operator responses. Prompt responses from the computer to the operator prevent boredom by maintaining a steady pace of task completion. Consistency in the time between user input and computer response is reassuring to the operator, while an unexpectedly long delay causes fear that a serious malfunction has occurred. Frustration is avoided when the operator can usually obtain his desired result and can also recover when necessary from incorrect actions. The remedy for confusion is twofold: logically structured operating commands and distinctly perceptible graphic displays.

10.3.5. Operating Procedures

The operating procedures for a graphics installation have three objectives: (1) accomplish work efficiently, (2) report results, and (3) protect accumulated data. Standardization, quality control, and equipment maintenance are procedures that contribute to efficient production.

Standardization is essential in achieving increased productivity with interactive computer graphics over manual methods. Drawings must be produced from a library of standard symbols following specified rules for graphic design. The procedures must be tailored to the application while remaining flexible enough to accommodate unusual assignments.

Quality control on the drawings produced with graphics is also crucial to a successful application. Many common drafting mistakes are eliminated by computer-assisted methods, but a graphics system actually introduces some new sources of error that must be controlled. On the positive side, computer-assisted drafting provides accurate measurements, consistent appearance for repeated symbols, presentation of drawings in different formats without redrawing, and correct transmittal of data to related reports. On the negative side, a computer-produced drawing is susceptible to typographical errors during data entry, to plotter problems such as smeared ink and skipped lines, to format errors caused by faulty plotter instructions, and to incorrect reports resulting from incorrectly assigned data base codes. All final plots should be screened by applying a quality control checklist that contains the potential errors mentioned above and other possible problems related to a particular turnkey system or application. Detailed checking of every drawing is too expensive and is not necessary. It is sufficient for each operator to quickly scan his own plots for obvious errors, with the supervisor making spot checks on one drawing out of fifty (or so) by comparing the final plot against the rough sketch and working notes. All quality control done within the graphics operation is in addition to the normal checking for technical content done by the person who receives the finished drawing.

Reliability is the probability that a device will perform without failure for a specified time period or amount of usage [22]. High reliability is indispensable for graphics hardware. An interactive system cannot make up for lost time after a breakdown by running extra hours overnight, as a batch-processing computer can, because the operators' idle time cannot be recovered. The average loss of available terminal time due to equipment failures and repairs should not exceed 5%. The ratio of available time to maintenance time is increased by scheduling preventive maintenance, stocking spare parts on the premises, and providing redundant equipment. The problem log (Figure 10.2) is another tool for improving graphics system performance. The supervisor uses the problem log to organize his efforts at obtaining solutions for all reported problems as well as to keep track of reliability over an extended period. When an incident occurs, the graphics operator fills out a problem log form and gives it to the supervisor, who makes a service call, notes the problem's source and remedy, and files the report. If a service call does not solve the problem, the supervisor transmits a copy of the problem log to the graphics system vendor for further action.

The two records that are the source documents for accurate reports concerning graphics operations are time cards by both manual draftsmen and graphics operators and a terminal usage log. Most companies already have labor cost codes that are used on time cards by all employees. The codes should be detailed enough to identify specific types of drawings, such as scaled and schematic. The labor charged to a drawing should include time spent asking questions and seeking reference material as well as the time spent on actual drafting or terminal work. However, the scope of each cost code must be consistent. For example, creative design leading up to a rough sketch must have a code that is separate from the code for formal drafting if one person does both tasks in the manual system and two individuals split the tasks under a graphics service-bureau arrangement. The usage log is the equivalent of a time card for the graphics terminals. A suggested form is shown in Figure 10.3. A supply of these forms should be kept at each terminal so the user can keep a continuous record of his sign-on and sign-off times and then calculate elapsed time rather than guess how long the work session lasted. If possible, the usage log should be implemented as an interactive screen display, so that the system can remind the operator to make entries and the computer can compile statistical reports.

Reports on operations serve several purposes. One major purpose is to determine the unit cost of drawings. This unit cost is used to prepare billings on completed work for outside clients, to do internal accounting, to make estimates on prospective future work, and to compare the efficiency of graphics methods to manual drafting. One common billing method is to set an hourly rate for use of a terminal, similar to the hourly rate for labor. This rate covers the expected return on capital investment and direct expenses such as maintenance and supplies. When used to generate billings to clients, both the terminal and labor rates include allowances for indirect overhead expenses and for profit. Another purpose of operational reports is to determine if the interactive computer graphics system is being used to its fullest capacity. The percentage of utilization is the total time listed on the usage log divided by the total number of available terminal hours.

IDENTIFICATION

TERMINAL NUMBER	OPERATOR'S NAME	DATE	DRAWING NUMBER	TIME WHEN WORK STOPPED	TIME WHEN WORK RESUMED	ELAPSED TIME

SYSTEM STATUS WHEN PROBLEM OCCURRED

WERE OTHER TERMINALS IN USE? _____
WAS PLOTTER IN USE? _____
WERE FILE OPERATIONS UNDERWAY? _____

DESCRIPTION OF PROBLEM

OPERATOR'S ACTION (JUST BEFORE PROBLEM):

COMPUTER'S RESPONSE:

OPERATOR'S RECOVERY PROCEDURE:

HAS ANY SIMILAR PROBLEM HAPPENED BEFORE?

CORRECTIVE ACTION

SERVICE CALL PLACED: DATE _____ TIME _____

VENDOR'S RESPONSE: DATE _____ TIME _____

NAME OF SERVICE REPRESENTATIVE: _____

DESCRIPTION OF REPAIRS: _____

SOFTWARE FAULT REPORTED TO VENDOR: DATE _____

VENDOR'S RESPONSE: DATE _____

DESCRIPTION OF RESPONSE: _____

Figure 10.2. Problem log.

TERMINAL NUMBER	OPERATOR'S NAME	DATE	PROJECT NAME OR COST CODE	DRAWING NUMBER	SIGN-ON TIME	SIGN-OFF TIME	ELAPSED TIME	TYPE OF PLOT (IF ANY)	FILE OPERATIONS (IF ANY)

Figure 10.3. Usage log.

Security measures are necessary because valuable data are accumulated within an interactive computer graphics system. Simple precautions prevent both intentional and accidental destruction of data. Operator identification codes limit interactive access to the files to guard against unauthorized changes to drawings. Accidental loss of data is prevented by frequently making copies of computer files, putting the copies in a safe place, and following rules on the length of time that the copies are retained. An orderly, permanent archive of computer files makes it possible for previous designs to be recalled as the basis for similar new designs.

In a stand-alone graphics installation, the computer, disk and tape drives, and plotter are all located near the graphics terminals and each operator is totally responsible for operating this equipment to do his own work. This stand-alone arrangement is convenient, but it is less secure than a computer-room installation in which all support equipment is operated by a few specialists in a restricted area away from the graphics terminals. Coordination problems between the graphics operators and the computer specialists are an inevitable disadvantage of the computer-room operation, however. A general guideline is that computer-room security is necessary only for a system with more than eight terminals.

10.4. ECONOMIC JUSTIFICATION

The potential benefits to a company from computer-aided drafting with an interactive graphics system consist of measurable economic results and intangibles. The intangibles include enhanced competitive status, structured methods for setting and maintaining standards, better use of manpower through reduced fluctuations in the work load, more flexibility in scheduling work, and improved continuity of work even with personnel changes. The measurable justification for graphics comes from the substitution of capital for labor. For sophisticated computer applications such as data base management systems and graphics systems, the capital investment includes both hardware and software. Computer systems are laborsaving because they require a lower ratio of labor to capital than the methods they displace. If the savings are measured relative to output, computer systems usually save both labor and capital [26]. For instance, the capital cost associated with manual drafting for drafting boards, chairs, office space, and so forth is reduced 50% or more with computer-assisted drafting, since half as many employees produce the same number of drawings.

Each company's business situation determines the impact of the savings in labor due to computer graphics. A company that is awarded a contract that is larger than those it normally handles sees computer graphics as a way of increasing the work capacity of its present staff. For a company that obtains work through project bidding, computer graphics reduces estimated drafting costs, and in many instances a graphics system pays for itself during a single major project. A company that previously hired temporary draftsmen to solve staffing problems uses computer-assisted drafting to reduce the number of employees without disrupting operations.

Ironically, inflation helps make an interactive computer graphics system an attractive investment. Most of the expense of installing a system is incurred at the beginning for equipment purchases, application testing, and operator training. Most of the savings occur later and continue indefinitely, in the form of a reduced labor requirement to produce the same work. In an inflationary economy, this is an ideal situation. The capital investment is made at today's prices. The savings accrue at tomorrow's wage rates, which will continue to escalate with inflation. In effect, investment in computer graphics acts to freeze a portion of labor expense.

Interest rates for debt fluctuate with the expected inflation rate, but even high interest rates do not cancel out the advantages of investing money now and paying back with less valuable money later. A capital investment also has income tax advantages since interest and depreciation are deductible. The element of risk in this computer graphics investment is the possibility of a general recession or a decrease in the firm's share of the work in its industry. The projection of the payback period for the initial investment, discussed later, is based on an assumed drafting volume. If the volume falls, the payback period will be longer.

Simple, well-chosen applications give the quickest return. Buying hardware for a single task where the projected payback period is short is a safeguard against obsolescence in a field of rapidly changing technology. It is also a recognition of the initial application as a learning experience. Once the equipment has paid for itself, if a switch to another type of system is indicated, that decision can be made without regret.

The tangible benefits of an interactive graphics system are measured by the financial results. These results are predicted by first establishing and classifying the cost of current procedures over a selected period as a basis for comparison, stating a set of assumptions about graphics, and then calculating the projected results. The different quantitative indicators of the economic benefits are productivity ratio, annual savings, return on investment, value ratio, and payback period. The following sample financial analysis shows how these indicators are calculated.

10.4.1. Financial Analysis: Assumptions

(1) The productivity ratio for computer-assisted drafting over manual methods is 2:1.

(2) The graphics system is operated on two shifts.
(3) The overall annual cost per employee is $44,000. (The same figure is used for manual draftsmen and graphics operators.)
This employee cost is calculated as follows:

Average hourly wage	$ 10
Burdens, 40% of wage	$ 4
(vacation, sick leave, payroll taxes)	
Indirect expenses, 80% of wage	$ 8
(supervision, office space, supplies)	
Total hourly cost	$ 22
Working hours per year per employee,	× 2,000
excluding vacation	
Overall annual cost per employee	$44,000

(4) The purchase price of a complete turnkey graphics system with four terminals, including installation, is $400,000.
(5) With 5-year straight-line depreciation and zero residual value, the annual depreciation charge for a $400,000 graphics system is $80,000.
(6) The annual fee for hardware and software maintenance is equal to 10% of the $400,000 purchase price of the system, or $40,000.
(7) It costs $60,000 in interest per year to borrow $400,000 at 15%.
(8) The cost of office space modifications to accommodate the system is negligible.
(9) There will be an initial 3-month period for operator training and standards development during which the productivity will average 1:1. This period is excluded from the calculation of annual savings. However, the calculated payback period includes this 3-month allowance.

10.4.2. Financial Analysis: Calculations

(1) *Annual Savings.*   The annual savings equals the cost of manual drafting minus the cost of computer-assisted drafting.

Manual drafting

16 employees × $44,000		$704,000
Computer-assisted drafting		
8 employees × $44,000	$352,000	
Depreciation charge	$ 80,000	
Maintenance fee	$ 40,000	
Interest	$ 60,000	
	$532,000	
Annual savings		$172,000

(2) *Return on Investment.* Return on investment is the annual savings divided by the capital investment.

$$\frac{\$172,000}{\$400,000} = 0.43 = 43\%$$

(3) *Value Ratio.* Value ratio is the total cost for a certain task using manual methods divided by the total cost for the identical task using computer graphics.

$$\frac{\$704,000}{\$532,000} = 1.3$$

value ratio $= 1.3:1$

Stated as a percent, the cost by computer graphics is about 75% of the cost by manual methods.

(4) *Payback Period.* Payback period is the total time required to recover the initial investment through savings in operational expenses.

Manual drafting
16 employees × $44,000 $704,000

Computer-assisted drafting
8 employees × $44,000 $352,000
Maintenance fee $ 40,000
Interest $ 60,000
                                                                                $452,000
Increase in cash flow $252,000

$$\text{Payback period (years)} = \frac{\text{capital investment}}{\text{increase in cash flow (annual)}}$$

$$\frac{\$400,000}{\$252,000} = 1.6 \text{ years} = \text{approximately 19 months}$$

Add the assumed start-up time of 3 months to find that the total time to recover the initial investment is 22 months.

10.4.3. Financial Analysis: Discussion

Productivity Ratio

Productivity ratio is defined as a comparison between the time required to complete a certain task using computer-assisted drafting and the time for the same task with traditional methods. This analysis assumes a low productivity ratio of 2:1 to demonstrate that a financial justification on drafting alone is possible. It is realistic to expect a productivity ratio of 4:1 or higher in repetitious drafting and an increase in efficiency of 10:1 or more when design or report-generator functions are added to drafting. At the time that a company is preparing the cost justification for its first graphics system, the company will have to rely on estimated productivity ratio figures obtained from talks with vendors and the vendors' existing clients.

Each application has a characteristic productivity ratio. The overall result for a graphics installation is the weighted average of the results for all applications. For example, the productivity ratio for creating a new map from field survey notes may be 4:1, while the comparison between revising an existing map manually and revising a computerized map may be 16:1. If 30% of a company's business is making new maps and 70% is updating existing maps, then the overall productivity ratio that company can expect to achieve is calculated as follows:

Express the ratio in decimal form, 4:1 = 0.25, 16:1 = 0.0625. Compute the weighted average, new maps + revisions = total business. (0.3)(0.25) + (0.7)(0.0625) = 0.119. The overall productivity ratio is 0.119, or slightly better than a ratio of 8:1. (Note, 8:1 = 0.125.)

Wage Rates

The merits of selecting the most experienced (and highest paid) workers as graphics operators as opposed to the assignment of the least skilled (and lowest paid) employees to the computer-assisted system are discussed earlier in Section 10.3.1, but it is important to note here that the average wage of the manual draftsmen and the average wage of the graphics operators are seldom identical. The financial analysis must be adjusted by substituting the actual wage rates in place of the assumed rate of $10 per hour and by making allowance for a second-shift pay differential, if any.

Initial Capital Investment

Graphics systems are priced within the reach of the companies they are designed to serve. The sample financial analysis is based on a fully equipped four-station system that costs about $400,000. This deluxe system includes a powerful minicomputer, a large capacity disk drive, a magnetic tape drive, a hard copy unit, a mechanical plotter, and four interactive terminals. A minimal system with one terminal and less support equipment sells for around $150,000 or rents for under $6000 per month including maintenance.

The vendor's sales representative confers with the client to determine the equipment and software required for a specific application. A turnkey graphics system is usually sold according to a published list of unit prices for its components. There is an additional charge for shipment to the user's site. If the vendor's standard terms are full payment due 30 days after acceptance testing at the factory, the customer must insist on a statement of his rights if the equipment is delayed or damaged in transit. Damage to one major component, such as the disk or plotter, can make the entire system unusable. The customer should defer full payment until after installation and the final acceptance test.

Direct cash sale is the only proposal most vendors of turnkey graphics systems can make because their firms do not have the money to finance equipment. However, customers can obtain graphics systems on 2- to 5-year full-payout lease plans arranged through third-party finance companies [27], and some vendors help clients arrange leasing plans through their established relationships with finance companies.

Depreciation

Depreciation is the systematic assignment of the cost of tangible assets to expense [28]. The annual depreciation charge is computed as the difference between the original cost of the asset and the estimated residual value divided by the estimated useful life in years. With 5-year straight-line depreciation and zero residual value, the depreciation charge for a $400,000 graphics system is $80,000 per year. The choice of this depreciation method, depreciation period, and salvage value is arbitrary and must be adjusted in accordance with a user's accounting policy. The depreciation period could be as long as 10 years or as short as 1 year. In 1-year depreciation, the purchase price is treated as a current expense instead of a capital investment. It is also possible to forecast a salvage value of 10 to 25% of the original price. The cost of office space modifications to accommodate the system is negligible. A turnkey graphics system is intended for use in a normal drafting room, not a computer-center environment. However, some minor changes in electric power connections, in lighting, in the arrangement of partitions, and so forth might be necessary.

Annual Savings

The computation of annual savings compares sixteen employees for manual drafting to eight employees for computer-assisted drafting. These numbers are derived from the assumption of a four-terminal graphics system working two shifts per day, which requires eight operators. Twice as many people (sixteen) are needed to produce the same drawings since a 2:1 productivity ratio is assumed.

The annual savings generated by use of computer techniques depends on both the efficiency and the utilization of the graphics system. To achieve the financial results predicted in the analysis, it is essential that a company have a sufficient work load, enough trained operators, and competent supervision to keep the system busy. There is a temptation to base a cost justification on two-shift utilization, then abandon that plan if providing staff, supervision, and suitable work assignments for the second shift becomes difficult.

The annual savings of $172,000 is a direct contribution to earnings for any company except a cost-plus contractor. Assuming that a company's profit margin is 5% of total sales, the savings is equivalent to over $3 million in additional sales every year.

Return On Investment

In the sample financial analysis, the 43% return on investment is profit. The cost of capital (assumed interest of 15%) has already been subtracted; however, income tax has not been taken into account. The savings through computer-aided drafting compared to manual drafting is the basis for calculating return on investment in the sample analysis. This approach assumes that the company realizes all the benefits as profit. Alternatively, part of the cost reduction can be passed on to the clients. The user company's accounting policy should make a distinction between recovering the actual costs for interactive computer graphics and obtaining the desired profit percentage. This distinction makes it possible to adjust the company's drafting rates to meet competition without losing sight of the graphics system's benefits.

The rate of return on investment is a measure of the expected cash inflow. The acceptance or rejection of a particular investment is decided by comparison of the present value of the expected net cash inflows to be generated by the investment with the present cash cost of making the investment. Rate of return is a more reliable basis for an investment decision than payback period because it takes into account the time value of money and it also considers the cash inflows generated after the payback period [28].

Value Ratio

Value ratio is a comparison that is calculated in terms of dollars rather than labor hours, which are used to determine the productivity ratio. The value ratio is equal to the total cost to accomplish a task using manual methods divided by the total cost to do the same task with a graphics system. In this sample analysis, the assumed productivity ratio is 2:1 and the calculated value ratio is 1.3:1. In other words, computer graphics cuts manpower headaches by 50% although the cut in total cost is only 25%.

10.4.4. Sensitivity Analysis

A *sensitivity analysis* is a study of the effect of any one variable on the projected financial results of a graphics system proposal. Figure 10.4 is a sample sensitivity analysis showing the relationship between the average hourly wage and the payback period. This sensitivity analysis is based on the same assumptions and methods as the preceding sample financial analysis. The chart shows how the average hourly wage values (column headings) are used to calculate the payback period for each hypothetical case. The results of these calculations, plotted on the graph, generate a curve that shows how the payback period for a graphics system becomes shorter as the cost of labor increases. This trend is especially meaningful during severe inflation because a graphics system is a capital investment made at present prices, which essentially freezes a portion of labor cost at present levels. It acts as a hedge against inflation during its useful life of 5 years or more.

A sensitivity analysis can also examine the effect of changes in the number of terminals, the number of shifts, and the productivity ratio. For a sensitivity analysis concerning the number of terminals, both the number of employees (manual draftsmen and computer operators) and the capital cost of the equipment (additional cost of each work station) must be adjusted. The financial results become more attractive as the number of terminals supported by a single system is increased, assuming full utilization. To calculate the sensitivity analysis regarding the number of shifts, only the number of employees is adjusted. It is unadvisable to plan on normal three-shift work because occasional overtime may be needed to handle peak loads or to catch up after problems.

The productivity ratio is a result, not a variable that can be directly controlled. However, it is still meaningful to do a sensitivity analysis on the productivity ratio to anticipate the annual savings or payback period. This can establish what ratio is the break-even point where the system begins to show a savings, or what ratio must be reached for the venture to be regarded as a success.

10.5. ADDITIONAL INFORMATION

There are many opportunities for learning about interactive computer graphics in addition to the operator training offered by system vendors. The sources of information concerning graphics include formal college courses, books, magazines, short courses, conventions, and exhibitions.

Many universities with strong computer science programs do not offer any

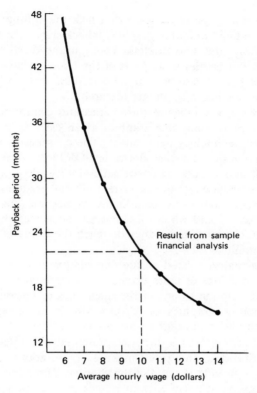

Average Hourly Wage (Dollars)	Annual Increase in Cash Flow (Dollars)	Time Required to Recover Investment of $400,000 (Months)	Payback Period Including Three-Month Start-Up Time (Months)
6	111,200	43.2	46.2
7	146,400	32.8	35.8
8	181,600	26.4	29.4
9	216,800	22.1	25.1
10	252,000	19.0	22.0
11	287,200	16.7	19.7
12	322,400	14.9	17.9
13	357,600	13.4	16.4
14	392,800	12.2	15.2

Figure 10.4. Sensitivity analysis: average hourly wage.

instruction in graphics, partly because they lack the appropriate equipment. However, outstanding computer graphics laboratories exist at Harvard and Cornell in the East, Utah and Brigham Young in the West, and at a growing number of other universities in all parts of the United States. These installations are, in many cases, also open to advanced students in fields other than computer science for interdisciplinary research.

A surprisingly large number of universities and community colleges offer formal course work in computer graphics as an elective in the paraprofessional engineering technology department. These courses normally deal with how to program a graphics display device in FORTRAN or BASIC, on an introductory level, and include extensive laboratory work producing drawings on a minicomputer-based graphics system. Upon graduation, engineering technology students are likely candidates to become computer graphics operators in industry, and while these courses do not attempt to cover the operation of commercial systems, they do teach the fundamental concepts in graphics programming.

The reference material listed at the end of this chapter includes books, periodicals, and citations of more extensive bibliographies that are available elsewhere. A subscription to one of the magazines or newsletters devoted to interactive computer graphics or CAD/CAM is an inexpensive way to become informed about what others are doing.

Short courses lasting 1 to 5 days are presented by professional societies, educational institutions, and profit-making organizations. A list of recent course offerings is given at the end of the chapter. These short courses are intensive and expensive. Course content ranges from a management overview of interactive computer graphics for industry to a deep technical presentation. One- and two-day tutorial sessions are also conducted at the beginning of the week preceding some major conventions. In judging a short course for value, the following points must be considered: (1) the instructor's qualifications, (2) demonstrations and field trips, (3) textbook or printed lecture notes, (4) the ratio of vendor presentations to instruction, and (5) the match between the course's content and the student's prior knowledge and area of interest.

Attendance at a well-chosen convention is a way to feel the pulse of graphics development by mingling with researchers, vendor representatives, and users. A list of graphics conventions and exhibitions appears at the end of the chapter. Most papers presented at computer conferences such as SIG-GRAPH and the National Computer Conference (NCC) deal with specialized topics in a technical manner; however, application reports and panel discussions dealing with user experiences are also featured. Other meetings, such as the American Institute for Design and Drafting (AIDD) convention and the IEEE/ACM Design Automation Conference, center on an application and emphasize graphics technology as it applies to that application.

The equipment exhibition is the most popular part of any major convention. The vendor's purpose in taking part in an exhibition is to establish his identity in the industry, not to provide detailed product information or actually close sales. Many firms schedule the release of new products to coincide with the dates of annual exhibitions. The visitor's interest in an exhibition is to gain a general knowledge of companies in the graphics industry and their product lines. A visitor who establishes a definite interest in a product during a show can call the vendor at a later date for further information. An exhibition is a convenient way to view many different graphics systems within a compact space and a short time, but the visitor must be wary of false impressions. A trip to the work place of an existing graphics user reveals more about the performance of a particular system than a demonstration at an exhibition.

APPENDIX: GRAPHICS INFORMATION SOURCE LIST

BIBLIOGRAPHIES

Calma Company, *Interactive Computer-Aided Design Considerations for Architects, Engineers and Constructors,* 1978, pp. 26–36.

National Technical Information Service, U.S. Department of Commerce, 2585 Port Royal Road, Springfield, VA, 22161. The following bibliographies are available for $28 (paper or microfiche copy):

Interactive Computer Graphics, Vol. 2, February 1976–January 1978. NTIS/PS-78/0223/4WC. One hundred fifty-one abstracts (seventy-four new) based on a search of the NTIS Data Base.

Interactive Computer Graphics, Vol. 2, February 1976–January 1978. NTIS/PS-78/0224/2WC. Two hundred and thirty-two abstracts (one hundred five new) based on a search of the Engineering Index Data Base.

Machover, Carl, "A Guide to Sources of Information about Computer Graphics," *IEEE Computer Graphics and Applications,* 1(1), 73–85 (1981).

Pooch, U. W., "Computer Graphics, Interactive Techniques and Image Processing 1970–1975: A Bibliography," *Computer,* 9(8), 46–64 (1976).

Schrack, G. F., "Current Literature in Computer Graphics and Interactive Techniques," *Computer Graphics,* **12**(4), 114–123 (1978).

BOOKS

Allan, John J. III, Ed., *Proceedings of the IFIP Working Conference on CAD Systems,* North-Holland, Amsterdam, 1977.

Chasen, Sylvan H., *Geometric Principles and Procedures for Computer Graphics Applications,* Prentice-Hall, Englewood Cliffs, NJ, 1978.

Foley, James D. and Andries van Dam, *Fundamentals of Interactive Computer Graphics,* Addison-Wesley, Reading, MA, 1981.

Giloi, Wolfgang K., *Interactive Computer Graphics,* Prentice-Hall, Englewood Cliffs, NJ, 1978.

Gruenberger, Fred, Ed., *Computer Graphics (Utility/Production/Art).* Thompson Book Company, Washington, 1967.

Hulbert, L. E., Ed., *Interactive Computer Graphics in Engineering,* The American Society of Mechanical Engineers, New York, 1977.

Nake, F., and A. Rosenfeld, Eds., *Graphic Languages, Proceedings of the IFIP Working Conference on Graphic Languages,* North-Holland, Amsterdam, 1972.

Newman, William M., and Robert F. Sproull, *Principles of Interactive Computer Graphics,* 2nd ed., McGraw-Hill, New York, 1979.

Parslow, R. D., and R. Elliot Green, Eds., *Advanced Computer Graphics (Economics, Techniques and Applications),* Plenum Press, London, 1971.

Parslow, R. D., R. W. Prowse, and R. E. Green, Eds., *Computer Graphics, Techniques and Applications,* Plenum Press, London, 1969.

Prince, M. David, *Interactive Graphics for Computer-Aided Design,* Addison-Wesley, Reading, 1971.

Rogers, D. F., and J. A. Adams, *Mathematical Elements for Computer Graphics,* McGraw-Hill, New York, 1976.

Ryan, Daniel L., *Computer-Aided Graphics and Design,* Dekker, New York, 1979.

Secrest, Don, and Jurg Nievergelt, Eds., *Emerging Concepts in Computer Graphics,* Benjamin, New York, 1968.

Siders, R. A., et al, *Computer Graphics: A Revolution in Design,* American Management Association, New York, 1966.

Walker, B. S., J. R. Gurd, and E. A. Drawneek, *Interactive Computer Graphics,* Crane Russak, New York, 1975.

Periodicals and Other Publications

Publisher	Title	Appearance	Cost	Notes
ACM/SIGGRAPH 1133 Avenue of the Americas New York, NY 10036 (212) 265-6300	*Computer Graphics*	Quarterly	$7 per year	Included in SIGGRAPH membership
	ACM Transactions on Graphics	Quarterly	$18 per year	Journal of technical papers
Anderson Publishing Company 4265 Avenida Simi Simi Valley, CA 93063 (805) 526-0764	*The Anderson Report*	Monthly	$48 per year	Newsletter, edited exclusively for the computer graphics industry
Byte Publications, Inc. 70 Main Street Peterborough, NH 03458 (603) 924-9281	*Byte*	Monthly	$18 per year	The small systems journal
Creative Computing P.O. Box 789-M Morristown, NJ 07960 (800) 631-8112	*Creative Computing*	Monthly	$15 per year	Applications and software for home computers
Mr. Ed Forrest 7209 Wisteria Way Carlsbad, CA 92008 (714) 438-1595	*Architects-Engineers-Constructors (AEC) Automation Newsletter*	Monthly	$36 per year	Professional newsletter, no advertising

Periodicals and Other Publications (Continued)

Publisher	Title	Appearance	Cost	Notes
Frost & Sullivan 106 Fulton St. New York, NY 10038 (212) 233-1080	*Computer Graphics Equipment, Software and Services in the Manufacturing Industry*	Report #490 dated 3/78	$775	Research report with analysis and forecast
Harvard University, Laboratory for Computer Graphics and Spatial Analysis 48 Quincy Street Cambridge, MA 02138 (617) 738-5020	*The Harvard Library of Computer Mapping*	1980 collection of eleven volumes	$50 first volume, $35 each additional volume, $250 set	
	The Harvard Newsletter on Computer Graphics	Twice a month	$125 (24 issues)	
	Harvard Newsletter Directory of Computer Graphics Suppliers: Systems, Hardware, Software, and Services	1980		
Hayden Publishing Co. 50 Essex St. Rochelle Park, NJ 07662 (201) 843-0550	*Computer Decisions* (The Management Magazine of Computing)	Monthly	Free to qualified subscribers	
IEEE Computer Society Service Center 445 Hoes Lane Piscataway, NJ 08854 (201) 981-0060	*Computer*	Monthly	$30 per year	Included in IEEE Computer Society membership
	IEEE Computer Graphics and Applications	Quarterly	$8 per year	In cooperation with the NCGA

Organization	Publication	Frequency	Price	Description
International Technology Marketing 120 Cedar Street Wellesley, MA 02181 (617) 237-2089	*Computer Graphics: A Study for Designers of Printed, Integrated and Hybrid Circuits* (1978)		$600 first copy, $100 additional copies	
	Computer Cartography: Worldwide Technology and Markets (1976)		$375	
IPC Science and Technology Press, Ltd. 205 E. 42nd St. New York, NY 10017 (212) 867-2080	*Computer Aided Design*	Alternate months	$83.20 (6 issues)	An international journal
Mini-Micro Systems P.O. Box 17041 270 St. Paul St. Denver, CO 80217 (303) 388-4511	*Mini-Micro Systems*	Monthly	Free to qualified subscribers	
Orr Associates, Inc. 21 Chambers Rd. Danbury, CN 06810 (203) 748-8044	*Computer Graphics Extravaganza*		$50	Primer, user experiences, system design articles, equipment vendor list

Periodicals and Other Publications (Continued)

Publisher	Title	Appearance	Cost	Notes
Productivity International, Inc. Publications Division P.O. Box 8100 Dallas, TX 75205 (214) 739-3056	*CAD/CAM Digest*	Alternate months	$18 (12 issues)	
	CAD/CAM Glossary		$28	
	A Survey of Commercial Turnkey CAD/CAM Systems		$85 per copy	Information from 15 vendors
ROM Publications Corporation Rt. 97, Box CD Hampton, CT 06247	*ROM*	Monthly	$15 per year	Computer applications for living
Times Mirror Magazines 380 Madison Avenue New York, NY 10017 (212) 687-3000	*Popular Science*	Monthly	$1.50 per copy	Frequent features on graphics for home computers
Ziff-Davis Publishing Company 1 Park Avenue New York, NY 10016 (212) 725-3500	*Popular Electronics*	Monthly	$0.50 per copy	Frequent features on graphics for home computers

Short Courses

Sponsor	Title	Length	Cost
ACM Italian Chapter Giorgio Valle, Chairman Instituto di Elettronica Facolta di Ingegneria Universita di Bologna Viale Risorgimento, 2 40136 Bologna, Italy	Introduction to CAD/CAM (international faculty, presented in English)	3 days	300,000 Italian lire
ACM/SIGGRAPH 1133 Avenue of the Americas New York, NY 10036 (212) 265-6300	SIGGRAPH conference tutorials: 1. Introduction to Computer Graphics 2. Introduction to Raster Graphics 3. Computer-Aided Design 4. Advanced Raster Graphics 5. Animation 6. Low Cost Graphics 7. User Interfaces to Graphics Systems 8. Graphic Design and Information Graphics	2 days	$120
AIAA Professional Study Series 1290 Avenue of the Americas New York, NY 10019 (212) 581-4300	Low Cost Computer Graphics (Personal Computers for Industry and University Use)	2 days	$250
The Center for Professional Advancement P.O. Box H E. Brunswick, NJ 08816 (201) 249-1400	Computer Aided Mechanical Design and Drafting	3 days	$425

223

Short Courses (Continued)

Sponsor	Title	Length	Cost
Continuing Engineering Education George Washington University Washington, DC 20052 (202) 676-6106 (800) 424-9773	Computer Graphics: Hardware and Software	3 days	$395
	Computer Assisted Makeup and Imaging Systems	5 days	$480
	Computer-Aided Design/Computer-Aided Manufacturing	3 days	$495
Engineering Society of Detroit (in cooperation with ACM/SIGGRAPH) 100 Farnsworth Detroit, MI 48202 (313) 832-5400	Computer graphics conference tutorials: 1. Computer Graphics 2. Architects/Engineers (A/E) Computer Graphics	1 day	$135
Frost & Sullivan, Inc. 106 Fulton St. New York, NY 10038 (212) 233-1080	Assessment and Forecast of Computer Graphics (panel discussion)	3 days	$575
	Understanding and Using Computer Graphics	3 days	$545
Graphics Utah Style (annual) c/o Hank Christiansen 1980 N. 1450 East Provo, UT 84601 (801) 374-5266	A Workshop on Interactive Computer Graphics with Emphasis on the MOVIE System	5 days	$500

Organization	Course	Duration	Cost
Harvard University, Laboratory for Computer Graphics and Spatial Analysis 48 Quincy Street Cambridge, MA 02138 (617) 738-5020	Harvard Computer Graphics Week (emphasis on mapping)	5 days	$300 registration fee and $85 per day
	Computer Graphics and Geographic Information Systems Seminars:		
	1. Selecting Computer Graphics Hardware	2 days	$495
	2. Computer Graphics: Update on Applications and Technology	2 days	$495
	3. Computer Graphics Hardware Update	1 day	$395
	One-Day State of the Art Briefings:		
	1. Business Graphics	1 day	$395
	2. Computer Mapping (Getting Started, Applications)	1 day	$395
	3. Computer Graphics (Applications and Technology)	2 days	$595
	4. Computer-Aided Design and Drafting	2 days	$595
IEEE Computer Society 5855 Naples Plaza Suite 301 Long Beach, CA 90803 (213) 438-9951	Interactive Computer Graphics (COMPCON preconference tutorials)	1 day	$65 (Text only, $25)
	Computer Graphics (Tutorial Week)	1 day	$100 (Text only, $28)
Integrated Computer Systems, Inc. 3304 Pico Boulevard P.O. Box 5339 Santa Monica, CA 90405 (213) 450-2060	Computer Graphics: State of the Art Techniques and Applications	4 days	$695 (Material only, $185)
	Computer Aided Design and Manufacturing	4 days	$695 (Material only, $185)

Short Courses (Continued)

Sponsor	Title	Length	Cost
National Computer Graphics Association 1129 20th St. NW Suite 512 Washington, DC 20036 (202) 466-5895	Conference tutorials: 1. Justification of Computer Graphics 2. Overview of Computer Graphics 3. How to Implement and Manage CAD/CAM Systems 4. Business Graphics 5. Architectural and Engineering Graphics System 6. Computer Graphics and Utility Companies 7. Printed Circuit Design and Manufacture	1 day tutorial 1 ½ day tutorials 2 through 7	$135 $85
Office of Continuing Studies Rensselaer Polytechnic Institute Troy, NY 12181 (518) 270-6442	Introduction to Computer Graphics	5 days	$495
University of California Extension Santa Cruz, CA 95064 (408) 429-2614	Annual Institute in Computer Science	1, 2, or 3 weeks	$400 per week
University of Maryland Conferences and Institutes Division University Blvd. at Adelphi Rd. College Park, MD 20742 (UCLA Extension, joint sponsor)	Applied Interactive Computer Graphics	5 days	$575
	Management of Computer Graphics	3 days	$450

The University of Michigan College of Engineering Ann Arbor, MI 48109 (313) 763-3459	Geometric Modelling and Computer Graphics	3 days	$295
University of Wisconsin Extension Department of Engineering 929 N. Sixth St. Milwaukee, WI 53203 (414) 224-4181	Design and Drafting Automation	2 days	$150

Conventions and Exhibitions

Sponsor	Name	Duration	Nonmember Cost	History
ACM Italian Chapter Giorgio Valle, Chairman Istituto di Elettronica Facolta di Ingegneria Universita di Bologna Viale Risorgimento, 2 40136 Bologna, Italy	EUROGRAPHICS International Conference and Exhibition	3 days		Annual since 1979
ACM/SIGDA and IEEE Computer Society-DATC, Joint Sponsors 1133 Avenue of the Americas New York, NY 10036 (212) 265-6300	Design Automation Conference	3 days	$85	Annual since 1964
ACM/SIGGRAPH 1133 Avenue of the Americas New York, NY 10036 (212) 265-6300	SIGGRAPH Annual Conference on Computer Graphics and Interactive Techniques	3 days	$120	Annual since 1974
American Federation of Information Processing Societies (AFIPS) 1815 North Lynn Street Arlington, VA 22209 (703) 243-4100	National Computer Conference and Exposition (NCC)	4 days	$75	

Organization	Event	Duration	Cost	Frequency
American Institute for Design and Drafting 3119 Price Road Bartlesville, OK 74003 (918) 333-1053	Convention and Design Drafting Exhibition	4 days	$175	Annual since 1959
Computer Aided Design IPC Science & Technology Press Limited IPC House 32 High Street Guildford, Surrey, England GU1 3EW	Conference and Exhibition on Computers in Engineering and Building Design	3 days		Annual since 1976
Computer and Automated Systems Association, Society of Manufacturing Engineers P.O. Box 930 20501 Ford Rd. Dearborn, MI 48128 (313) 271-1500	CAD/CAM	3 days	Exhibition only $3	Annual since 1973
Engineering Society of Detroit (in cooperation with ACM/SIGGRAPH) 100 Farnsworth Detroit, MI 48202 (313) 832-5400	Computer Graphics Conference and Equipment Display	3 days	$175	Annual since 1975

Conventions and Exhibitions (Continued).

Sponsor	Name	Duration	Nonmember Cost	History
IEEE Computer Society 5855 Naples Plaza Suite 301 Long Beach, CA 90803 (213) 438-9951	COMPCON, IEEE Computer Society International Conference	3 days	$65	Annual since 1962
Massachusetts Institute of Technology Cambridge, MA (617) 253-1000	Conference on Computer Graphics in CAD/CAM Systems	3 days		Annual since 1979
National Computer Graphics Association 1129 20th St. NW, Suite 512 Washington, DC 20036 (202) 466-5895	NCGA Conference	3 days	$245	Annual since 1980
ONLINE Cleveland Road Uxbridge UB8 2DD England	Computer Graphics 80 (10 Years After Computer Graphics 70) International Conference and Exhibition	3 days	195 British pounds	

CHAPTER 11

Application Survey

This chapter is a survey of current applications for interactive computer graphics, organized under headings that represent major industries or fields. The variety of applications prevents this discussion from being exhaustive or detailed, and in some cases the full impact of graphics in an area is obscured by the division into categories. For example, energy applications fall into a variety of industrial classifications: mapping in oil exploration, modeling and drafting for the design and construction of power plants and refineries, and control panel displays used in the operation of power generating equipment and power distribution networks.

11.1. ARCHITECTURE / ENGINEERING / CONSTRUCTION

Three-dimensional computer graphics in architecture can create a realistic-looking view of a proposed building and a series of these views can even simulate movement around the building and its surroundings and through its interior spaces. Less spectacular but equally significant results are obtained through the application of two-dimensional computer graphics during detailed design development. This phase demands carefully coordinated work by several disciplines communicating through overlay drawings, an approach made even more effective by the computer's ability to hold the design data as separate layers, to combine the layers in any conceivable way on the screen or as a plot, and to make revisions by one discipline immediately available to all others. Typical layers include the basic building structure, interior partitions, the power system, the telephone system, light fixtures, ducting, plumbing fixtures, and furnishings. During the construction documentation phase that follows detailed design, an interactive graphics system multiplies the productivity of an experienced drafter, especially on drawings with standard components grouped into typical layouts. A computer graphics system with effective data handling also saves labor in preparing nongraphic data related to the design, such as estimates, purchase orders, and construction bills of material.

Architectural space planning is an orderly approach to locating multiple buildings on a site, rooms inside a building, or equipment within a room. Figure 11.1 is an example of space planning during the design of a hospital to determine the arrangement of equipment in an operating room. Space planning is most vital during the early design stage to ensure that the structure will suit the intended functions. Computer graphics techniques make it feasible to produce high-quality presentations of proposed layouts and alternatives for the building's owners and the users so they can work closely with the architect to achieve the most satisfactory space usage. Space planning with computer graphics also has ongoing advantages in facilities management, equipment inventory, and building remodeling.

In civil engineering, a computer graphics system that produces perspective drawings of proposed highways helps create safer designs. These drawings take into account a description of the natural terrain and include details of proposed landscaping and signposting. The perspective drawings can be viewed individually or they can be filmed in sequence to produce dynamic simulations. Using the drawings, the highway design is reviewed for potentially dangerous places where the length of the driver's uninterrupted line of sight along the road falls below a safe minimum, such as in hilly areas and on curves. Poor design is easily discovered and corrected during this review [29]. Other graphics applications in civil engineering include the use of automated drafting techniques to produce drawings of excavations, concrete foundations, and steel structures. Interactive graphics is a useful tool in the design of mine shafts with respect to test data concerning the location of ore or coal deposits.

In mechanical engineering, geometric descriptions of parts or structures for stress analysis using the finite element method are commonly prepared with the help of graphics techniques. Some popular uses for graphics in electrical engineering related to the design and construction of industrial plants, electrical systems in vehicles, and electrical machinery are wiring diagrams, logic diagrams, and one-line diagrams. Electrical engineering is an application area where an interactive computer graphics system multiplies the efficiency of a designer or drafter because the drawings are schematic rather than scaled, standard symbols make up almost all of the drawing content, and there are multiple drawings that are repetitions of each other with only minor variations.

The design of chemical plants and refineries involves extensive use of in-

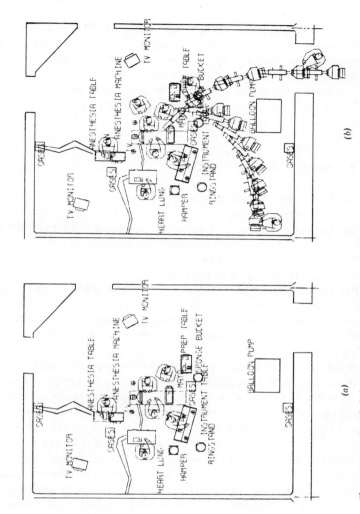

(a)

(b)

Figure 11.1. Detailed drawing of operating room with clearance test for portable X-ray uit. (a) Layout stored in computer. (b) Copy modified to check movement. Courtesy of Stewart Design Group, Boston.

233

teractive graphics by multiple engineering disciplines. Computer-assisted drafting of flow sheets (symbolic process diagrams) is the main application in chemical engineering. Drafting applications in mechanical design include scaled pressure vessel drawings, double-line scaled piping plans, and isometric-view piping diagrams. Interactive graphics also assists in the production of instrument drawings, electrical diagrams, and project scheduling charts.

11.2. DESIGN / MANUFACTURING

Automation of the design and production process is more complete in electronics than in any other industry. In integrated circuit design, the locations of components to be interconnected are digitized from a sketch, and then an automatic routing program generates the connecting lines. The ease with which the computer can make changes by moving elements on the drawing encourages the designer to find the optimal utilization for space on the chip. Photoplotting converts the integrated circuit drawing directly into the masks needed to manufacture the semiconductor device. Computer graphics is also an important tool for the design of both the electronic logic and the physical component assembly of computers and other complex electronic equipment.

The transportation industries, which include aerospace, automotive, and ship building, use computer graphics extensively to meet a variety of requirements. Sculptured surfaces are designed, analyzed, and manufactured for aircraft fuselages, aircraft wings, automobile bodies, ship hulls, ship propellers, and engine turbine blades. A multitude of components for wiring, piping, and structural reinforcement are arranged within the restricted volume defined by these complex curved surfaces. Human factors studies are done to consider the safety and comfort of the occupants of cars and planes, using computer graphics to test the interaction between a model of the human figure and a proposed vehicle design. Performance studies involving computer graphics are used for the evaluation of a whole simulated vehicle and for modeling the operation of subsystems in detail so the movement of components can be traced. The transmission gears shown in Figure 11.2 are an example of a vehicle subsystem.

Jewelry manufacturers use interactive graphics to create three-dimensional models of new products. This allows the designer to better visualize the piece of jewelry and to let others inspect its appearance before the item is crafted in precious metals and stones. Bottles, packaging, glassware, china, silver, flatware, fixtures, telephone sets, toys, furniture, and other products are designed with greater efficiency and accuracy using the assistance of a

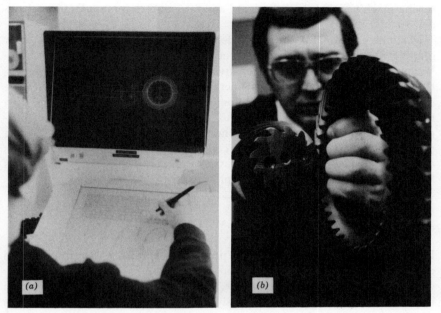

Figure 11.2. Gear model. (a) Simulated operation. (b) The resulting manufactured parts. Courtesy of Computervision Corporation.

graphics system for visualization and computations. Molds and dies for plastics, glass, and metal are produced directly from the computer design by generating tapes for numerically controlled (N/C) machine tools.

Computer graphics minimizes the waste of materials in the cutting of parts from sheet metal, plastic, cloth, and leather by optimizing the pattern layout. After the pattern designer draws a figure on the graphics screen, the computer calculates its area, circumference, or other characteristics. This design assistance is most important in the garment industry, where the computer calculates patterns for the entire range of sizes from the original design.

Computer graphics is an essential tool for designers of artwork, fashion, wallpaper, textiles, rugs, carpeting, lace, embroidery, and similar products, since complex patterns involving many small figures are automatically generated by the computer system. These patterns can be displayed in any combination to determine the overall effect, and many alternative designs can be tried in less time than is required to draw a single pattern by hand. This computer assistance stimulates the designer's imagination. The computer design leads directly to production through control programs for industrial sewing machines that do embroidery and for looms that manufacture fabrics and rugs.

Machine components can be modeled using three-dimensional computer graphics. One modeling package for CAD/CAM applications is Syntha-Vision, developed by the Mathematical Applications Group, Inc. In SynthaVision's volume element input method, items chosen from a set of twelve distinct primitive solid shapes are combined to form a geometric description that can then be accessed by other user-supplied program modules for purposes such as engineering analysis and N/C tape generation. The modeling package includes graphics functions capable of producing both line drawings and photographic-type shaded images, as shown in Figure 11.3. Boeing has licensed SynthaVision to model complex aircraft parts [30, 31].

11.3. BUSINESS MANAGEMENT

Financial graphs must be easy to prepare, accurate, and attractive. An excellent tool for this job is a desk-top minicomputer system (Figure 11.4) in conjunction with a felt-tip pen plotter. This computer system can be operated by the same person who has previously calculated the financial statistics and drawn the graphs by hand.

Production of critical path method (CPM) diagrams and other schematic charts for planning and scheduling work is another application of interactive computer graphics in business. The data are entered as a graphic network on the screen by the person responsible for project planning, and then the logic of the network is analyzed by the computer to derive nongraphic data such as the scheduling dates.

Computer-generated, full-color 35-mm slides (Figure 11.5) for management presentations, training classes, and advertising are available from service bureaus at prices that are competitive with conventional slide sources. An operator interactively creates lettering and artwork, and he directly converts collections of numbers into line graphs, pie-wedge charts, and bar charts. The bar charts can use ordinary rectangular bars, or an unusual effect can be created by scaling some symbol in proportion to the value being illustrated.

11.4. CARTOGRAPHY

Mapping systems based on computer graphics are used in applications as diverse as urban planning and oil exploration. The input data for a computer graphics map is typically either conventional surveying field data or locations

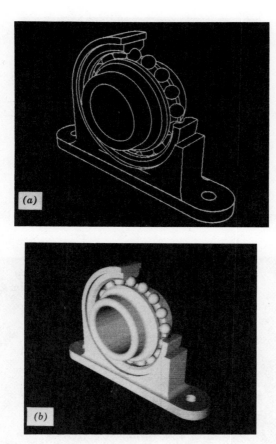

Figure 11.3. SynthaVision solid object model, perspective view. (a) Line drawing. (b) Shaded image. Courtesy of Mathematical Applications Group Inc. (MAGI).

digitized from an existing map. All information is recorded as real world units so that data from many sources may be combined into one meaningful data base. If each coordinate point is stored as a forty-eight bit binary number, then a position on the earth's surface can be located relative to any other position with a tolerance of ⅛ inch. A map covering a smaller area can be even more accurate.

A number of municipal and county governments have systems for geographic records management that produce tax maps, subdivision maps, and other graphic output, as well as maintain related nongraphic information. Utility companies use computer graphics systems to record cartographic data on property right-of-way arrangements, production installations, and dis-

Figure 11.4. Personal computer, with integral keyboard and screen. Courtesy of Compucolor Corporation.

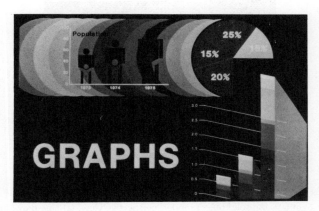

Figure 11.5. Computer-produced 35-mm slide. GENIGRAPHICS® slide courtesy of the General Electric Company.

tribution facilities for the purposes of inventory valuation, maintenance scheduling, and expansion planning.

The petroleum industry uses computer graphics in oil exploration activities to produce geological and topographic maps and well log analyses. Graphics also helps in mapping pipeline routes for natural gas transmission companies. In forestry, computerized maps containing data obtained from aerial survey photographs are used to measure areas having particular tree species, soil types, and other characteristics. Meteorological instrument readings are presented visually by using computer-generated shading, cross-hatching, and other patterns to identify areas of rain, fog, snow, or other weather conditions.

11.5. HEALTH CARE

Treatment planning is one broad application area for interactive computer graphics in health care. Radiation treatment planning involves selecting and positioning hypothetical radiation beams until an adequate dosage pattern covers the tumor area. Orthodontic treatment planning utilizes visual presentation of the expected changes in a patient's face as different corrective procedures are tried.

In another medical application, stereotaxic brain surgery, an interactive graphics system assists the surgeon in locating the exact area related to the patient's complaint by matching the patient's actual responses to electrical stimulation with anatomical landmarks on a map outlining various internal brain structures having specific bodily functions [32]. Figure 11.6 shows the computer display of a map with superimposed response symbols.

Interactive graphics is used in medical research to reconstruct anatomical structures from data provided by computerized tomographic X-ray scanners or by manually digitizing serial tissue sections. Another application is cell area measurement based on a digitized image of the cell's perimeter. In dental research, X-ray films and plaster dental models are digitized to provide data for a study in which computer graphics helps orthodontists evaluate growth patterns of the lower face and their relation to tooth development in children and adolescents.

11.6. SCIENTIFIC RESEARCH

Almost any collection of scientific data is more meaningful when displayed graphically. The ability of a computer graphics system to plot several measured variables as a function of time or against each other gives researchers the opportunity to observe complex relationships, and the speed of the computer system makes it practical to graph the results of computations based on a series of parameter values or varying conditions. The researcher can interact with the display to fit models representing theory to the graphs of observed data. For example, interactive computer graphics is used in biochemistry to help determine the precise structure of proteins, enzymes, and other complex biological molecules [33]. Crystals of the substance under investigation are bombarded with X rays to produce a diffraction pattern that is an electron density map, showing the location of atoms as density

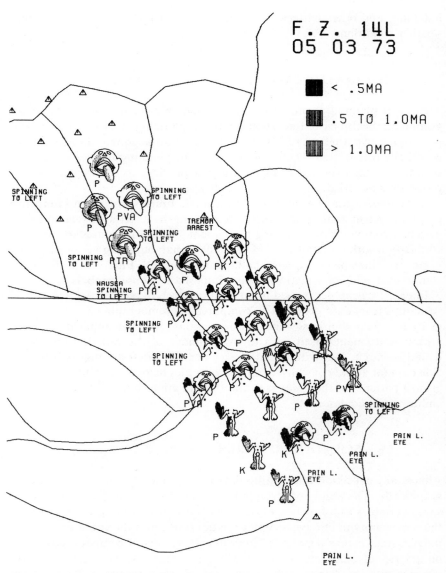

Figure 11.6. Computer display of symbols for patient's response to electrical stimulation of the brain, with atlas template shown in background. Courtesy of Peter A. Hawrylyshyn, Mount Sinai Hospital, Toronto, Canada.

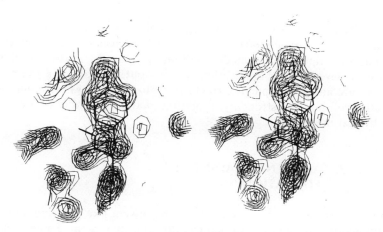

Figure 11.7. Stereoscopic views of an electron density map with superimposed stick model. Courtesty of Edgar F. Meyer, Texas A & M University.

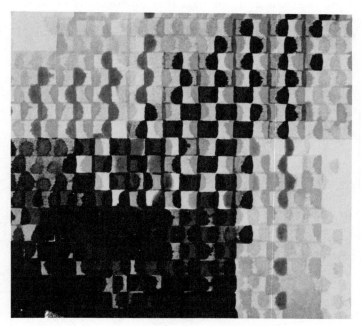

Figure 11.8. Computer art: Matrix Multiplication by Frieder Nake, 1967. Reprinted, with permission, from ''Computer Graphics and Art'' by Charles Csuri, *Proceedings of the IEEE,* April 1974. © 1974 IEEE.

peaks. The researcher views stereo displays of both the electron density map and a proposed atomic model of the biological molecule on a screen (Figure 11.7) and manipulates the model until an optimum fit to the experimental data is achieved. Other applications for computer graphics in the physical sciences are analysis of particle tracks in high-energy physics, simulation of galactic evolution in astronomy, spectrum analysis in radioastronomy, and geophysical modeling in geology.

11.7. ART / ENTERTAINMENT / EDUCATION

Computer art "is a medium for artistic expression like painting and it will eventually produce a rich tradition of cultural achievement. Some artists are producing significant work and in the future we are likely to see various directions, styles or points of view about art. Computer art is encountering many of the reactions and problems that photography faced in the early nineteenth century. In fact, photography and even film were not accepted as an art form until well into the twentieth century" [34]. Figure 11.8 is an

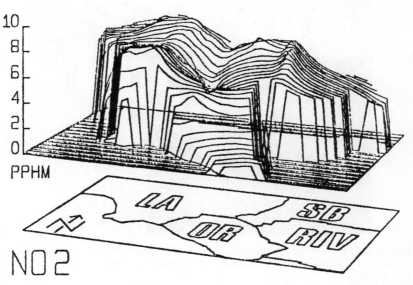

Figure 11.9. Frame from computer animated film, *The Tainted Sky*. Courtesy of Kent R. Wilson, University of California at San Diego.

example of the work of Dr. Frieder Nake, a mathematician, computer scientist, and artist who is one of the pioneers in computer art.

Interactive computer graphics is also emerging as a means of creating animation for research, education, and entertainment. A computer film surpasses conventional visual aids in giving the audience an intuitive grasp of a complicated situation. For example, Kent Wilson's computer-animated film, *The Tainted Sky,* illustrates the chemical and meteorological interactions that produce complex patterns of air pollution over an urban region (Figure 11.9). It is based on air quality data from the Los Angeles Basin. Detailed information on animation that is beyond the scope of this book can be found in the references, which include an overview of the current research activity in animation techniques [35], a description of a method for animation of three-dimensional objects [36], and a method of computer animation that is comparable to the traditional hand-drawing techniques using overlays of two-dimensional drawings, separated into multiple planes to create the effect of three-dimensional depth [37]. In the future, computer graphics may replace the highly labor-intensive methods of animation that produced Walt Disney's classic movies and cartoons. Graphics systems capable of producing dynamic images also have an important role as training aids through the simulated operation of ships, planes, and spacecraft.

Electronic games utilizing television displays are introducing millions of people to the fascination of using an interactive input device to make something happen on a screen. Most of these games are individually owned units kept in the home, but institutions such as schools, libraries, and museums also offer public access to computer graphics through games. The Boston Children's Museum has been providing this service since 1971, with the goal of providing museum visitors with an "environment for discovery" by allowing them to interact with a computer by playing one of a number of games such as checkers and tic-tac-toe [38].

References

1. William M. Newman and Robert F. Sproull, *Principles of Interactive Computer Graphics,* 2nd ed., McGraw-Hill, New York, 1979.

2. Ruth M. Davis, "Evolution of Computers and Computing," *Science,* **195**(4283), 1095–1102 (1977).

3. Robert F. Sproull and Elaine L. Thomas, "A Network Graphics Protocol," *Computer Graphics,* **8**(3), 27–51 (1974).

4. Evans and Sutherland Computer Corporation, *Picture System 2 User's Manual* (Document #901129-001 NC), 1977.

5. M. David Prince, *Interactive Graphics for Computer-Aided Design,* Addison-Wesley, Reading, MA, 1971.

6. Wolfgang K. Giloi, *Interactive Computer Graphics,* Prentice-Hall, Englewood Cliffs, NJ, 1978.

7. Robert M. Dunn and Bertram Herzog, Eds., "Status Report of the Graphic Standards Planning Committee of ACM/SIGGRAPH, Part II: General Methodology and Proposed Standard," *Computer Graphics,* **11**(3) (1977).

8. Raytheon Company, *Electronic Progress,* **18**(2) (1976).

9. R. C. Hillyard and I. C. Braid, "Characterizing Non-Ideal Shapes in Terms of Dimensions and Tolerances," *Computer Graphics,* **12**(3), 234–238 (1978).

10. Richard E. Parent, "A System for Sculpting 3-D Data," *Computer Graphics,* **11**(2), 138–147 (1977).

11. A. R. Forrest, "A Unified Approach to Geometric Modelling," *Computer Graphics,* **12**(3), 264–269 (1978).

12. Norman Badler and Ruzena Bajcsy, "Three-Dimensional Representations for Computer Graphics and Computer Vision," *Computer Graphics,* **12**(3), 153–160 (1978).

13. Donald P. Greenberg, "An Interdisciplinary Laboratory for Graphics Research and Applications," *Computer Graphics,* **11**(2), 90–97 (1977).

14. H. J. Borkin, J. F. McIntosh, and J. A. Turner, "The Development of Three-

Dimensional Spatial Modeling Techniques for the Construction Planning of Nuclear Power Plants," *Computer Graphics,* **12**(3), 341–347 (1978).

15. Herbert B. Voelcker and Aristides A. G. Requicha, "Geometric Modeling of Mechanical Parts and Processes," *Computer,* **10**(12), 48–57 (1977).

16. J. A. Brewer and D. C. Anderson, "Visual Interaction with Overhauser Curves and Surfaces," *Computer Graphics,* **11**(2), 132–137 (1977).

17. I. E. Sutherland and R. F. Sproull, "A Clipping Divider," *Proc. AFIPS FJCC 1968,* Thompson Books, Washington, 1968.

18. D. F. Rogers and J. A. Adams, *Mathematical Elements for Computer Graphics,* McGraw-Hill, New York, 1976.

19. James F. Blinn, "Simulation of Wrinkled Surfaces," *Computer Graphics,* **12**(3), 286–292 (1978).

20. William M. Newman and Robert F. Sproull, *Principles of Interactive Computer Graphics,* McGraw-Hill, New York, 1973 (pages 283–332 contain material omitted from 2nd ed.).

21. R. H. Ewald and R. Fryer, Eds., "Final Report of the GSPC State-of-the-Art Subcommittee," *Computer Graphics,* **12**(1–2), 14–169 (1978).

22. American National Standards Institute, *American National Standard Vocabulary for Information Processing* (ANSI X3.12-1970), New York, 1970.

23. David C. Evans, "Keynote Address," *Computer Graphics,* **8**(1), 5–9 (1974).

24. Donald J. Humcke and David P. Kent, "Ergonomics of a Large Interactive Graphics Operation," *Computer-Aided Design,* **9**(4), 262–266 (1977).

25. James D. Foley and Victor L. Wallace, "The Art of Natural Graphic Man–Machine Conversation," *Proc. IEEE,* **62**(4), 462–471 (1974).

26. Herbert A. Simon, "What Computers Mean for Man and Society," *Science,* **195**(4283), 1186–1191 (1977).

27. Charles M. Spiridon, "Leasing at the Low End," *Computer Decisions,* **7**(12), 34–35 (1975).

28. Glenn L. Johnson and James A. Gentry, Jr., *Finney and Miller's Principles of Accounting, Introductory,* 7th ed., Prentice-Hall, Englewood Cliffs, NJ, 1970.

29. Thurber J. Moffett, "Building Highway Systems with Computer Graphic Simulations," *Proc. IEEE,* **62**(4), 429–436 (1974).

30. _____, "The Faster 3-D Way to Computerized Design," *Business Week,* November 21, 1977.

31. _____, "Computer Makes 'Photos' of Parts Yet-To-Be," *Design News,* January, 1978.

32. P. A. Hawrylyshyn, R. R. Tasker, and L. W. Organ, "CASS: Computer-Assisted Stereotaxic Surgery," *Computer Graphics,* **11**(2), 13–17 (1977).

33. D. M. Collins, F. A. Cotton, E. E. Hazen, Jr., E. F. Meyer, Jr., and C. N. Morimoto, "Protein Crystal Structures: Quicker, Cheaper Approaches," *Science,* **190**(4219), 1047–1053 (1975).

34. Charles Csuri, "Computer Graphics and Art," *Proc. IEEE,* **62**(4), 503–515 (1974).

35. Edwin Catmull, "The Problems of Computer Assisted Animation," *Computer Graphics,* **12**(3), 348–353 (1978).

36. Ronald J. Hackathorn, "ANIMA II: A 3-D Color Animation system," *Computer Graphics,* **11** (2), 54–64 (1977).

37. Marc Levoy, "A Color Animation System Based on the Multiplane Technique," *Computer Graphics,* **11**(2), 65–71 (1977).

38. _____, "Bursting at the Museums," *Computer Decisions,* **7**(3), 44–45 (1975).

Index